THE WTO PRIMER

THE WTO PRIMER

TRACING TRADE'S VISIBLE HAND THROUGH CASE STUDIES

Kevin Buterbaugh
Richard Fulton

First published in 2007 by
PALGRAVE MACMILLAN™
175 Fifth Avenue, New York, N.Y. 10010 and
Houndmills, Basingstoke, Hampshire, England RG21 6XS.
Companies and representatives throughout the world.

PALGRAVE MACMILLAN is the global academic imprint of the Palgrave Macmillan division of St. Martin's Press, LLC and of Palgrave Macmillan Ltd. Macmillan® is a registered trademark in the United States, United Kingdom and other countries. Palgrave is a registered trademark in the European Union and other countries.

ISBN-10: 0-230-60020-4 (hardcover)
ISBN-13: 978-0-230-60020-1 (hardcover)

ISBN-10: 0-230-60021-2 (paperback)
ISBN-13: 978-0-230-60021-8 (paperback)

Library of Congress Cataloging-in-Publication Data is available from the Library of Congress.

A catalogue record of the book is available from the British Library.

Design by Scribe Inc.

First edition: January 2008

10 9 8 7 6 5 4 3 2 1

Printed in the United States of America.

To Karen and Sara and Mom, inspirations all. —Rich

To Claudia for providing me the support to write. —Kevin

TABLE OF CONTENTS

LIST OF FIGURES

Chapter 1

Introduction

The World Trade Organization (WTO) may well be the least known and least understood component of the contemporary international political economy. The role it plays in the interplay of international trade is central and significant. Yet, other elements of the system like the World Bank or the International Monetary Fund are more visible even though their scope is narrower and their impact less telling. This text is an attempt to provide a primer for the study of the WTO that allows the reader to explore this significant organization.

It is true that a great deal has been written on or about the WTO, but most of the writings are one of two types: (1) technical tomes written for the expert and the practitioner or (2) polemics, either for or against what is perceived to be the impact of the WTO. Examples of supportive polemics can be found published by advocates of an organization centered on promoting a mission of globalization of international trade through unfettered flows of trade.[1] Protectionism is the enemy, and gradualism is counterproductive. On the other hand, the negative polemicists see the organization as the chief culprit in worldwide economic and environmental impoverishment and as an organization that serves a narrow set of elite and corporate interests.[2]

The technical texts on the WTO are useful but often stiff and narrowly focused on the technical operations or legalese of the organization. These are primarily written for experts and practitioners who need to thread their way through the hundreds of pages of rules and regulations that make up the maze of agreements that are the working elements of the WTO. Over the decades, the specific trade negotiations have added volumes to the texts of the agreements. They were negotiated piecemeal; tariffs and rules of trade were established individually by commodity or by bilateral agreements that became universal by way of the Most Favored Nation principle. This has produced pages upon pages of very specific conditions on which tariff levels and nontariff barriers can or cannot be set on commodities and, of late, also on the delivery of services. Experts, lawyers, national policy leaders, and economic diplomats all need to have the reference points detailing these specific items. Thus, texts explaining the rules of the game and providing the specifics for the process of playing the game are necessary but not very accessible to students whose interests and needs are only in the broader picture.

The polemical book is more widely available but does not provide the foundations for reasoned dialogue. The polemic either unduly praises the organization or, more likely, attacks it as an evil arm of an amorphous concept called globalization. Many of its arguments are not without merit, but they are made in an attempt to directly affect public policy, and not as foundations for understanding the internal logic and operation of the WTO.

THE CONTEXT OF INTERNATIONAL RELATIONS

This text provides a reasoned appraisal of the WTO through an approach that places the organization within the framework of competing theories of international relations and organization.

The contemporary world of free trade was founded on Adam Smith's liberal postulate that the free marketplace, through unfettered competition, produced an invisible hand that guided rational economic decisions. Smith believed that left alone by government, individuals (and states) would make self-interested economic choices, and that these would lead naturally to the society as a whole benefiting. He was attacking the prevailing view of mercantilists that argued that states are in competition for international trade, and what benefits one will necessarily harm the other: "Each nation has been made to look with an invidious eye upon the prosperity of all the nations with which it trades, and to consider their gains as its own loss."[3] To the contrary, Smith believed that free trade benefits all through the invisible hand of individual choice. In the realm of international trade, that meant interference with the free flow of trade (tariffs, for example) was to be condemned. Smith's orthodox liberalism remains the bedrock of the approach to international trade incorporated within the WTO. The continuing theme of the WTO remains: let the "invisible hand" of competition control the flow of the international political economy, not the heavy and visible hand of government regulation.

Table 1.1   Theoretical views on trade and international organization

Theory	Basic view
Liberalism	Both state and nonstate actors are important.
	The marketplace sets conditions of international trade by limiting the role of government and maximizing the role of individuals/enterprises.
Neoliberalism	Shares the core assumptions of liberal theory, but also recognizes the importance of institutions for cooperation and the reflection of state interests in the creation of rules and institutions.
Mercantilism/realism	States set policies to maintain economy/security by protecting indigenous enterprises through tariff and nontariff means.
	Contemporary *neomercantilism* supports trade to build the economy but is defensive in protecting the state's economic base.
	States often will fail to cooperate even when all can experience gains, as each seeks to gain relatively more from a deal than partners.

Even Smith, however, taught that the invisible hand does not always lead to productive results. He believed there were three limited conditions that required government to interfere or impinge on individuals and the market: (1) to provide for the national defense including retaliation against unfair trade practices, (2) to protect individuals within the state from injustice and oppression, and (3) to provide public services that individuals could not provide on their own (public goods). By public goods, he meant public works like roads, bridges, and port facilities plus institutions like police and fire departments.[4]

Given their continuous struggle with the mercantilist assumption that the state must protect its productive units with tariff and nontariff barriers aimed at external trade forces, the inheritors of Adam Smith's views, so-called trade neoliberals, have had to embrace a fundamental paradox. They have had to concede that in order to champion and maintain an international free trade environment, they would have to embrace an increasingly specific set of rules of the game. In the post–World War II era, the accumulation and increasing regularization of rules was accelerated under an arrangement among, first, the major trading states and, later, most all states called the General Agreement on Tariffs and Trade (GATT).

By adopting this complex set of rules, the world trading community committed itself to an ever increasing movement toward a more authoritative governing body to substantiate and legitimize enforcement of those rules. All the while, neomercantilists, whose instincts are for protectionism, interjected exceptions to the rules in an attempt to protect specific national economic interests. The subsequent development of the WTO, then, is the net result of the necessity to provide for Smith's exceptions to government control—national defense (unfair trade practices), protection against injustice (violations of free trade agreements) and oppression (the use of trade as an economic weapon), and even the provision of "public goods" in the forms of a dispute settlement body and rule of law.

Our text is designed to explore the development and formation of the WTO as the visible hand of trade in the international political economy. It traces the growing willingness of self-interested countries to cooperate in fielding a system of trade freed, as much as possible, from state-centered mercantilism.

Growing trade openness in the post–World War II era provided the beginnings of an international trade regime dominated by the search for a set of nearly universally agreed rules of the game. This developing regime first took the form of the GATT, and it depended mostly on specific, mutually agreed tariff reductions with only a decentralized set of Dispute Settlement Procedures (DSP).

Discontented with the ad hoc character of these agreements, GATT participants began to desire a stronger and more permanent structure, the WTO, eventually inaugurated in 1995. The WTO was designed to more specifically commit states to an institutionalized system of oversight and enforcement of agreed upon free trade rules. In addition, it was pledged to expand the scope of the agreements beyond tariff reductions and into hitherto uncovered areas of concern like protection of patents and copyrights, trade in agriculture, and service industries. As a main theme, this text will trace the politics and practices that accompanied the development of these liberalizing trade rules and structures.

As a second theme, the text will demonstrate the nature of trade decision making. Specifically, the text is interested in how decisions reflect not only the clash of states over the nature of the international political economy but also the clash of domestic interests over the nature of the resultant globalization of decision processes and outcomes. Robert Putnam outlined the relationship between domestic and international policy making in the mid–1980s.[5] His book concentrated on the emerging foundations of cooperation in international relations through an analysis of a series of power summits of the dominant political—economic states (the so-called G-7 consisting of the United States, Canada, Germany, France, Great Britain, Italy, and Japan). His conclusion that domestic as well as international politics were important in explaining the outcomes of summits applies to the creation of the GATT and WTO and the conflicts that take place within them.

Any balanced approach to an understanding of the growing influence of the WTO as the repository of international trade rules needs to take into account the effect domestic politics has on the decisions of member states. As Robert Putnam puts it simply, "From a political point of view, international economic co-operation can usefully be conceived as a two-level game."[6] In the first level, all policy, including foreign policy, begins within the decision processes of domestic politics. Internal social groups provide both support and opposition to external free trade policies. The second level is the international arena of state decision making itself. Helen Milner, who built her work on Putnam's two-level game theories, has stated that "social groups such as labor organizations, capitalists, multinational corporations, import-competing firms, and ethnic groups [have] identifiable preferences about international economic policy that often translate into national policy."[7] The more domestic groups that have definable interests, she continues, the more likely such groups are to affect the definition of state interest in foreign policy actions. Certainly this has proven the case when we see the activities of the antiglobalization movement.[8]

As a study by James Shoch concerning recent American administrations illustrates, institutions within the domestic arena such as political parties can also make an impact on foreign policy.[9] He demonstrates for the Reagan, Bush, and Clinton administrations the impact of divided government (differing party control of executive and legislatures) on trade policies. Partisan politics as significant domestic influences must be taken into consideration if we are to understand the decisions that are made affecting the myriad international trade issues (from clothing to gambling) increasingly adjudicated within the GATT/WTO.

Clearly, "international cooperation may be fostered by domestic pressures or blocked by domestic opposition."[10] The process encompasses this two-level game: one played within the domestic political arena and one within international diplomacy, both levels, of course, being played both serially and simultaneously. This also means that the policy maker has the difficult task of finding a winning set of issues or points that can gain both the acceptance of international actors and domestic actors simultaneously. Leaders may also attempt to use one level of the game to affect their bargaining position in another. Thus, a leader may mobilize support domestically in order to prevent certain options from being viable internationally, or vice versa.

The text's discussion of the hard negotiations during the Uruguay Round of negotiations that led to the actual formation of the WTO reveals the complex interplay of the two-level game. Even more pertinent, we have included relevant case studies in this book that demonstrate the dynamics of the two-level process as the WTO tries to work out the application of rules within its newly created structures. For example, domestic special interests and party influences play a significant role in the determination of state policies in, of all places, a study of what some call "the great banana war" (Chapter 5) and in the case of scientific-political controversy over international trade in beef (Chapter 6). And the politics of admissions into the WTO reflect this two-tiered process as well (Chapter 7 on China's accession).

Beyond the purely internal impact of domestic forces, a challenge to a wide array of globalization symbols (the WTO, the International Monetary Fund, the World Bank) has come from the mobilization of transnational coalitions of domestic social and economic interests. The Seattle meeting of the WTO described in Chapter 8 illustrates the explosive potential of these coalitions. Many domestic interests found themselves cooperating with or melding into transnational networks that, while still anchored within domestic politics, used international cooperation in an effort to magnify their media exposure to influence the outcomes of domestic agendas. Seattle would be no surprise to Putnam. He concluded in 1984 that "one might discover transnational alliances, tacit or explicit, in which domestic interests pressure their respective governments to adopt mutually supportive policies."[11] And this is what the antiglobalization and anti-WTO groups were attempting to do in 1999 and have continued to attempt since.

The arena of international trade, then, remains open to conflicting motivations. Realist theory in international relations, also called mercantilism, predicts that states will pursue their own interests in order to gain an advantage in areas of international trade at the expense of others. Trade liberals, on the other hand, assume that all states have some comparative advantage (areas of trade within which they can compete better than most) that they can exploit in a system of free trade and therefore all come out winners. Leaders of most states today, developed or developing (though these latter often reluctantly), assume that an increased interdependency of the global economy dictates some degree of participation in a free market international economy.[12] But most still want to adjust the mechanisms of the international political economy to reflect the needs of their own political situation—domestic as well as international.

The fundamental questions remain: when, why, and how are states going about the business of cooperation in international economic affairs? It seems obvious that the answer is that "the probability of co-operation depends on the mixture of compatible and incompatible goals of the various players."[13] Where, then, is the source to be found of the compatibility of state interests that has translated mutually "compatible and incompatible goals" into the formation of the WTO commitments? Many have perceived the United States as the fulcrum of cooperation in the immediate post–World War II era because of its hegemonic position—its dominance of economic and political power within the "free world" community.[14]

The text takes this assumption as its third theme. American decision makers championed free trade at the end of World War II because it brought economic benefits to the country—that is, it was in the national interest. Moreover, it was in the interest of the United States to spread this system globally and to use its hegemonic status to do so. The Bretton Woods (1949) agreements that established the International Monetary Fund, the World Bank group, and the beginning discussions that were to result in the GATT were the product fundamentally of American diplomacy. This centrality has persisted, which is why we focus on American policy in our discussion of the development of the GATT/WTO.

The liberal trade environment of the nineteenth century produced unprecedented economic growth. The Great Depression of the 1930s brought that growth to a screeching halt. Protectionism and anti-immigrant feelings were perceived, rightly or wrongly, to be the cause of this deep economic decline.[15] American-led Western leadership championed trade liberalization (particularly in tariff reductions) as a way of guaranteeing that economic collapse would not recur in the postwar era. These same leaders had suffered through the depression and the war that followed and were determined not to repeat what they saw as their protectionist roots. Because economic prosperity was produced in the period of American dominance after the war, the assumption persisted that trade liberalization linked to American hegemony was the foundation of this prosperity. Japan and the states of the emergent European Union continued to follow the American lead even as they became its main trade competitors.

As American hegemony declined in the latter part of the century, some theories predicted a decline in international cooperation. What could rescue the trend toward greater cooperation in this time period, Putnam argued, was "if a few large states [took] collective responsibility for leadership of the world economy."[16] This, Putnam claimed, was in fact the lesson from game theorists; small groups find it easier to solve policy problems, particularly if they dominate the arena within which they operate. In the realm of international trade, Europe and Japan, as well as the United States, were this small group of cooperative powers, at least through the early years of the new millennium.

Our review of the development of the GATT, with its central decisions revolving around the relationships among the United States, European Union, and (intermittently) Japan, reflects this observation. These three actors have accounted for 70 percent of international trade through recent decades and have created the trade patterns that led, through a progressive series of rounds of negotiation, to increasingly effective agreements and eventually more formal structures of regulation.

Cooperation does not mean compatibility, however. Growing trade conflicts among the three economic power centers witnessed challenges to American predominance. Out of these conflicts of interest in specific areas of trade policy has grown a dichotomy characterized by (1) an increasing cooperation among the three in trade liberalization while (2) each has maintained important policy elements based on self-interested protectionism. As it turns out, this dichotomous pattern is not limited to the big three but holds true for virtually all of the participants in the WTO.

Early postwar negotiations that created and expanded, step by step, the tariff limitations that are the heart of GATT produced a series of exceptions to the tariff rules with the effect of limiting free trade in favor of protectionism. These exceptions were granted because of pressures from richer states that were trying to insulate particular domestic industries. Later rounds, while aimed at the development of the GATT agreements by adding nontariff barriers to the equation, produced additional exceptions made in order to encourage the participation of developing states. These concessions allowed, for one thing, poorer countries to be exempt from certain rules, particularly to allow developed states to give the less developed favorable tariff rates on their basic exports while allowing them to protect emerging domestic industries. Even with these steps, the invisible hand of major state trading had the tendency of marginalizing the less developed, which means that social justice, even economic national defense, could only be achieved by help from a demonstrably visible hand. The developing states were promised concessions under GATT agreements that could, in practice, only be fulfilled later under the stricter structure of the WTO.

Contemporary developing states feel the need for protectionist exemptions to protect their emergent industries—agricultural, manufacturing, technical, and service, not unlike those used by America in its formative years of economic modernization, as we shall see. Adam Smith-like limited exceptionalism continues to be negotiated by developing states as their overwhelming numbers within the soon-to-be nearly universal WTO membership increases their collective influence. If they are to become active participants in a free trade environment guided by invisible hand assumptions, they feel that the visible hand must be augmented by positive aids to their early development efforts. They also want better representation in the processes of decision making and to reduce the influence of the most powerful.

The series of early GATT and later WTO exceptions and loopholes continue to fly in the face of the underlying free trade philosophy of the GATT/WTO, of course. Even more disruptive to the growth of confidence in the early GATT was the fact that the organization had no formal structures, only a series of agreements. This meant that any rule implementation was completely dependent on mutual policing of important rules by the participating states themselves. The GATT established only a regime, a voluntary cooperative relationship, and left significant elements of protectionism extant within the arrangements and left whole areas of trade outside the agreed upon set of rules. In order to produce more certainty and enforceability of the rules for this international trade regime, states saw the necessity of a more intrusive organization. It was left to the Uruguay Round to invent the WTO, which brought into focus the difficult process of negotiating a stronger organizational framework and working structure to accommodate new rules of enforcement.

The Uruguay Round took years to complete. As part of this, all previous GATT agreements and codes were folded into the final WTO. Yet even with the successful formation of the WTO, much was left undone, including the need to accommodate a continuing set of demands to expand free trade agreements to such areas as agriculture, intellectual property, service industries, and the protection of labor and the environment.

The 2000 Seattle meeting was supposed to begin a new round of negotiations. Its failure emphasized the point that the international community must set priorities among the variety of untouched issues pressing on world trade and then work to find mutually agreeable solutions. The consequent meeting in Doha, Qatar initiated a new round of negotiations. Its task proved not to be easy given the increased demands for social justice from both developing states and a variety of active internationalized interests. Its first meeting in Cancun, Mexico, in 2003 ended without an agreement on priorities or objectives for the round. The round continues to struggle to find common ground. Still, if there is a consummation of the round, the probable conclusion will be an expansion of the agreements, for it seems that the more the agreements are expanded, the more they must expand. The expectation is that this contemporary round will last for some years.

Ironically, by the turn of the twenty-first century, the very success that led to the WTO treaty has helped to create challenging factions among third world coalitions and transition (former communist) states that have complicated this round of negotiations.[17]

These relatively new and increasingly effective players in the game, including the huge political economies that are China and India plus the growing potential of Russia when it is finally admitted, produce an increasing number of centers of economic power that will make cooperation more difficult. This contemporary round of negotiations will challenge Putnam's admonition that small groups of powers maintain the stability of the international political economy. As the number of players increases, the chances of them cooperating is lessened, and the chances of free riding or shirking responsibilities goes up.

CONCLUSIONS

From this introduction, it is clear that the road to free trade has not been, nor does it continue to be, free of many obstacles. Since nearly all trade is conducted within the context of states, the remedies for hindrances to free trade remain fundamentally in the realm of relations between states. These relations are conducted either on a bilateral or multilateral basis; and indeed, the multilateral agreement processes usually turn on the politics of decisions made through bilateral negotiations.

The complex fabric of bilateral economic relations is, in today's world, being transformed into patterns of regional and global free trade arrangements. The WTO is moving toward becoming the overriding center for principles, rules, regulations, and obligations that direct an increasingly globalized trade. It is becoming more and more the central visible hand of international trade. The goal of this organization is to minimize the hindrances to international free trade by being the foundation for an integrated, rule-based system of international trade relations. Bilateral relations and regional multilateral relationships are to be placed within the confines of the umbrella guidelines of the WTO.

The following chapters will explore the development and present state of GATT/WTO as it pursues agreement on global international free trade. Part I begins with Chapter 2, designed to follow the development of the post–World War II international trade system from the establishment of the GATT regime through its first eight rounds of negotiations. What comes through in this discussion is that the step-by-step approach to establishing a stable set of agreements toward international trade, given all its faults, was a successful way to establish confidence in and enthusiasm for international free markets. Chapter 3 explores the contentious Uruguay Round of GATT negotiations. It highlights the United States' central role in molding the rules and structures of the WTO. For the first time, the international trade regime was anchored in a formal treaty with an organization to administer it and a dispute settlement system with some teeth. Chapter 4 describes the mission and structure of the WTO itself, including its dispute settlement arrangements. Here are embodied the unique aspects of the WTO agreement as an effective organization. Chapter 4 also covers some challenges and issues that have arisen for the WTO since its creation.

Part II of the text provides a series of case studies dealing with controversies surrounding the WTO and complaints brought before the WTO for settlement. These, more than anything else, help to explain the complexity of the problems surrounding the establishment of a global free trade environment. The cases were chosen specifically to illustrate the fundamental interactions within the WTO. Important criteria used for case selection were that (a) it had to discuss a substantive issue, (b) it should illustrate the processes and politics of the WTO, (c) it should involve participation by diverse international actors and interests, and (d) it should illustrate internal and external power interactions.

Chapter 5 examines an early dispute brought before the WTO dispute settlement system. Though seemingly trivial, this conflict over bananas between the United States and European countries turned out to be a test case of the dispute settlement processes within the WTO. It intertwines domestic politics, lesser developed state relations with their former colonial masters, large state diplomacy, and conflicts of interest among developing countries. At stake were not only bananas, but also precedent. Chapter 6 centers on the continuing controversy over the use of hormones in the production of beef. Involved are health, safety, and environmental questions as legitimate concerns of states in their international trade dealings. The question is, do states use these concerns as covers for protectionist policies? And who should decide what is a legitimate health, safety, or environmental regulation, and how should this decision be made? This case also raises the important question of sovereignty and how trade affects it. Once again, major states clash since U.S./Canadian beef was banned in Europe.

Chapter 7 uses the important case of China's desire to join the WTO to describe the WTO accession process. China obviously represents a major entry into the modern international trade system. This case not only looks deeply into China's (and by extension, other transition states') necessity to make significant domestic changes in order to meet international standards, but also into its need to make bilateral trade obligations across the world to gain support for entrance. Accession illustrates the hard bargaining that must take place before new members are added to the organization.

Chapter 8 demonstrates two diametrically opposed trends in globalization. First, the Seattle meeting analyzed here was an attempt to begin a new round of negotiations to expand the reach of the WTO. The conference's failure illustrates that the by then 143 participating states were not ready to negotiate the types of commitments necessary to inaugurate a new round. At the same time, the meeting showed what needed to be accomplished in order to continue the expansion of free trade: lessons hopefully learned to prosecute the consequent Doha Conference. A second insight is into the increased public opposition to globalization and the diverse organizations that symbolize pursuit of that opposition. The street demonstrations and the worldwide media attention precipitated by the Seattle meeting of the WTO set out a pattern of domestic and transnational group exposition of issues that continue to challenge.

Chapter 9 presents an account of the attempts of the WTO to rescue its expansion plans through a new round of negotiations now called the Doha Round. While the round was successfully launched in Doha, Qatar, in its first meeting designed to set the foundations of a new accord, it stumbled badly. The consequent Ministerial Meeting in Cancun, Mexico was nearly as large a disaster as Seattle was. Clearly, the WTO has serious problems that continue to plague its further expansion and the development of a more liberal trade regime. This chapter also illustrates the complex dealings of states within the WTO. We see lesser developed states opposing the more developed; we see conflict among the developed; and we see conflicts among the lesser developed. We also see state positions being affected by domestic constituencies.

Chapter 10 brings conclusions on lessons learned and on the prospects and future of the WTO by defining the newer, more contentious areas of negotiation left incomplete or on the periphery of present GATT/WTO agreements. How the WTO handles these issues will define the ability of the WTO to accomplish its fundamental long-term goal. The chapter also summarizes lessons from the various case studies and shows us how these illuminate various theories of international relations and organizations.

This book, then, is the story of the evolution of the WTO as it has navigated the rough waters of international politics in the second half of the twentieth century and into the twenty-first. The successful formation of the organization was not inevitable, nor does it have a guaranteed lease on the future. In fact, the more it tries to fulfill its specific mandates, the more it accumulates resistance, up to and including outright opposition to its existence.

PART I

HISTORY AND DEVELOPMENT OF THE GATT/WTO

CHAPTER 2

THE GATT ROUNDS

The nature of the international political economy is found somewhere in the relationship between the state and the marketplace. Yet both the state and marketplace are mechanisms of product, service, and resource allocation. Markets often have much of their structural reality within the state, but they operate independently through economic imperatives of their own, and these market forces have grave difficulties with physical boundaries.

The history of international trade in the modern era is one of contrasting national policies. State policies, even in the days of relative laissez-faire, have had a tendency to focus a high priority on national economic development. This means that a strong motivation has existed to limit the competitiveness of foreign goods in favor of fostering native industries. Through most of the eighteenth and nineteenth centuries and into the twentieth, the mechanism for this form of protection was the *tariff*: a monetary tax on imports that increases the cost of goods in relation to internally produced equivalents.

It is true, of course, that tariffs are not used exclusively, not even primarily in some time periods and places, for protectionism. Tariffs have historically been used as an important source of income for governments. This was particularly true in earlier eras before income and sales taxes. As states found these new sources of income, however, the need for tariffs was minimized for all but the poorest. Thus, it is from the nineteenth through the twentieth centuries that the reduction of tariff rates was the premier method for opening national markets to foreign goods. The key to sustaining increased free trade is to maintain balanced benefits in this process, a concept called *reciprocity*—each government gives similar levels of concessions in order to balance the benefits from the agreements made.

This chapter explores the development of an international free trade movement motivated largely by the goal of solidifying peace and spreading economic development and growth across national boundaries by means of multinational negotiations and agreements. In short, it deals with attempts to liberalize markets in a world still dominated by states.

Our focus will be the development of the General Agreement on Tariffs and Trade (GATT) as the early manifestation of and still the foundation document of the WTO. Roger Gilpin, a major international political economy scholar, has said,

"The GATT . . . provided the institutional basis for trade negotiation in the postwar [World War II] era."[1] Yet others note that the GATT lacked institutional integrity and acted fundamentally by means of a series of negotiation conferences that set *codes* (principles of action), but without an enforcement arm.[2] In fact, the GATT was rather weak as an international organization anchoring its worth on the setting of codes, voluntary compliance, and providing continuity for negotiation forums. At base the GATT was really not an international organization at all since its foundation legal documents were intergovernmental agreements by definition, lacking in formal enforcement structures rather than the more binding agreements set by treaties.

Nothing of the magnitude of the GATT can exist only on paper, however. It either falls apart and dies, exists but becomes moribund, or can "over the four decades of its existence . . . evolve into a de facto world trade organization."[3] The evolution of the GATT could not progress with only a skeletal structure and a voluntary code of conduct. There would arise an inevitable point when the GATT would have to reform or lose momentum in its quest to establish a secure global free trade environment.

That point came in the 1990s when the combination of (1) the collapse of the Soviet empire (ending the Cold War); (2) the increased integration and effectiveness of the European Union (EU); (3) the rise of multiple competitive world trading states, including the Newly Industrialized Countries (NICs); and (4) the relative decline of American hegemony simply demanded a stronger trading system. The resultant WTO was designed to be the core of that system.

The purpose of this chapter is to provide a condensed overview of the four-decade–long development of the GATT as it approached its transformation into the WTO. In pursuit of this story, this chapter will (1) outline the conditions of world trade up to the postwar formation of the GATT; (2) survey its early rounds of successful tariff reductions; and (3) examine the increasing complexity of the GATT by exploring the transforming Dillon, Kennedy, and Tokyo Rounds.

Note during this narrative that each time the GATT contractors felt the need for increased expansion or expanded influence, they called for negotiation sessions that were called *rounds*. The early rounds were single sittings of negotiations among GATT participants; they were in essence a single meeting in the same place over a short period. Later rounds each consisted of an extended series of negotiations with several meetings over a period of years. Each round lasted longer than the previous round, as each attempted to subdue increasingly complex issues and mechanisms of trade protectionism.

THE ENVIRONMENT THAT CREATED THE GATT

The General Agreement on Tariffs and Trade was an integral part of the reformulation of the international environment fashioned after World War II—largely through U.S. leadership. It was planned to act alongside two other multinational agreements that were attempts to establish an order for the world economy. Combined, these were to be known as the Bretton Woods organizations—the World Bank and the International Monetary Fund. While not specifically linked to the other two in the end, the mechanism that was to become the GATT certainly was conceived at the time as an equal partner.

The important thing to establish at this point is that U.S. policy was at the center of the formation of the postwar economic system for the noncommunist world. The end of the war found the United States with the only intact industrial economic infrastructure. All other major world trading states were in ruin wholly or in major parts. American *hegemony* in this period came not just from its political, military, and nuclear superiority, but also from its economic dominance. The United States accounted for half of the total economic output in the world at this time. It is not unreasonable, then, to discuss the state of the world trading system leading up to the formation of the GATT from the perspective of American policies.

Alfred Eckes begins his book on American foreign trade policy by stating that "from colonial times the 'Spirit of Commerce' has inspired and shaped America's relations with the world."[4] Even though George Washington's farewell warning of "foreign entanglements" led the way toward a political and psychological isolationism, on the whole, early America believed in free trade because it needed to have the markets of Europe open to its goods (particularly agricultural goods, an interest that persists in U.S. policy to this day). Eventually, the free trade tendencies of early American policy had to be compromised because of the political strength of domestic industries that demanded protective tariffs. By the end of the nineteenth century, half of all imports went untaxed, but the other half saw targeted duties aimed at competitors to import-sensitive U.S. manufacturers. A series of bilateral agreements were made with major trading partners on the basis of reciprocity, but more often than not these agreements were a result of U.S. pressure. High tariffs brought protection, but sometimes with the cost of some alienation from major partners. Clearly this would not do in the long run.

Trade developments mirrored the success of political parties that championed competing ideas on trade policy. The Democratic Party had a strong tradition of freer trade policies going back to the 1840s. It saw tariffs as a revenue-only device. From the 1860s to 1934, the Democrats and the muckraking press attacked Republicans for bowing to corrupt import-sensitive industries to maintain high tariffs. From Lincoln to Hoover, on the other hand, the Republicans believed in the use of targeted duties to encourage economic development by protecting domestic industries. The policy seemed to have succeeded along with the Republican Party's electoral fortunes; it succeeded not only as the dominant policy, but also as a spur to development. As a result, U.S. GDP grew significantly faster than free market British GDP from the 1870s up to World War I.

This is particularly interesting given today's arguments over the effect of protectionist national policies. Poor countries proclaim that they need special protection for their emerging industries. Thus, they argue for, and to some degree obtain, pledges of special dispensation from trade codes that preclude or minimize high tar-iffs. A strong argument can be made that these very same protectionist tariff policies enabled American industries to develop and prosper in the forty years spanning the nineteenth and twentieth centuries. The same can be said for protectionism in much of Europe at the same time, particularly in Germany and Russia, each of which demonstrated high tariffs alongside high domestic growth. In Asia, even more dras-tic efforts at national protection took place, particularly in Japan. However, it should be remembered that foreign trade remained a relatively small part of the economies of major states at this time—less than 10 percent for the United States well into the late 1940s.[5]

At the turn of the century, Congress closely controlled trade policy, limiting flex-ibility on the part of the executive.[6] Disillusionment with Wilsonian international-ism, including a significant movement toward liberalization of trade policy, led Congress and the country toward more restrictive trading policies from the 1920s to the early 1930s. The free trade Wilson administration had gone too far. The reaction brought Republican victories that brought a period of success for protectionism.

The most protective period in American history happened during the time between the Forney-McCumber Act of 1921 and the Smoot-Hawley Act of 1930 (the congressional reaction to the Great Depression).[7] Though it increased protec-tionism, the Forney-McCumber Act also shifted some important responsibilities for trade policies directly to the president. It allowed the president for three years to uni-laterally retaliate against any unfair foreign trade practice. He could place penalty duties on goods or even exclude goods from countries he found discriminating against American exports. This resulted in an emphasis on bilateral trade negotia-tions with exclusive reciprocity (deals that affix only to the signatories, excluding other countries) rather than providing an opening for multilateral trade negotiations (MTN) that would give favorable reciprocity to all traders, as Wilsonian Democrats wanted. Of some interest for today's WTO debates is the fact that this act also placed protections for intellectual properties in the hands of the administration.

The State Department opposed any aggressive use of the act, however. Its primary concern was in the political arena, and it felt that aggressive trade protectionism made it harder to further American political interests.[8] This was to begin a pattern of trade enforcement views the State Department would maintain well into the 1970s.

As it turned out, the Smoot-Hawley Act played the part of the enduring protec-tionist villain. It has been blamed for the rise of fascism, of radicalism in Japan, and thus for planting the seeds of World War II. Forever after, it has been pointed to by free trade advocates as the prime example of the harm done by trade barriers. Critics claim that this act created a domino effect in international trade—state after state retaliating with their own "beggar thy neighbor" protectionist policies plunging the world into deep depression and war. Others claim, with some justification, that the act's tariff levels were no higher than earlier bills, but that it was the environment that doomed its application. The economic situation of the time was, to be sure, complex with many elements converging to make for disaster. The Smoot-Hawley

Act, whether culpable in and of itself or not, had become the symbol of counterproductive trade policies.

If it did nothing else, however, the act stimulated reformers to begin to plan for free trade reform. Chief among these reformers was Cordell Hull working early in the 1930s with a group of second-line foreign service officers in the U.S. State Department. Hull associated free commerce with peace. He became a significant advisor to and secretary of state for President Franklin Roosevelt. As Democrats came to control Congress and the presidency after 1932, their traditional free trade outlook combined with Hull's tireless leadership to produce a significant change in U.S. policies. The first thing Secretary Hull did was navigate an "emergency" program through Congress that would bring about the most important change in the "institutional history of U.S. trade policy"[9]: the transfer of policy power from the Congress to the executive on a more permanent basis. Hull consequently passed this power on to a group of technocrats.

The Reciprocal Trade Agreement Act of 1934 (RTA) granted to the executive the right to raise or lower tariffs by as much as 50 percent from the 1930 levels. Hull used this act to establish an interdepartmental Committee on Trade Agreements (CTA) to administer a policy of both bilateral reciprocal agreements and multilateral trade agreements. This secretive group (even Congress did not know its composition for some twenty years) set the basis of U.S. policy on trade. Trade policy was taken out of congressional politics, which had limited its flexibility, and into the realm of free trade technicians.[10]

Earlier reciprocal agreements had limits set on them by Congress; they tended to be extortionate in tone. The CTA would expand agreements so that bilateral agreements would apply to all trading states that did not discriminate against American products in each area of agreement. Quickly, the United States made multinational trade treaties with some forty-eight nations.[11] These policies led in a direct line to the trade environment of today.

THE ITO AND THE FORMATION OF GATT

Parts of international trade theory postulate that trade liberalization should be a smooth process when there is a hegemonic state driving the process, and this was the role played by the United States after World War II. Indeed, at a seminal conference in a small New Hampshire town in 1944, the United States, Canada, and Great Britain led the way in establishing what became known as the Bretton Woods System. Following the lead of British economist John Maynard Keynes, these war victors searched for a balance between the interests of states and the need for a stable international marketplace by establishing what was to become known as "embedded liberalism."[12] States were to pledge themselves to liberal economic policies, retaining control over domestic economies but agreeing to participate in multinational agreements for collective coordination of the international political economy.

The result of the conference was the Bretton Woods System. It "was based upon three pillars: economic development, monetary stability, and trade."[13] The World Bank supported the first pillar, the International Monetary Fund the second, and an International Trade Organization (ITO) was to be formed to support the third.

In September of 1945, America sent a proposal to Great Britain based on a State Department publication entitled "Proposals for the Expansion of World Trade and Employment," closely following a 1937 secret memo written by Leo Pasvolsky of the Hull State Department group. It outlined three basics of American policy: (1) use tariffs as the major trade regulator (thus minimizing nontrade barriers), (2) lower tariff rates, (3) establish an unconditional most favored nation (MFN) principle.[14] Discussions to perfect this view continued in the bowels of the State Department from 1943 to 1945. A fourth principal was added to place a ban on most quantitative restrictions on imports.[15]

These discussions, transmitted especially to the United States' British partner, became the basis for negotiations for an international trade policy.[16] There were some compromises made for European countries to allow for some quantitative barriers to trade and for the United States to recognize its already healthy agriculture supports system. The United States also insisted on an escape clause "to permit countries to take temporary action to prevent sudden and widespread injury to the producers concerned."[17] Significant loopholes in the system, you will note, were envisioned from the very beginning. Still, the United States was committed to multilateral negotiation on freer trade. As early as 1945, the United States used its foreign aid resources as a means of gathering commitments to nondiscriminatory trade from Great Britain, Belgium, Czechoslovakia, France, Greece, the Netherlands, Poland, and Turkey.[18]

In 1946 the UN Economic and Social Council (ECOSOC) convened a conference in London to deal with the international trading order. The Smoot-Hawley Act was a still-potent motivator of this conference pushing most major trading states to reinvigorate trade in the postwar era on the foundation of free trade assumptions. Objections continued, of course, to the application of broad principles that might in any way negatively impact specific national interests. The necessity for loopholes to accommodate these interests was compelling. Most exceptions to general codes were aimed at protection of domestic industries and protecting the balance of payments in major European countries. Momentum was building for an international trade agreement, a broad one if not a perfect one. And the United States came to champion the creation of an International Trade Organization as the third pillar of institutionalized stability in the international political economy.

A charter for an ITO was drawn up at a Geneva conference in 1947 and presented at another UN sponsored conference (UN Conference on Trade and Employment) held in Havana in 1948. Building on the series of negotiations from 1943 to 1947, fifty-seven countries signed the charter and proceeded to submit it to their respective ratification processes. The U.S. negotiator, Will Clayton, had made several concessions to gain charter approval. He acceded to language that seemed to allow expropriation or nationalization of foreign property under "just" circumstances. He also compromised on the use of import quotas under certain circumstances and on voting rules within the ITO. The latter was remarkable given the American hegemonic position, for the United States agreed to a one-state, one-vote system for decision making in the ITO. Unlike its UN stance, it was willing to give up its veto powers. The assumption was that American power and general agreement on a consensual decision-making environment would not make this concession significant.[19]

On the whole, the charter gave the ITO "broad powers to regulate tariffs, quotas, labor standards, investments, monopolistic practices, and commodity prices."[20] Granted that language in some sections specifically defined several loopholes and an escape clause, this represented a significant transfer of power to a multinational organization. And exactly because of that it would be difficult to pass through the legislatures of major countries.

This was to prove especially true of the United States. Few thought that any ratification from Congress would come easily; there were too many controversial elements within the ITO charter. The question of giving up sovereignty to an organization run on principles of equality of input alone would be daunting in postwar America. Even free trade supporters like the National Foreign Trade Council opposed the ITO treaty. Besides, the Cold War was heating up, displacing attention toward military and political affairs. The State Department was losing credibility over the supposed "loss of China" to the communists. The Marshall Plan also gave the Americans the feeling that they had a right to demand a more independent role in international economic affairs since they were paying for it.

If the ITO was an American idea, so was the creation of an interim set of agreements to jump-start an immediate lowering of tariff barriers. This urge had been a general one among major traders, so specific negotiations to this end had begun at the 1947 Geneva meeting. In Havana, the delegates finalized an alternate document that was to serve as an interim agreement until the ITO came into being. In fact, this agreement was made even before the conclusion of the ITO negotiations and did not depend on the successful conclusion of the ITO treaty for implementation. This significant document was the GATT.

The GATT was to emerge as the fundamental document guiding international trade relations for most of the rest of the century. It was signed as a temporary measure on October 27, 1947, to go into effect on January 1, 1948. Such a measure could not become immediately operational if it were in treaty form, of course. This meant that the document had to be worded in such a way that it would not require the approval of the U.S. Congress. The mechanism for its legitimization for the United States was the Trade Agreements Act of 1934. This act, you will remember, allowed the president to unilaterally make agreements on the lowering of tariffs as long as they contained reciprocity for American goods.

The U.S. Senate could not muster the two-thirds vote to approve the ITO treaty, and since President Truman became increasingly involved with the war in Korea and could not expend the energy needed to get the treaty passed, the treaty was quietly withdrawn in 1950. The ITO was never to see the light of day again.

GATT PRINCIPLES

The core document of the GATT outlined principles and procedures but had no organizational framework. There was a small administrative bureaucracy, expanded and made permanent in 1951 and then augmented with a Council of Representatives in 1960, but neither had powers to enforce tariff and nontariff barrier commitments within the document. The only additional structural element dealt with the processes of decision making and governance by signatories themselves—which were incidentally called "contracting parties" instead of members because there was no formal organization of which to be a member. Only with the WTO treaty in 1995 did the GATT agreements become part of an international organization with formal membership.

The founders of GATT were interested in broad-based principles of fair and *freer trade* (not completely *free trade* since they institutionalized many exceptions to free trade). But they were also convinced, as Secretary Hull was, that the interdependence that came with integrated trade agreements reduced the risk of war. The preamble to the GATT spells out the central concerns. It says the founders "recogniz[e] that their relations in the field of trade and economic endeavor should be conducted with a view to raising standards of living, ensuring full employment and a large and steady growing volume of real income and effective demand, developing the full use of the resources of the world and expanding the production and exchange of goods."[21] Within these broad goals, specific tariff reduction and elimination of discriminatory treatment in trade were the immediate targets.

Two things emerged from the GATT agreement. First of all, the agreement spelled out a series of principles that were to guide the contracting partners. These were not legally bound within an organization; therefore they were designated "codes of conduct" or simply "codes." Second, the states signing the agreement (twenty-three in 1947–48) made a series of specific binding agreements to lower particular tariffs.

There are four driving core principles that are the foundation of the GATT agreement: (1) nondiscrimination or the most favored nation principle, (2) tariff reductions and binding, (3) national treatment, and (4) prohibition of protective measures other than tariffs (with exceptions).

MOST FAVORED NATION

Article I of the GATT provides for this basic concept. In trade arrangements, states make agreements with other states regarding the conditions under which they will trade specified goods with each other. This principle states that any agreement in which one contracting partner grants another country "more favorable treatment" (meaning they receive the best deal offered in that category) requires that state to immediately and unconditionally give the same treatment to imports from all signatories to the GATT. This is called nondiscrimination because GATT partners cannot sign agreements that favor nonsignatories over signatories or some signatories over others.

Note that what this principle does is broaden the access of goods to markets in a sweeping manner on the basis of bilateral negotiations. If the United States makes a deal with Russia that lowers the tariff on vodka, that tariff rate must be made available to all importers of vodka—Polish, Finnish, or whoever, if they belong to GATT. Since there are literally tens of thousands of goods traded in the international marketplace, it would be a nightmare to negotiate freer trade positions with each country on each product. Most favored nation treatment becomes the touchstone for lowering tariffs on huge numbers of goods by way of singular negotiations. Multilateral negotiations might also be involved with some products, but even then there is no need for universal participation by GATT signatories in order to allow each to benefit from the deal made.

This MFN, or nondiscrimination obligation, applies to all facets of trade, including customs duties, charges of various types and kinds that are connected to importing and exporting, as well as any internal policies affecting the valuation of an import or export. This includes any taxes or charges a state may wish to levy, as well as any licensing and regulatory policies.[22]

TARIFF REDUCTIONS AND BINDINGS

Fundamentally, this principle concerns transparency in national trade policies. Countries undertake commitments to openly state their maximum import duties or other regulations or barriers on specified types of goods. There are to be no hidden rules, practices, or agreements. Trade policies are to be reported to GATT and these reports distributed through GATT internationally.

These commitments, often referred to as "bindings," can come about from bilateral or multilateral negotiations where a country agrees to adjust its tariff policies or practices. Through MFN these agreements become applicable to all GATT signatories. You begin to see how GATT becomes a major conduit for the expansion of equitable and fair treatment of products across the international political economy.

Early in the GATT process, developing countries shied away from this code because they often did not have a schedule of bindings on any of their goods. The concept of reciprocity limited or prevented these countries' participation in GATT until they were given specific exceptions to this rule—thus the limited number of original signatories (twenty-three in Geneva/Havana). The Kennedy Round of negotiations in 1967 gave special status to developing countries so they would not have to follow all of the disciplines of GATT. As we will see, this became a problem when some of the previously developing countries, the NICs, became effective competitors to the major trading states in several sectors.

NATIONAL TREATMENT

This code compliments the MFN rule by extending the equality of treatment of imported goods to the domestic marketplace. Not only is there a guarantee of equality of treatment as goods come into the country, but the principle applies to what happens to the goods while in the distribution process internally. National treatment means you must treat foreign goods the same as domestic goods once they have crossed the frontier and satisfied the obligations accompanying entry into the domestic market. You cannot put taxes or regulations on imported Japanese cars that do not apply equally to American cars.

Clearly, the GATT principles prefer tariffs as the singular control mechanism of states to regulate international trade. Protection of the domestic industry or supplier should only be given at the frontier, not after the goods enter the domestic marketplace.

PROHIBITION OF NONTARIFF BARRIERS

This principle has proved to be a bit more problematic. The tariff code principles in Part 1 of the agreement are articulated, even though several exceptions are specified as well. Since tariffs are preferred as the protectionist mechanism, then other means should be barred. The GATT does try to eliminate steps other than tariffs in Part 2 of the agreement. For example, quantitative restriction on imports and exports are generally banned by Article XI of the agreements. Indeed, most of Part 2 of the agreement attempts to discourage such nontariff measures as custom regulations, import licensing, direct subsidies, and antidumping duties.[23]

But safeguard exceptions (claims by states of the need for special protections or *safeguards*) are included in the article to allow contracting partners to protect their economies. Thus, specific broad areas allowed for protection include the right to adopt measures to protect a country's ability to feed itself and measures used to shield industries in danger of collapse, to defend against dumping, or to attack balance-of-payments problems. The most frequently used of these loopholes has been the balance-of-payments clause, as its language is sufficiently vague to allow countries with trade imbalances to easily use it as an excuse for protectionist measures.

Besides the Article XI safeguards, the agreement recognizes exceptions for Britain's special arrangements with its former colonies as well as, importantly, an exception for trade agreements permitting common markets and free trade areas to act collectively toward the outside, while granting special relations within the pact. In the beginning, the United States accepted this latter arrangement because it wanted to encourage the formation of the European Coal and Steel Community as a means for postwar European recovery on a cooperative basis. As time went on, the exception expanded in recognition of the special conditions created by the formation of the European Community (which evolved into a singular trading area under its revised EU charter).

A couple of points must be made before we continue on to a description of the various rounds that expanded or redefined the GATT. Parts 1 and 3 of the GATT agreement were meant to be strictly adhered to by the contracting partners. States were to buy into these principles without reservations. Many elements of Part 2, however, provided a great deal of wiggle room within the subsequent Protocol of Provisional Application (PPA), the operational document for the GATT agreement. Part 2 asks signatories to implement "to the fullest extent not inconsistent with existing [national] legislation."[24] This became the ultimate loophole for states, particularly allowing them to avoid nontariff barrier discussions in the early rounds of GATT negotiations. With little in the way of enforcement capability, states could interpret on their own what "inconsistent" would mean in specific circumstances. The PPA had a "grandfather clause," for example, which allowed states that had contradictory laws already on the books to continue to apply them. You can see why early GATT success came mostly in the area of tariff reductions. Still, it is important to realize that these successes were dramatic.

TARIFF REDUCTION ROUNDS

The twenty-three states that signed the core protocol negotiated in Geneva and finalized in Havana pledged themselves to the codes of conduct described above. This was not the end of the negotiations, however. These states, essentially the industrialized OECD (Organization for Economic Cooperation and Development) members, were serious about tariff reductions and did not just want to establish some principles; they also wanted to negotiate substantive reductions on specific goods. The GATT turned out to be an extended and long agreement because it expanded on its base principles by inclusion of numerous bilateral and multilateral agreements between states to reduce tariffs on specific goods. The end result was a web of some two hundred amendments and additions to the GATT by states making specific tariff reductions on particular goods. States were not bound to participate in all or any of these side agreements, but the agreements became part of the GATT system. By this method, the Geneva Round brought concessions through item-by-item negotiations on some forty-five thousand tariff lines covering about half of world trade: "The GATT Accords, therefore, are a cluster of treaties, codes, side agreements, and understandings with varying members and coalitions of members participating in each."[25] It is fair to say that some of these might even be interpreted to contradict or be in conflict with the basic code.

Given the nature of the MFN provisions, this process significantly spread the lowered tariffs between contracting partner states. The results were dramatic in this first round; for example U.S. tariffs received an average reduction of 21.1 percent. Results were not so impressive from the following three rounds of negotiations, all of which concentrated on fine-tuning tariff relationships and lowering rates. These rounds were designed to admit new partners and to increase pressures for tariff reductions. All three rounds, Annecy (France) 1949; Torquay (UK) 1950–51; and Geneva 1955–56, were single sitting rounds.

In Annecy, six countries joined the GATT and entered into several of its side agreements. However, not much progress was made; average reductions were modest. The British Commonwealth as well as Western Europe simply refused to address many protectionist tariffs: "Economics took precedence over diplomatic strategy."[26] At Torquay, the British wanted a one-sided agreement to protect its empire, and this again kept significant across-the-board progress from occurring. Though reductions were minimal, three new countries joined, and 8,700 tariff concessions were made among partners, mostly in marginal products.

The second Geneva Round took place in the shadow of American bilateral concessions to encourage the emerging Japanese export economy. Though the Geneva GATT agreements added one country, its tariff reductions were modest for all. Average U.S. reductions were only 3.5 percent, but the United States had already made an unbalanced agreement with Japan that would eventually reverberate within domestic politics. The major trading states had reduced their weighted average tariffs to 15 percent by the mid-1950s, however. And they benefited greatly from the subsequent large increase in total international trade.[27] Trade grew faster than the average GNP; the figures for 1950–75 showed an average 8 percent increase in world trade as opposed to an average 4 percent increase in GNP—that trend was to continue into the 1990s. Yet some sectors of the U.S. economy were being hurt by cheap imports. Chief among these were large employers like textiles, steel, and automobiles.

During the last years of the Eisenhower administration, political pressures began to grow for protection of import-sensitive industries. Though Eisenhower himself seemed to be aware of this, the administration and its State Department continued to make Cold War politics the higher priority. Between the 1930s when the Reciprocal Trade Agreements Program gave the president great discretion in making tariff reductions and when Eisenhower left office, U.S. tariffs had been reduced by 80 percent.[28] Containment of communism as a priority policy had targeted the recovery of Western Europe, the integration of World War II enemies into the international economy, and the denial of technology to the Eastern Bloc. Trade's role was to be the vehicle for these political/strategic goals. Since international trade was only 4 percent of U.S. GNP, the U.S. government thought that the encouragement of imports was an easy way to help its friends without having to resort to extensive direct foreign aid.

The tariff reductions in the first four rounds of GATT negotiations came relatively easily. Nontariff barriers (NTB) were slowly growing throughout the world, however, and the United States' relative open-door policy began to chafe on American politics. The world was taking advantage of U.S. policies by raising NTBs while U.S. policymakers preferred in these early years to ignore the violations of NTB rules embedded in Part 2 of the GATT.

THE DILLON ROUND (1960–61)

The United States called for the Dillon Round (Dillon was under–secretary of state and originated the idea) as a means of dealing with the trade repercussions of the formation of the European Economic Community (EEC). Although the GATT allowed for regional organizations and exceptions for their united trade policies, the EEC was getting more aggressive in its external tariff policies. Furthermore, the planning for its highly subsidized Common Agriculture Policy (CAP) began to put American agricultural exports in some peril. Agriculture, an original GATT exception, raised its cumbersome head. And it proved to be too difficult a subject to be successfully dealt with.

Bilateral negotiations between the United States and the EEC were augmented by multilateral negotiations in the larger environment of this GATT round. There were thirty-nine countries in the GATT by now, and the Dillon meetings facilitated modest tariff reductions covering 4,400 goods. These were to be the last of the relatively easy areas of reductions. Further progress needed to attack products more central to national incomes.[29]

President Kennedy was eager to salvage the Dillon Round, so he agreed to waive limitations on a number of import-sensitive items and to let agriculture lie. Interests hit by this action such as steel, machine tools, firearms, and woven fabrics were furious. Trade Commission findings of concessions on specific goods noted that a legal peril point had been crossed. Congress established peril points as tripwire demarking points for American producers when trade threatened their industries. These findings were ignored. In addition, Kennedy had simply acquiesced to the new EEC discriminatory Common Agriculture Policies, angering even his own Agriculture Department.[30]

The State Department's policy favoring Cold War politics over trade convinced Kennedy to end the Dillon Round, leaving a stalemate with the EEC. Domestic U.S. interests were not pleased, nor were key members of Congress. Trade liberalization as the thrust of U.S. policy in the postwar era was increasingly coming under fire. Economic interests and Congress were tiring of U.S. concessions being met with nationalist policies from Europe and Japan while American Cold War perceptions and priorities continued to guide trade policies.

THE KENNEDY ROUND (1963–67)

The bill that authorized American participation in the Kennedy Round, the Trade Expansion Act, was passed in January 1962. The authorization to negotiate was for a five-year period. It envisioned a strategy to improve "free world" access to U.S. markets and to get access to Europe's agricultural market. The act gave the president the ability, for the first time, to slash duties *across the board*, rather than product by product, in conjunction with the other OECD countries. Flexibility and a residue of Cold War goals dominated thought behind the bill. Still, there were compromises. Congress demanded that all nontariff agreements required congressional approval.

Even more importantly, the bill took chief responsibility for trade negotiations away from the State Department and gave it to a newly created Special Trade Representative (STR). The president still had the final say, and the bill gave him broad powers in tariff areas, but trade now had an independent voice within the administration. U.S. negotiators for the first time had no other responsibilities in the area of foreign relations; trade could stand on its own within the administration in the struggles over policy. This round produced some significant tariff reductions, but its main importance was to come in redirecting the GATT negotiations toward non-tariff barriers and the accommodation of developing countries' special needs.

Item-by-item tariff reductions had proven to be increasingly burdensome as a means for tariff reductions. The OECD countries agreed to a strategy of an across-the-board formula of reductions, at least for industrial products. This change allowed negotiations that produced a tariff reduction of 36–39 percent on sixty thousand products. Duties were slashed on some 64 percent of dutiable goods, concentrating on those items in which Europe and the United States accounted for 80 percent of world production. The largest cuts, 80–93 percent, were in machinery and transportation equipment, while chemicals, iron, steel, and textiles saw lower reductions.

We need to point out that agriculture was left, as it had been from the beginning, to item-by-item negotiations, negotiations that proved to be limited in their success. Tropical products (coffee, tea, cocoa, bananas, and oil seeds) were but slightly touched by tariff reductions. Nontropical products did not do much better. Average agricultural tariff cuts were only 20 percent—with several exceptions. Special negotiating groups had been set up independently to deal with dairy products and with meat. The Kennedy Round itself could not penetrate these protected areas.[31]

Though the new President Lyndon Johnson was a devoted free trader, he became increasingly pressured to take more seriously the operationalization of reciprocity within the GATT agreements. The United States had given up too much for too little in return, it was argued. On top of this, increased opposition to further concessions came from not only Republicans in Congress but some Democrats as well. These concerns along with escalating quarrels with Europe contributed to the elongation of negotiations.

By 1967, congressional authorization was running out, domestic legislation dominated Johnson's priorities, and Vietnam was taking center stage. Europe was refusing compromise on agricultural access, and Japan was stonewalling on access to its markets. A decision had to be made on the Kennedy Round negotiations. Fearful of cascading protectionism, Johnson gave in and signed the agreement. The 1962 authorization gave the administration complete discretion in negotiating the round, but this was to be the last GATT negotiation that did not need to go before Congress for approval.

There were significant successes besides the tariff cuts. Nontariff barriers were opened for the first time to serious discussion; though not much progress was made, the cat was out of the bag. In one area, *antidumping* (the selling of goods below domestic or production costs, flooding a market with cheap goods), a specific code was negotiated. It pledged contracting partners to specific antidumping rules, though domestic political opposition in America, even to the point of congressional legislation, kept this code from being effective in the short run.

The question of what to do with the problems of developing countries was also raised at these negotiations. The explosion of new states as a result of the collapse of colonial empires brought renewed emphasis on these issues. Few of the problems were solved, but three articles were added to the GATT basic agreement in 1965, becoming Part 4. These allowed for special treatment and protectionist exceptions for developing countries. Fundamentally, Part 4 waived the rule of reciprocity in negotiations between less developed and developed states. This encouraged more states to join the GATT; the number reached forty-five during the Kennedy Round with an additional twenty-nine shortly thereafter. A subsequent 1971 General System of Preferences document was added to these agreements to help the poorer states.[32] It would take a couple of decades, however, before significant general tariff preferences would be given to developing countries by industrial countries. Only in 1974 did the United States establish even this possibility into its law.

"Developing countries" was not well defined in the new Part 4, and the agreement allowed for many unbalanced tariffs. It even permitted Newly Industrializing Countries (e.g., South Korea, Singapore, Brazil) to use NTBs, which they did successfully, to protect and support specific sectors of their economies. Subsequently they used these sectors to enter and compete in markets in Europe, North America, and eventually even Japan. Consequently, developed states began complaining that the NICs were unfairly using the vagueness of the GATT's wording and various developing country exceptions to unfairly compete against them.

Europe, Japan, and some developing countries came out of the round with some advantages. The United States was hurt in several areas, particularly in its inability to open markets to its agricultural sector and to stem the flow of imports that increasingly created balance-of-payments problems. Even though the average tariff for all products entering industrial nations was down from around 60 percent in the 1930s to 6.2 percent after the Kennedy Round, sectoral differences remained. For example, finished manufacturing goods were only down to 9.4 percent.[33] National differences remained as well; the United States had lowered its tariff on automobiles from 6.5 percent to 3 percent, while Canada, the EEC, and Japan all kept theirs at 10–15 percent.[34] These variations resulted in a backlash in the United States against trade liberalization.

In the 1968 U.S. presidential elections, both candidates pledged remedies for ailing industries, including an attack on nontariff barriers and the imposition of import limitations. The victor, Richard Nixon, was no friend of the GATT. The U.S. Trade Commission, moribund for years, began to recommend use of the GATT escape clauses to give relief to industries that brought complaints before it—and Nixon paid attention to these reports. Trade laws were enforced more under his administration than ever before. Congress had become more aggressive as well, willing to give Nixon more retaliatory authority in the growing trade conflicts with Europe and Japan.

THE TOKYO ROUND (1973–79)

To this point in time, "The Kennedy Round was the high point of the postwar movement toward trade liberalization."[35] By the early 1970s, however, unsettled long-term problems combined with new short-term unfair trade practices left GATT vulnerable. Patrick Low and others provided a long list of developments that had the tendency to weaken support for the GATT: The 1955 waiver the United States gained for its agriculture subsidies, thus the basis for removal of agriculture from GATT negotiations; sectoral protectionism, for example the development of the 1973 Multifibres Arrangement; extra legal import charges increasingly used by the United States and Europe; EEC exceptions being accepted without challenge; special colonial/post-colonial state relations with European powers; creation of free trade areas to avoid GATT disciplines; increased bilateral "voluntary" quota agreements; Nixon's use of protectionist retaliatory measures.[36] The Multifibre Arrangement proscribing textile flows was particularly damaging because of textiles' centrality to many states' trade and because it set a precedent for cartel-like agreements in areas like steel, shipbuilding, and automobiles. Patrick Low would add to this list the intriguing observation that the success of GATT in lowering tariffs had encouraged countries to search out evasive nontariff barriers to exploit.[37]

When, in February 1972, the European Community (EC) publicly declared an interest in a new round of multinational trade negotiations, the United States and Japan agreed. A call went out to join a GATT Ministerial Conference in Tokyo in 1973 that attracted the bulk of the world's trading countries. The negotiations were to cover tariffs, nontariff barriers (with specific attention to the safeguard system) in manufacturing and in agriculture, tropical products, and codes for preferential treatment for developing countries. This round of negotiations was to be a substantial one, at a minimum, dealing with trade problems in a more sweeping manner by use of the more efficient across-the-board approach. In the end, ninety-nine countries representing nine-tenths of the world's trade participated.[38]

The Tokyo Declaration, the formal call for the round, envisioned final agreements by 1975, but negotiations were slow to get started, delayed along the way, and complex. Consequently the round of negotiations lasted until 1979. Once again, as with most postwar trade negotiations, the key to decision making during this round centered around the virtually bilateral relations between the EC and the United States. Japan, the third major trading power, was relatively passive. The nine members of the EC had a difficult time developing a unified negotiating position. The entry of the United Kingdom (UK) into the EC (1972) and France's resistance to further concessions within EU decision making complicated the process. It took until February of 1975 before an agreed-upon directive could be approved to guide the EC negotiators.

Also, "developing country strategy became more concerted and strident in the Tokyo Round."[39] Newly Industrialized Countries (NICs) had increased their impact on international trade, and the United Nations Conference on Trade and Development (UNCTD), created in 1964, gave a united, though external, political voice to developing states in the GATT. The Tokyo Round would find developing countries' efforts concentrated on gaining promised trade concessions from the rich states.

The process of gaining authorization to negotiate further trade agreements was not easy in the United States either. Antiliberalization forces continued to gain strength, and the Nixon administration had plunged the political system into chaos over the series of difficulties called the Watergate scandals.

The political weakness of the presidency left room for Congress to put significant restrictions on the Tokyo Round negotiations. Congress was not about to make the mistake it had made when it gave carte blanche to the president in negotiating the Kennedy Round. This time there would be assurances that Congress, and indeed many sectors of the U.S. political economy, could play an active role in the negotiation process.[40]

Nixon's initial 1973 authorization proposal to Congress asked for broad authority to negotiate tariff reductions, which had become a traditional part of the GATT process. Congress had little problem with this. It was in the arena of nontariff barriers that Congress, especially the Senate, was cautious. The Senate did not want to give to the executive what it perceived to be its constitutional responsibilities over foreign trade legislation. In turn, the Republican administration wanted to guarantee foreign powers that they could negotiate in good faith without finding domestic opposition at the end of the process. Compromise was necessary.

A complex consultation system was established to keep Congress and major trade constituencies informed throughout the negotiations. Members of Congress joined negotiation delegations, and key committees were periodically briefed. Private sector committees, twenty-seven in total covering a variety of industry sectors, were created under an umbrella organization called the Advisory Committee for Trade and Policy Negotiations. It was to give an advisory opinion on the final product of the negotiations.[41] Consultation was to be extensive, if cumbersome.

Of great importance for the credibility of U.S. negotiators, given this domestic scrutiny, was the addition of the so-called *fast-track authority* to the compromise. Congress would be informed ninety working days before final agreements were signed, leading to specific committee consultations. After the final agreements were formally presented to Congress, it would have sixty days to vote on the agreement package. There were to be no amendments; Congress (both houses needed for nontariff portions) votes yes or no, up or down on one vote (greater detail of fast-track authority can be found in the next chapter in the discussion of the Uruguay Round ratification process).[42]

The pragmatic effect of this arrangement was that agreements had to be made no later than March 1979 if the authorization deadline of January 5, 1980, was to be met. The Special Trade Representative, placed in the President's Cabinet by the 1974 Authorization Act, set a timetable for concluding basic agreements by early 1978. Similar rules were in effect for the later Uruguay Round as well. One scholar has argued that the extensive consultation and openness was the reason for the relatively easy success of both the Tokyo and the Uruguay Rounds within Congress.[43]

Congress finally passed the authorizing Trade Act of 1974, and President Ford signed it in January 1975. Since 1973, the administration had been negotiating without authorization. Obviously, the 1975 date envisioned in Tokyo was unrealistic from the start. To complicate the round's timetable further, the United States was in the throes of pre-election politics. This led to delays until a new administration took power in 1977. Worldwide concern about these delays led to the "Downing Street Declaration," where major trading states (OECD particularly) met to discuss the delays, pledged to uphold liberalization principles, and reaffirmed the need for the Tokyo Round.

In the interim, the GATT secretariat maintained movement within the round by establishing a series of committees to deal with its issues. Seven groups were set up: (1) tariffs, (2) nontariff matters (with subgroups to cover the many code areas under consideration), (3) agriculture, (4) safeguards, (5) the "sector approach" (toward elimination of all barriers in specific sectors), (6) tropical products, and (7) special and differential treatment for developing countries.[44] These laid the groundwork for negotiation toward a final agreement.

TOKYO ROUND RESULTS

The results of the Tokyo Round were impressive given the hits taken by the international economy during the 1970s. The oil crisis of 1974 brought recession to major countries. Accompanying this was a period of high inflation and unemployment in the United States and Europe. Exacerbating these trends for many was the decade-long surge in Japanese exports. The condition of the international political economy brought protectionist pressures to all the major trading states, especially the EC and the United States. One scholar of the period concluded that "free trade ideals were left behind, victims of domestic regulatory practices, the influence of protectionism, and, above all the Cold War. . . . [while] at the level of tariff bargaining, Americans usually gave more than they received. At the level of defending cherished principles and goals, they were forced into wholesale retreat."[45]

Perhaps because of rather than in spite of this, agreement on *tariff reductions* was reached early in 1977. Both the EC and the United States were pledged to further the across-the-board method of tariff reductions (with a list of exceptions, of course) as a means of furthering the long-term trends toward minimal tariffs. They quarreled over the formula for reductions, however.

The EC wanted what it called a harmonizing formula, one that would provide for larger percentage cuts in those tariffs that were highest. The United States opposed this, fearing the formula would harm some of its industries. Besides, the United States worked out the formula in simulation and found that EC tariff reductions would be less under the formula than those for the United States. The United States counter-offered an across-the-board 60 percent reduction in tariffs.[46]

The EC still liked a harmonized formula. In the end, the Swiss provided the compromise, a weighted formula. It was a bit complex, and it had no foundation in economics, but it sold to the two giants because the bottom-line cuts averaged 40 percent (before exceptions), which fit the targets for both.

After the formula was applied, the average overall rate for nine industrial states was 34 percent of pre-Tokyo rates, creating an average tariff of 4.7 percent. U.S. tariffs were cut 31 percent to an overall average of 6.4 percent.[47] The across-the-board compromise not only included the formula, but the ability for product-by-product deals between individual countries that would, under the MFN concept, make these agreements in effect multinational. In the end, a few agriculture agreements added to the industrial products created reductions for twenty-seven thousand tariff lines covering 75 percent of industrial country duty-bound lines. Once more, significant progress had been made in the straight tariff reduction area.

As expected, nontariff barrier issues were not solved so easily. The final agreement provided sections that dealt with three nontariff areas:

1. establishment of six codes
   —four of a technical nature
   —two of a broad/major nature
2. four "framework" agreements for developing countries
3. separate economic sector agreements
   —dairy
   —bovine
   —civil aircraft

The four *technical codes* covered the areas of customs valuation, import licensing, technical barriers to trade, and antidumping. Administrative practices had restricted trade by the use of *customs valuation* and *import licensing*. Although used extensively by developing countries, these techniques were not foreign to major trading countries; for example, Congress kept alive the manipulative American Selling Price (ASP), one of nine methods of valuing goods coming into the country that had been ostensibly killed in the Kennedy Round. Under pressure from the chemical industry, Congress refused to let it go. The Tokyo agreements set a code that established five valid methods, one primary and the other four secondary, to be used in descending order. The primary method was to use the transaction value (actual price plus importation costs) for the valuation. Only special circumstances should spark use of the others. Though complex, this agreement tended to limit manipulation in this area.

The code on *licensing procedures* spelled out the necessity for neutrality in application of licensing rules and equality in administration of those rules. Because of the fast-track process, Congress had to accept these two codes as part of the "package" of the Tokyo Round agreements.

The code on *technical barriers to trade* was an attempt to assure nondiscrimination and granting of national treatment with respect to standards, technical regulations, testing methods, and certification systems.[48] Product standards in regards to health, safety, environmental protection, packaging, and labeling had increasingly become means of limiting imports. This code argued for international standards to be adopted to eliminate these problems, though it did not articulate specific ones. It did approve procedures for notification of national standards and transparency in processes in order to allow for international input into domestic decisions. Governments were to advise importers, especially developing countries, on how to meet requirements. National governments were to discourage subnational units from setting restrictions as well. These problems did not go away, however, as illustrated by state and local laws in the United States and EC members setting their own standards.

The revised *antidumping* code differed from the Kennedy Round agreement in the technical, though controversial, area of how states determine injury from import dumping. The code required proof of injury to a domestic producer by means of evidence on volume of the imports plus the effect on prices. If injury was found, the code said that settlement should be equal to the injury and no more. A dispute settlement mechanism was placed within the agreement. We explain this process later in the chapter.

The two *broad/major codes* dealt with government procurement and subsidies and countervailing duties. The *government procurement* issue is the only one of these codes that was excluded from the original GATT agreements on nondiscrimination (Article III). The Tokyo code established for this touchy issue was two-fold: first, a general set of universal principles was agreed to, and then the code allowed for negotiations between countries on the actual application of the principles. The general principles pledged countries to nondiscrimination against foreign suppliers in government procurement and to transparency in the processes of procurement: "It contained detailed rules relating to such matters as describing the technical specifications for a product, publishing notices on bidding opportunities, qualifying as a possible supplier, determining the time allocated for submitting bids, awarding contracts, furnishing knowledge about bids and reviewing complaints."[49]

Besides agreeing to the principles, each signatory would provide a list of specific items they were willing to include under the rules. In this way, negotiations would set the actual availability of sales to foreign entities. These lists were provided in the annexes to the code agreement, as were purchasing entities of participants. This code was a major breakthrough for access to government purchasing by foreign firms.

Since EC countries and developing countries tended to have larger government pen-etration in their economies, the United States was pleased with this code as it prom-ised the potential for opening more markets for its firms.

The area of *subsidies and countervailing duties* provided a much more complex problem since the major negotiators for both the EC and the United States had dif-ferent concepts as to what was or was not a reasonable subsidy. The basic GATT agreement already permitted subsidies to domestic producers if they did not produce "serious prejudice to the interests of any contracting partner" (Article XXIII).[50] However, under U.S. pressure, tighter rules were created governing direct subsidies, but the exception areas remained large. In particular, agriculture remained an excep-tion as it had been since 1947 when the United States demanded that it be placed outside of GATT rules.

The area of indirect subsidies, such as tax breaks for exports or price supports, was another story altogether. Neither the EC nor the United States was willing to agree on how much detail should be included as to what a reasonable subsidy was and what was not. The wording of the agreement left room for interpretation. In one area, though, it was clear. In order to get rid of a U.S. law that brought automatic countervailing duties (retaliatory tariffs) when foreign subsidies were claimed, the Tokyo agreement outlined strict rules for issuing them. Fundamentally, the rule said that "material injury" had to be proved before the duties could be imposed.

Agriculture was the primary area of concern for the United States in its relations with the EC. The United States pushed hard for specific limitations on subsidies from the EC under its Common Agriculture Policy. In the end, the subsidy section was so vague that the Subcommittee on International Trade of the U.S. Senate Finance Committee concluded, "The code does not contain specific criteria with which to measure subsidies and determine when they are excessive."[51]

While enforcement difficulties would continue, the agreement did set more spe-cific settlement procedures than were extant in GATT for subsidy claims and coun-terbalancing duties. Indeed, the same basic formula was used for dispute settlement of all the codes within the Tokyo Round. The process said that first, conflicting par-ties were to hold bilateral consultations over the problem. If they could not work out their differences, a committee was to be formed of the code's signatories. (Note that not all GATT signatories signed all of the new codes under the Tokyo Round nego-tiations.) An expert panel would hear the case and report to the committee. The committee (in effect a committee of the whole) could then make recommendations to the parties involved or even approve countermeasures if violations were found and there were material injuries proven. Since the vote was to be on a consensus (thus unanimous) basis, it became a political problem as to whether or not the GATT could enforce its code.

Encouragingly, one scholar discovered that up to 1984, of the 159 disputes brought formally before the GATT (before and after the Tokyo Round), in only 8 did the disputants refuse to comply with the panel recommendations.[52] These numbers show an overall success of the dispute settlement system, though unanimity did allow some very high profile cases to go unsettled. Many disputes never reached the formal complaint stage because of the problematic nature of the GATT enforcement procedures; others were solved politically early in the conflict process. The ambiguity of this point led to the need for reform in the Uruguay Round.

The four *"framework" agreements* were designed specifically to aid in the incorporation of developing countries into the GATT disciplines. This agreement, separated out for a separate "framework" of negotiation, provided a contractual basis for favorable treatment of developing countries, especially by developed countries. Called the Enabling Clause, this portion of the agreement gave a permanent legal foundation to granting of tariff preferences under the Generalized System of Preferences. Special provisions for developing countries gave them permission to make arrangements that were not based on reciprocity with either developing countries or industrial countries. These arrangements were all to be voluntary. The GATT accepted these and other special conditions in exchange for pledges from developing country partners to become more active in the GATT. It proved difficult for developing countries to find substantive concessions, however, and it was another decade before developing countries would become aggressive in their GATT, by then WTO, participation.

The other three framework agreements covered (1) rules on use of trade restrictions to compensate for balance-of-payment problems, (2) exceptions for protection of infant industries in developing countries, and (3) sections on rules to expedite dispute settlement and for transparency within the trading system. The cumulative effect of these provisions was the opportunity for developing countries to foster and maintain economic stability and growth outside usual GATT rules.

Developing countries were still not satisfied with the outcome of the Tokyo Round. Too many of their key products were not covered by the general agreements. Agriculture, textiles, and basic minerals all had special regimes that discriminated against developing countries or made it impossible for them to compete equitably. Developing countries had to continually argue for preferential treatment and more programs of economic and investment aid on the part of the world's major traders.

This leaves us with the round's attempts to deal with *special sector* side agreements. The sectors addressed seriously were dairy products and bovine meat. The only progress made was to set up consultation and exchange of information procedures among dairy councils and bovine councils. There were some protocols established in an attempt to set minimum export prices on select dairy products, but they proved ineffective. When the general topic of agriculture arose, the United States, Australia, and New Zealand tried to push for substantive agreements but got only a generalized statement that came in the form of a recommendation to contracting parties "to further develop active co-operation in the agricultural sector within an appropriate consultative framework."[53]

The only successful sectoral negotiation was a side agreement between the United States, the EC, Japan, Sweden, and Canada on the complete elimination of tariffs on aircraft and component parts by the beginning of 1980. The implications of the agreement were that countries should not use any inducements to have their governments buy only from domestic firms. Also, national setting of separate standards was limited in the agreement to eliminate this nontariff mechanism.[54] To oversee the agreement, a committee on trade in civil aircraft was established. It was, all in all, a successful freeing of trade within this sector.

The major unfinished business of the Tokyo Round concerned the provisions for *safeguards* in Article XIX of the GATT that allowed for emergency protection if an import seriously threatened a domestic industry. This concerned the concept of nondiscrimination, or most favored nation; that is, imports in the same category must be treated the same. The EC pushed hard with U.S. neutrality to indicate in the code that rather than getting emergency protection from all country imports, specific countries could be targeted. This allowed a targeting of protection from a specific unfair source. Developing countries saw this as a threat and lobbied long and hard against it. In the end, no new code on safeguards emerged from the round.

The Tokyo Round ended with some agreements that were viable, others that looked good but did not change behavior significantly, and some that were not successfully addressed at all. Ample room remained for dissatisfaction with the state of multinational agreements represented by the GATT. Most of the codes targeted the OECD countries and left the developing countries dissatisfied and still outside the mainstream of the GATT. International circumstances continued to challenge the rule of law concepts of the GATT, plus the problems of nontariff barriers and developing country equity had grown to the point of muddying the waters of international free trade.

CONCLUSIONS

Step by step, the GATT process produced significant reductions in tariffs across increasing sectors of the international economy. Early negotiation rounds were very successful in this respect. However, the explosion of membership brought the need to deal with economies that were unable to compete effectively under a liberalizing trade regime. Free trade was not always fair trade.

In addition, as tariff barriers fell, states found ways to placate their domestic producers who found foreign competition daunting. Their response was a bevy of often creative nontariff barriers. While the Tokyo Round began to attack the problems, increased complexities left large holes in the GATT system exploited by these nontariff actions. Lastly, the growth of international trade as a percent of major state economies thrust into the mix new areas of concern—service industries for example. The need for further and more complex negotiations toward a more mature system became increasingly obvious.

CHAPTER 3

THE URUGUAY ROUND AND THE CREATION OF THE WTO

The WTO was born in January 1995. This milestone in the contemporary international political economy was the result of the long and winding road, the Uruguay Round, that lasted almost twelve years. Officially, the Uruguay Round began in 1986 and was scheduled to be completed in 1990. However, conflicts between the United States and EU as well as others led to the round being extended almost an additional four years. Many times the round was on the brink of failure. In the end, all parties had devoted so much time, effort, and political capital to the negotiations that failure may well have spelled the end not just to the extension and reform of the GATT, but perhaps even to the GATT itself. Success came not so much with a cheer as with a sigh of relief. A milestone had been reached by the end of the Uruguay Round, but all parties were to bear the scars of the process.

The Uruguay Round created a new system for international trade. It expanded dramatically the coverage of the GATT, especially in the areas of services, intellectual property, and domestic policies of states affecting investment and agriculture. More importantly, it created for the first time a formal organization, the WTO, to help oversee and administer the GATT system. As part of this, the WTO was given the power to settle disputes between parties to the agreement. Many have said that these changes were the beginning of a truly integrated world economy with the WTO as its linchpin.

Interestingly, as the round began, creating a world trade organization was not one of the participants' goals. It was almost an afterthought. A formal organization for the GATT was proposed only late in the round, briefly disputed, and then accepted. It was not until after the round was over that the significance of the WTO was recognized by GATT members.

In order to understand the WTO, we must first understand where it came from, and this requires us to examine the Uruguay Round. That is the focus of this chapter. The following chapter will examine in more detail the structural aspects of the WTO—its functions, organization, and role in administering the GATT. We begin with the context surrounding the beginning of the Uruguay Round, then move on to an examination of the positions of major countries or blocks of countries on issues within the round. We then examine the negotiation process leading to the creation of the round and within the round itself. And finally, we examine ratification of the Uruguay Round by the United States since its failure to ratify would have scuttled the agreement.

Before moving to an examination of the round, we need to keep in mind several of the overall concepts and themes laid out in Chapter 1 of this book. Free trade is seen by liberals, as well as most economists, as beneficial to all those participating in it. Free trade allows the law of comparative advantage to operate, leading to specialization among countries and greater efficiency in production. The postulated result is higher growth rates and better standards of living for all. This would seem to imply that free trade agreements create no losers and are thus politically easy to make and negotiate. If all countries win from liberal agreements, then there should be little opposition to them, right?

Wrong. We must also remember that the world is divided into states. Each of these states has a desire to survive and protect its interests. Free trade is often an obstacle to achieving these desires because the benefits of free trade are not always shared evenly. In trade, some states will win more than others. This can create or exacerbate imbalances of power between states, leading some states to perceive risks to their interests and security. Because of this, states have a natural tendency to pursue, to one degree or another, mercantilist strategies. A state will seek to insure that any gains from free trade benefiting another state will be offset by larger or similar gains for itself.[1]

In the GATT, this can be seen in the norm of reciprocity. At its simplest, the norm leads to the expectation that a state is expected to equally exchange trade concessions for the trade concessions gained from others. For example, if the United States lowers a trade barrier for Japan (allowing X value of goods to flow into the United States), Japan is expected to lower a barrier to one of the United States' products, allowing a similar value of goods into Japan. In reality, the norm is more complex, but states expect overall to receive about as much as they give to others in the form of concessions.

Not only must states worry about their interests in relation to other states; they must also worry about domestic interests. Freer trade is not painless. The law of comparative advantage works by eliminating noncompetitive industries within a country so that the resources used for those industries can be transferred to other industries that are more efficient and competitive. In the long run, more jobs and new industries are supposed to be created by this adjustment. In the short run, people are thrown out of work, and industries die. The people in these threatened industries and the industries themselves can be expected to resist free trade, and they do. For a state to successfully overcome this pressure it must be able to show that for each loss sustained, it has obtained a benefit. Here we see the value of reciprocity. Each state can turn to its citizens and say, here is what I obtained for you. In this way, domestic support can be built to overcome the resistance of those who will lose from free trade.[2]

Reciprocity may facilitate the making of free trade agreements, but paradoxically it can also make it more difficult to negotiate them.[3] This is especially true as the number of participants in multinational negotiations increases. In the Uruguay Round, more than one hundred countries were involved. Attempting to provide assurances of universal reciprocity in such a context becomes almost impossible.

The GATT's second major norm, nondiscrimination, only compounds the problem.[4] This norm requires all members of the GATT to treat all other members equally—most favored nation (MFN) treatment. If two members lower barriers to each other, they must lower them equally to all other GATT members as well. Nondiscrimination makes it possible for countries to free ride on the trade concessions of others. Instead of reciprocating with lower trade barriers, a country merely waits for other GATT members to lower their barriers to each other, knowing that when they do so, they must lower them for it as well. In the Uruguay Round, many countries waited until the bitter end to make any trade concessions in order to protect themselves from the free riding of others.

States, in seeking solutions to collective problems, may also create multilateral institutions or organizations. However, each state will seek to fashion the international organization or institution in a way that reflects its own interests.[5] The competition between states may lead to the creation of institutions and organizations that are not able to act or function well. Diverse interests also may make compromise difficult, if not impossible. In the sections that follow, we will see these conflicts play out through the Uruguay Round.

Lastly, it must be remembered that creating an open and competitive trade arena does not make all trading states equal. The ability to access the arena and to compete within it is affected by a variety of resources, and the wealthier states seem to have more of these resources than the poorer states. These differences lead to opposition to free trade agreements, as we saw in our discussion of the Tokyo Round. National and nongovernmental entities have also increasingly challenged the foundation principles of the GATT because of these perceived inequities.

THE CONTEXT OF THE ROUND

The 1970s and early 1980s were times of economic difficulty for many developed and developing countries. The first oil shock in the 1970s led to several problems— the worst of these being stagflation. This was a combination of low growth, high inflation, and high unemployment within developed countries—the United States, Canada, Western European countries, New Zealand, and Australia. Stagflation persisted throughout the 1970s and into the 1980s for most of these countries. The second oil shock in 1979 and 1980 worsened an already vexing problem as most developed countries also began running large trade deficits due to their dependence on foreign oil.[6]

In 1979 the U.S. Federal Reserve Board reacted to these economic problems by raising interest rates significantly. When interest rates rise, demand for products generally falls, leading to less pressure on prices, thus easing inflation. The Federal Reserve Board's actions initially had little effect. Inflation continued to rise in the

United States throughout 1979 and reached a high of 16.8 percent in January 1980. In reaction, the Federal Reserve Board continued to raise interest rates throughout 1980 and 1981. In January 1981, the federal funds rate reached a high of 19.1 percent. Interest rates for things like car loans, mortgages, and so on were often ten to twelve points higher than the federal funds rate.[7]

High interest rates eventually resulted in the deepest economic recession for the United States since the Great Depression. U.S. Gross Domestic Product (GDP) in 1980 shrank 0.2 percent, grew by 1.9 percent in 1981, and shrank 2.5 percent in 1982. Unemployment went from 5.9 percent in 1979 to 9.7 percent in 1982.[8] The decline in output and significant increase in unemployment eventually had the effect that the Federal Reserve Board wanted: inflation began to be tamed in the U.S. economy. The deep recession in the United States led to a significant reduction in imports into the United States. Making bad conditions even worse, these actions plunged the world into a recession and led to a debt crisis among the developing countries that further reduced worldwide demand for products.

Banks in the developed countries had accrued large cash surpluses throughout the 1970s as oil-producing states sought places to deposit their newfound wealth. The banks took these "petro dollars" and loaned them to developing countries at high rates of interest. Repayment of these loans was dependent on exports. As the world slipped into recession, developing country exports declined, making repayment difficult, if not impossible, leading developing countries to threaten to default on their loans. A mass default by developing countries could have led to the failure of many large U.S., European, and Japanese banks. This could have rippled outward eventually crippling the domestic economies of developed states and the international economy as well. The global economy seemed on the brink of a catastrophe.[9]

Not surprisingly, these troubles stressed the system of trade created by the GATT. GATT members began feeling increased domestic pressure to close or protect their markets as it became difficult to politically justify allowing unrestricted imports when jobs were disappearing at home. However, GATT members were forbidden from using the easiest form of market protection—tariffs. As part of GATT membership, the developed countries had bound (limited) their tariff rates. Raising these rates would seriously violate the treaty and open the country to retaliation from other GATT members.

Instead of raising tariffs, GATT members found other ways to protect their markets—ways that were not prohibited by the GATT or that fell within gray areas covered by the GATT. These methods were mostly nontariff trade barriers (NTBs).[10] Many countries, for example, forced trade partners to "voluntarily" restrain their exports or face some form of economic retaliation. The United States used these "voluntary restraints" extensively, especially in the areas of steel and automobiles. Other countries relied on things like border inspections or health and safety regulations to delay imports or stop them completely. The use of these measures had gradually emerged since the Kennedy Round and tended to undermine the GATT and the international trade system. These measures, coupled with the worldwide recession, led to a decrease in world trade between 1979 and 1982. The volume of world exports grew 5.2 percent in 1979, 2.9 percent in 1980, and shrank 0.6 percent in 1981 and 2.2 percent in 1982.[11]

The use of NTBs to protect markets also led to more disputes between GATT members, putting stress on the GATT dispute resolution process and leaving many to argue that the process was endangered. The GATT dispute resolution process required consensus. Thus, a single country, including the country found in violation of the GATT, could block action by refusing to accept the dispute settlement. This resulted in many complaints about unfair trade practices but little punishment to those using them, especially to the major states. As a result, many countries began questioning why they should be a part of the GATT in the first place.[12] What is the point of participating in an agreement if no one has to abide by it?

Agriculture also became a serious trade problem in the late 1970s and early 1980s. EC policies were a major cause of this problem. The EC developed a Common Agriculture Policy (CAP) in the early 1960s. As part of this policy, the EC began subsidizing the production of grains. By 1980 these subsidies turned the EC from a net importer of grain to an exporter. In 1974 the EC imported 12.3 metric tons of grain more than it exported; by 1980 the EC was exporting 3.8 metric tons more grain than it imported, and this grew to 19.6 metric tons by 1984. EC policy led to a huge surplus of grain in the world market, causing prices by the mid-1980s to collapse.[13]

Other grain-exporting states felt compelled to help their farmers by creating similar policies to those of the EC. In some respects, a grain subsidy arms race ensued. One country would increase its subsidies to make it easier to export, and competing countries reacted by increasing their subsidies. Failure to do so would have led to the loss of export markets. By 1986 it was estimated that 40 percent of the subsidies given to grain producers in the United States was done so merely to offset the effect of grain subsidies by other countries, and that the total cost of subsidies to the EC, Japan, and the United States (the three countries that relied most heavily on them) was $102.9 billion, $54.1 billion, and $88.1 billion respectively.[14] All major grain-exporting countries saw increases in the levels of support given to farmers during this period. Agriculture was seen as veering out of control. For many countries, agricultural policies were becoming budget busters, and something needed to be done.

INTERESTS OF MAJOR PARTICIPANTS

Having examined the context leading up to the call for the Uruguay Round, it is time to explore the interests of the major actors or groups of actors involved in it.

THE UNITED STATES

The United States was the lead country in pushing for a new round of negotiations. By the early 1980s, the United States had lost much of the postwar comparative advantage it had held in major industrial goods like steel, automobiles, and electronics.[15] Japan in particular became a competitor in these sectors, first penetrating U.S. markets, then dominating them, and in some cases pushing U.S. firms out of them. The open market policies of the United States had by the mid-1980s caused the country to move from the world's largest creditor to the world's largest debtor. The United States began experiencing record trade deficits as imports flowed in at a far faster rate than its exports flowed out. Graph 3.1 shows the U.S. Merchandise Account Balance from 1970 to 1986. As one can see, 1975 was the last year that U.S. exports exceeded imports. By 1986 imports exceeded exports to the tune of $131.9 billion.

This change in economic fortunes motivated the United States to push for expansion of the GATT into economic sectors where it remained strong. The first of these

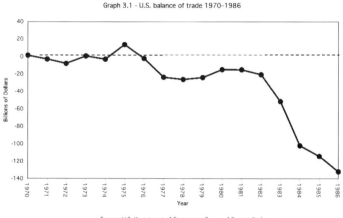

Graph 3.1 - U.S. balance of trade 1970–1986

Source: U.S. Department of Commerce: Survey of Current Business
- NIPA Tables (1929-1999)

Graph 3.2 - U.S. balance of services trade 1970–1990

Source: U.S. Department of Commerce: Survey of Current Business - NIPA Tables (1929-1999)

was in the area of services. U.S. service exports increased from twelve billion dollars in 1970 to eighty-three billion dollars in 1985. Service exports also exceeded service imports throughout this period. Graph 3.2 shows that the U.S. balance of trade in services increased dramatically between 1970 and 1990. Beginning in 1974, the United States ran a surplus in services trade, and generally this surplus grew during the period. Many countries prohibited or heavily restricted foreign firms from providing services within their borders. The United States hoped to open these markets for its firms and believed that once opened, its firms would have a competitive advantage.[16]

Not only did the United States want to open international markets in services, it also believed that the GATT needed new and stronger protections for intellectual property.[17] U.S. multinational corporations had developed long lists of trademarks, patents, and copyrights. Keeping rivals from stealing these items was essential for U.S. firms to remain competitive, since it was believed that some countries, particularly the Newly Industrializing Countries (NICs) like South Korea, had caught up with the United States by stealing U.S. technology and ideas. Expanding the GATT into the area of intellectual property would prevent countries from stealing U.S. technology in the future and allow U.S. firms holding intellectual property to force those wanting access to it to pay license fees or royalties which would then flow back to the United States in the form of higher corporate profits.

A third interest was expansion of the GATT into the area of investment policies.[18] Many countries placed restrictions on the investments of foreign firms within their borders. These regulations consisted of things like requiring firms to reinvest profits from the investment within the host country, requiring the use of some local content, or requiring that a certain percentage of the investment's products be exported out of the host country. The United States believed that these regulations hurt U.S. Multinational Corporations (MNCs), and it wanted rules added to the GATT that would control and limit what member countries could demand.

A fourth interest was to force the Newly Industrializing Countries (NICs), South Korea, Singapore, and Taiwan, for example, to pull more of their weight within the GATT. Now that the NICs were becoming as rich as the United States, EC, Canada, and so on, they should open their markets to the developed world and stop abusing exceptions placed in the GATT to help poor countries develop in order to gain unfair trade advantages. The United States wanted to create new rules that would more strictly define which countries could use the various exceptions for development.

Finally, agriculture was a key issue for the United States. U.S. farm subsidies reached record levels by the mid-1980s. It is estimated that the total costs were eighty-eight billion dollars in 1986.[19] At the time, the United States was running record budget deficits and was in the midst of a spending spree that added four trillion dollars to the national debt between 1980 and 1992. Many in both Congress and the president's administration saw cutting farm programs as a means for balancing the budget. In order for the United States to reduce farm subsidies, it had to force others to reduce their subsidies as well. Otherwise, American farmers would find themselves underpriced in the international agricultural marketplace, and while farmers made up a very small fraction of the U.S. economy, they were well organized politically.

The GATT allowed a variety of policies and practices in the agriculture sector that were not allowed in the manufacturing sector. The United States hoped to close these loopholes in the round. In particular, the United States hoped to force either an international freeze on export subsidies or ban them entirely. It also hoped to reduce the use by members of import quotas and health and safety regulations to exclude some agricultural products from their markets. Finally, the United States wanted to force countries to phase out subsidies for agricultural production because of the vicious circle they created. Subsidies encourage overproduction that leads to decreasing prices, which requires a larger subsidy.[20] The United States believed its farmers had a comparative advantage in agricultural production. A world with no barriers to agricultural trade, including no subsidies, would be a world in which American farmers would out compete foreign rivals. Thus, the United States entered the Uruguay Round with a "zero-option" package that called for the complete freeing of agricultural markets within a short amount of time—less than ten years.

THE EUROPEAN COMMUNITY

The EC shared with the United States a desire to expand the GATT into the area of services. Several countries within the EC rivaled the United States in services exports—particularly financial services, insurance, and banking. By lowering trade barriers to services, these countries would be able to increase substantially their exports of services, helping not only themselves but the EC as a whole.[21] The EC also agreed with the United States that intellectual property needed more protection within the GATT. Like the United States, the EC had many large multinational firms with huge stakes in intellectual property. Failure to protect these stakes would allow firms in other countries to steal this property and eventually challenge EC firms in their home markets.[22]

One area where the EC diverged from the U.S. position was in the area of controlling unilateral actions within the GATT. Starting in the late 1970s and early 1980s, the United States began using two sections it had placed into its trade laws—Super 301 and Special 301—to punish countries it believed were in violation of the GATT. The EC believed that this form of unilateral activity undermined the GATT and needed to be corrected in a new round of negotiations. The EC threatened to create its own form of Super 301 and Special 301 to protect itself from the United States if the GATT was not expanded to control these types of self-protective policies.[23]

The most important area of EC-U.S. divergence was agriculture. The EC relied extensively on quotas, variable tariffs, and export subsidies to control its agricultural market through its Common Agricultural Policy. A new round of negotiations would open all of these policies to attack. The EC was bent on protecting them because of the highly organized and politically powerful farm organizations that depended on these policies in member states.[24] The EC was willing to discuss some agricultural reforms within the GATT, but the community wanted to include measures that allowed for the controlling of international agricultural markets—perhaps even a formal agricultural quota system giving each member of the GATT a specific percentage of the international market.[25] The EC's ideas flew in the face of what the United States and other major agricultural exporters were advocating. In the end, the EC offered little in the way of proposals for reform. Instead, it simply reacted to what other countries offered and did its best to resist anything that would lead to significant changes in or the dissolution of its CAP. Agriculture would turn out to be a central issue in the Uruguay Round negotiations.

THE CAIRNS GROUP

This was a group of fourteen developed and developing countries that united to insure that a new round of negotiations would lead to significant agriculture reform within the GATT.[26] By forming a coalition, these countries were able to exert more power over the negotiations. Together, their populations were as large as the EC, United States, and Japan combined. Furthermore, they accounted for about the same amount of export and import activity as the EC and United States. In the agricultural sector, the group accounted for 25 percent of world trade.[27]

All these countries relied heavily on agricultural exports. They also relied far less extensively on farm subsidies, export subsidies, and other farm policies to stimulate production and enhance farm incomes. The domestic policies of some members of the group actually made it tougher for farmers to produce, not easier. Yet, the farm sectors in each country were some of the most productive in the world. At first, these countries had been able to compete internationally without the policies used by the EC, Japan, and the United States, but this was becoming impossible by the mid-1980s. Export subsidies and production subsidies had become so high in the EC and United States that Cairns Group members were forced to respond with their own policies or lose access to their export markets. In some cases, policies of the EC, United States, and Japan had so distorted agricultural markets that Cairns Group members were actually importing some agricultural products that they otherwise would have been exporting.[28]

The Cairns Group wanted to see export subsidies eliminated under the GATT. The group also wanted agricultural quotas to be reduced if not eliminated, and the group called for rollback and relief from these distorting policies while negotiations were taking place. Finally, the Cairns Group called for "tariffication" of agricultural policies. This meant that GATT members would have to transform all policies that protected agricultural products into a tariff with a similar effect. Tariffs are more transparent than other forms of protection, and exporters can more easily deal with them. The Cairns Group was willing to allow any changes to be phased in over ten years, and they were not opposed to allowing some protections to continue to exist, a major contrast with the zero-option plan presented by the United States.[29]

THE DEVELOPING COUNTRIES

The Uruguay Round was the first round of negotiations where developing countries had a significant influence. India and Brazil were the two most active developing countries before and during the Uruguay Round and were essentially the voice of most developing country interests. As a group, the developing countries shared several common interests. The first was a general opposition to including services within a new round of negotiations.[30] The developing countries feared that opening their markets to foreign service providers would make it impossible for native service industries to develop. Most developing countries did not possess developed banking, financial, insurance, accounting, or other service industries. There was little chance native providers of these services would develop if foreign multinationals were already present in their markets. Developing countries were also opposed to including discussion of investment policies and measures. They believed that development required them to use rules regulating how foreign firms invested and what they did with their investment. Without rules, foreign firms might do little to enhance the local economy.

Developing countries particularly wanted better access to developed country markets.[31] Developed countries had used safeguard provisions placed within the GATT to protect their markets from developing country competitors. Developing countries wanted to weaken these safeguard provisions and place more constraints on their use. The developed countries had also succeeded in closing their markets to developing country textile production through a formalized Multi-Fibre Arrangement (MFA).[32] The MFA placed import quotas on sixty categories of goods into U.S. and EC markets and assigned developing countries specific portions of these quotas. Developing countries saw these quotas as denying them the ability to develop and grow their markets. Developing countries believed that any new round of negotiation had to include discussion of the MFA, its integration within the GATT, and its eventual elimination.

A third interest was restricting unilateral action by GATT members to open the markets or punish the conduct of other members. Developing countries were particularly concerned with the Super 301 and Special 301 trade laws of the United States. They believed that the United States' economic strength allowed it to use these laws as weapons to wring advantageous trade conditions from them.

A fourth interest of the developing countries came in the area of tropical products. Developed countries had over the years erected extensive quotas and tariffs on tropical agricultural, forestry, and mineral products. Developing countries wanted to see these reduced. A more significant problem in this area was that tariffs were usually higher within developed countries on refined or finished tropical products than in their primary state. Developing countries felt this was to encourage the creation of industries refining tropical products in the developed countries while discouraging their creation in the developing countries. Developing countries hoped to include within a new round of negotiations rules reducing these high secondary tariffs. In doing so, they hoped that refining, canning, and distilling industries would develop within their borders allowing them to export products with a higher value than the raw commodities they had been producing and exporting.[33]

Finally, developing countries, particularly India, Brazil, and some African countries were opposed to including intellectual property in a new round of negotiations. Developing countries complained that the long length of patents and copyrights made it more difficult for developing countries to obtain the technology they needed to develop. They also opposed some of these protections on humanitarian grounds. Patents, in granting a monopoly for a proscribed period of time, allow companies to charge far higher prices for a product than they otherwise could. In the area of pharmaceuticals, this meant that often developing country citizens could not afford to purchase drugs to fight diseases, condemning them to suffer and possibly die needlessly. Developing countries argued that they should be allowed to copy technology essential for the protection of life whether covered by patent or not.[34]

In addition, many developing countries saw the patenting of biological or genetic products as illegitimate since they are seen as natural, not something that is created. Moreover, they feared that allowing the patenting of seeds, plant extracts, and so on would deny their farmers and citizens the right to reuse seeds in planting or deny access to traditional medicine. Finally, patents were seen by many poorer states as a form of robbery. MNCs enter developing countries, study traditional medicines, determine the active ingredients in them, and then patent the findings.[35]

JAPAN

Having the second largest economy in the world, one would think that Japan would have been a significant player in the Uruguay Round. However, this was not the case. Japan was more a reactive than an active participant. This does not mean that Japan did not have interests; in fact Rapkin and George (1992) argue that the reason for Japan's passiveness was that its fundamental interest was to insure that its ban on imports of rice into the country was protected in any agreement reached.[36]

After World War II, Japan initiated a complex agriculture policy to help stimulate domestic production and guarantee good incomes for farmers. As part of this policy, Japan banned imports of rice into the country. Exceptions were made only when local harvests were not enough to meet demand. The agricultural control policies and rice import ban created a strong domestic political constituency for the programs that became so strong, that by the 1980s none of the major political parties in Japan were willing to oppose them.[37] Thus, negotiators for Japan in the Uruguay Round found their hands tied. Their major bargaining chip, the rice policy, was removed from the table. Without chips, one cannot effectively play the game. Negotiators instead pushed the idea that an exception should be added to the GATT to allow countries to pursue self-sufficiency in food.

Besides the protection of its rice market, Japan agreed with Europe that the GATT needed to be expanded to reduce or eliminate the U.S. ability to act unilaterally on trade issues. Japan throughout the 1980s had been the target of U.S. efforts to limit automobile, steel, and other imports. Many of these efforts ended with Japan conceding to "voluntary" ceilings on imports because it feared U.S. action under Super 301 and Special 301.

Finally, Japan wanted to see the dispute settlement procedures of the GATT strengthened. As one Ministry of International Trade and Industry official stated, "Rules and principles are more important to a country without strong political power, than to countries that have such power."[38] A dispute settlement system based more on rules and laws than strength would allow Japan to challenge the policies of other states and know that when it won these challenges, other states would have to comply with the decision no matter how strong they were. Japan's perception of weakness belied its economic strength.

PRELUDE TO THE ROUND

Many economists and free traders argue that the only way to maintain a free trade regime like the GATT is to keep it moving and to keep it moving at an ever faster pace—much like a bicycle.[39] Up to a point, the faster one rides a bike, the more stable the bike is. A slow moving bike is a bike that will easily spill. When applied to the GATT, this means that a free trade regime must be constantly expanded and deepened, otherwise forces working against open markets will topple it. In the early 1980s, the free trade bicycle was beginning to wobble due to the various problems in the international economy and trade system. The United States was the first country to begin calling for a new round of negotiations in the early 1980s in order to expand and deepen the treaty. The United States believed that the GATT needed some new momentum if it was not to fall—a position that would repeat itself during the later Doha Round.

The United States convinced GATT members to agree to a ministerial meeting in November 1982 to discuss the problem of "new protectionism." A long list of issues was presented to GATT members for their consideration. The issues ranged from expanding the GATT into agriculture and services, to the workings of the dispute settlement process, and to the rolling back of several new forms of protection that had emerged during the previous years. There were so many issues that there was no way to address each one properly during a single meeting.

The biggest problem, however, was not the number of issues, but rather the lack of consensus on what to do about them. The developing countries opposed launching a new round of negotiations to expand the GATT. They believed that the developed countries had failed to live up to previous commitments and could see no reason to expand the treaty until the elements already in place were implemented and enforced. The developed countries themselves could not agree on what should be done. Some countries, like the United States and Australia, believed that agriculture had to be dealt with in a new round. The EC opposed this idea on the grounds that it would force the reform of its Common Agricultural Policy. Japan feared a new round of negotiations would lead to the labeling of its industrial policies as unfair barriers to trade.

Conflicts between GATT members spilled into public view, leading many in the press to comment that the GATT itself was in serious trouble and perhaps dead. The head of the EC trade delegation said that the November meeting had been "badly prepared, badly organized and should never have been held at this time."[40] Most observers felt the November meeting was a fiasco.

Nevertheless, the ministerial meeting did produce a declaration, although two prominent members, Australia and the EC, refused to sign it. This declaration laid the groundwork for the opening of the Uruguay Round, but not until four years later. It began by stating, "The multilateral trading system . . . is seriously endangered."[41] It then called for members to roll back any actions they had taken that were inconsistent with the GATT and to refrain from creating any new policies that distorted or obstructed trade. More importantly, the document created a study program and designated groups and committees to begin research on various issues facing the GATT. These groups were to perform research on the issues and report at the next GATT ministerial meeting in 1984. The most important groups dealt with agriculture, services, dispute settlement, safeguards, textiles and clothing, and intellectual property. The work of these groups became instrumental in expanding the GATT into agriculture, services, and intellectual property during the Uruguay Round. The groups defined the issues, determined measures of barriers to trade in each sector, and helped create a common language with which to negotiate.

In response to the perceived failure of the 1982 GATT Ministerial Conference, GATT Director General Arthur Dunkel took the unusual step of commissioning a panel in November 1983 to investigate and report on problems affecting the international trade system. The seven members of the panel were given the mandate to "identify the fundamental causes of problems afflicting the international trading system and to consider how these may be overcome during the remainder of the 1980s."[42] The panel was chaired by Fritz Leutwiler, head of the Swiss Central Bank, and had six other members from developed and developing countries. The panel met five times during 1984 and released a report in early 1985. Fifteen recommendations were made; one was a call for a new round of negotiations to strengthen the multilateral trading system. Most developed countries welcomed the report; many developing countries did not. Dunkel received a barrage of criticism from developing country governments for commissioning the report on his own. In the end, the report seemed to help clarify some of the major issues confronting the GATT and its membership, but it had little effect on spurring action to expand and reform it.

The United States continued its efforts after the failed 1982 Ministerial Conference to begin a new round of negotiations. The United States succeeded in getting the 1983 G-7 summit meeting to make a joint statement calling for new GATT negotiations. In February 1984, the U.S. Trade Representative William Brock brought together the trade ministers from Japan, Canada, and the EC for discussions on a new round of trade negotiations and the issues that would be its focus. This group of countries became known as the Quad. Later in 1984, Brock invited ten additional developed and developing countries into the discussions of the Quad. It was essential that developing countries were included in the discussions since they made up a majority of GATT members. Without their support, no new round of negotiations would be possible. The United States also succeeded in convincing the Organization of Economic Cooperation and Development (OECD) to make a statement in support of a new round of GATT negotiations during its 1984 meeting.[43]

Throughout 1984 the United States pressed the EC to come out strongly in favor of a new round of negotiations, but the EC was divided on the issue. Several members favored a new round, but others, particularly France, opposed one. France worried that the EC's Common Agricultural Policy would come under fire since French farmers received a large share of CAP subsidies and were well organized and politically active. France was also heavily engaged in restructuring its economy away from a statist or dirigiste model to a more market-oriented one. This change was creating significant opposition in France to greater openness to international market forces. In addition, France wanted new trade negotiations to be linked to negotiations over the international monetary system. In 1985, French resistance led to U.S. Secretary of State George Shultz's warning, "We intend to move forward in trade, we hope on a multilateral basis. But we'll do so on bilateral terms if we have to . . . excluding the French from the resulting benefits of reductions in trade barriers."[44] France was eventually convinced by other EC members of the need for a new round of negotiations. However, its opposition to agricultural reform under the GATT would become a reason for the round lasting beyond 1990.

The GATT Council met in the summer of 1985 and for the first time fully debated a new round of negotiations. Several of the larger developing countries, in particular India and Brazil, strongly opposed the idea because they believed that the developed countries had still not fulfilled prior round commitments within the GATT. They also did not like the idea of expanding the trade agreement into services and intellectual property. The United States proposed that a meeting of senior-level trade representatives from all GATT members be called to lay the groundwork for a new round of negotiations. With India and Brazil opposing this suggestion, the United States took the unprecedented step of calling for a vote by mail on the issue from all GATT members. The United States argued that if a majority wanted a meeting, then those opposing could stay home if they wished. By calling for a vote, the United States succeeded in getting what it wanted. A senior-level meeting was scheduled for the fall of 1985. At this meeting, it was agreed that a new round of negotiations was needed and would be started in the fall of 1986.

THE URUGUAY ROUND

After years of haggling, the Uruguay Round was finally set. However, beginning is not completing. That would take another seven years of negotiations. To make the narrative of the Uruguay Round easier to follow, we have broken it into four stages. The first deals with the opening of the round at Punta del Este. The second examines the round during its first four years. The third examines the round from 1991 to 1994. And finally, we examine the crucial ratification stage of the round by the United States.

PUNTA DEL ESTE

Punta del Este is a resort town in Uruguay. On September 14, 1986, it became the venue for the opening conference of what would later be labeled the Uruguay Round. The site was chosen to reflect the growing power and importance of developing countries within the GATT. The task of the conference was to create a declaration that would articulate the various areas in the GATT to be reformed, expanded, or changed during the round of negotiations. Three draft declarations were presented at the conference. One draft, the Swiss-Colombian draft, was supported by forty-eight member countries, most of which were developed and industrialized. This text placed the "new issues" of services, intellectual property, and trade-related investment measures, as well as agriculture, at the center of a new round of negotiations. India and Brazil led a group of nine countries that opposed the inclusion of services, intellectual property, and trade-related investment measures. These countries believed that the issues were outside GATT jurisdiction, and they developed their own draft declaration excluding them. Finally, Argentina offered a modified version of the so-called Swiss-Colombian text.

During a week of tough negotiations, the three drafts were melded into a single document. Debate over inclusion of the "new issues" in the round proved to be the most difficult issue at the conference with the United States, India, and Brazil, the central disputants. The United States made it clear to India and Brazil that it would walk away from the round if the new issues were not included. The round would end before it had even begun. This stance led India and Brazil during a night meeting to eventually agree to a compromise. The new issues would be included in the round, but at the same time separated from it. The issue of services would have its own negotiation track and its own committee to supervise it. It would not be a part of the other negotiations on more traditional trade issues. Intellectual property and trade-related investment measures would be included in the general round of negotiations, but any conflicts in these areas would be kept from spilling into more traditional trade areas. This meant that if negotiations on intellectual property hit a snag, they would not disrupt negotiations on tariffs and nontariff issues. Countries were not to link what happened in negotiations over new issues as they regularly linked negotiations among old issues.

On Saturday, September 20, 1986, the meeting at Punta del Este ended with the adoption of a formal declaration laying out the aims and rules of the new round of negotiations. The declaration contained two sections. The first dealt with negotiations on goods, the traditional purview of the GATT. It created a Trade Negotiation Committee to oversee the round and fourteen separate subjects of negotiation: (1) tariffs, (2) nontariff measures, (3) tropical products, (4) natural resource-based products, (5) textiles and clothing, (6) agriculture, (7) GATT rules and articles, (8) safeguards, (9) Multilateral Trade Negotiation agreements and arrangements, (10) subsidies and countervailing measures, (11) dispute settlement, (12) trade-related investment measures, (13) intellectual property protection, and (14) the functioning of the GATT system. Separate negotiating groups, each with a chair, were created for each topic. Section 2 dealt with negotiations over services for the creation of a General Agreement on Trade in Services (GATS). A separate committee was created to oversee this issue.[45]

1986–90

At the end of the Punta del Este meeting, the trade ministers of the various countries announced their intent to get the round off to a quick start. Previous rounds had often bogged down or gone sluggishly until a formal deadline was reached in the negotiations. Only then would the various parties become serious about bargaining and making commitments. It was hoped that the Uruguay Round would be different, that a good pace could be kept, and that by the end of four years the round would be completed. To this end, the first set of meetings for the round was called for October 1986. Each negotiating group was brought together to craft a work schedule, and by the end of April 1987, every group had met at least once to discuss and begin negotiations. One hundred and fifty additional meetings would be held by these groups between 1987 and 1988.

A trade dispute between the EC and United States in late 1986 and early 1987 began to complicate matters. The EC added two members in 1986, Spain and Portugal, that resulted in a reduction of $430 million in grain exports to Spain from the United States due to the EC's Common Agricultural Policy. Farmers in the United States immediately protested to the U.S. government. The Reagan administration responded by threatening to impose 200 percent duties on a list of European exports including wine, brandy, and cheese if the EC did not maintain the market access that had existed for U.S. exports before Spain and Portugal entered the community. Negotiations brought a compromise that continued market access for U.S. grain for four more years. It was thought (erroneously as it turned out) that the Uruguay Round would be completed within this time frame and that the agricultural negotiations within it would make the conflict moot.

Congress did not give the U.S. president fast-track negotiating authority for the round until 1988, which further complicated international negotiations. Without this authority, most countries were wary of making deals with the United States. The fast-track process takes place when Congress agrees to vote a treaty up or down with no possibility for making amendments. Without fast-track authority, Congress could make countless changes, a possibility that would undermine the credibility of the president in negotiating with foreign countries.

In order to maintain the pace of negotiations, the United States proposed that a midterm meeting be called for 1988 with the hope that a package of early agreements could be adopted at this meeting. In particular, the United States wanted to pass early agricultural reforms as well as agreements dealing with services. By harvesting fruit early, it was hoped that the end of the round would be less complicated and contentious. It was also hoped that early success in the round would pave the way for success down the road as GATT members began to see the benefits derived from the early harvest of agreements.

The midterm gathering was held in Montreal on December 5, 1988. When the session opened, it seemed a substantial early harvest was going to be possible. During the meeting, progress was made on a draft agreement for eleven of the fourteen major areas under the Trade Negotiating Committee. Negotiators agreed on an overall target for tariff reductions (30 percent) and to reduce substantially barriers to trade in tropical products and natural resources. They also agreed to initiate periodic country reviews under the GATT to determine how well members were complying with them. Members had also largely agreed on a new dispute settlement process.

These agreements went for naught, however, as a dispute between the United States and EC led to the complete unraveling of the Montreal meeting. The United States demanded that the EC agree to the zero option for agriculture. This meant that at some point in the future, all trade-distorting agricultural policies would be eliminated. The United States refused to negotiate on any short-term changes in agriculture policies until the EC agreed on the long-term goal of the zero-option plan. The EC, in turn, refused to accept the zero option. It was willing to make some short-term changes in agriculture policies, but it was not willing to countenance the eventual elimination of them. The Cairns Group attempted to mediate a compromise between the two but failed. At one point, the Australian trade minister, Michael Duffy, commented in frustration, "The United States and European Community really do deserve one another. They're a pair of rippers. I think we're staring down the barrel of an all-out farm trade war."[46] The unwillingness of the EC and United States to bargain led to the trade delegations from South America to walk out of the meeting. If there was no agreement on agriculture, there would be no agreement on anything at Montreal.

The Uruguay Round was suspended for four months after the Montreal meeting in order to break the agriculture deadlock. A series of meetings were held in Geneva between the United States and EC with the director general of the GATT as mediator. An agreement was forged whereby the United States and EC agreed to the goal of "substantial progressive reductions in agricultural support and protection sustained over an agreed period of time, resulting in correcting and preventing restrictions and distortions in world agricultural markets."[47] Each side could interpret this to mean what they wanted. For the United States, it meant the zero option; for the EC, it meant small short-term changes in policy. In essence, the EC and United States agreed to disagree so that negotiations could continue in other areas of the round. This also meant that agriculture remained a problem that would be left for later in the negotiations. However, the compromise did facilitate the adoption of agreements when the round resumed in April 1989.

After Montreal, Arthur Dunkel, director general of the GATT and chair of the Trade Negotiation Committee, laid out a timetable for the round. He wanted governments to finish presenting their proposals within each group by the end of 1989. Between January and July of 1990, Dunkel wanted the negotiating groups to narrow the differences between country proposals and to develop general agreement on their issues. From August to December 1990, each of the fifteen negotiating groups would refine the agreements and place them in the proper legal language. Adoption by GATT member states would then take place at a meeting concluding the round early in 1991 in Brussels.

In most areas progress was made toward final agreement. However, in some of the groups wide disagreement remained. In 1990 the United States began moving away from its earlier support for an agreement on services. It began to question whether it wanted to give MFN status to all signers of a new services agreement. The United States feared free riders. It believed that many states would attempt to exploit the opening of the U.S. service market while granting no access to their markets. This led to a U.S. demand that the signing of a services agreement be conditioned on reductions in barriers to services trade. Countries failing to reduce barriers would not be allowed to sign or would not have to be recognized by those making reductions. Due to domestic industry opposition, the United States also began to question whether it really wanted to open its air and marine transport markets. The weakening of U.S. support led many to question whether a services agreement was still possible.

In April 1990 a new issue arose. Canada proposed the creation of a world trade organization that would supercede the GATT and its secretariat. Canada hoped to place the GATT on a more permanent organizational footing. The structure administering the GATT was a temporary expedient created in 1948 that had become permanent by default. When the GATT was created, it was to be administered by the International Trade Organization (ITO), but the U.S. Congress refused to ratify the treaty creating the ITO. Thus, the GATT became a treaty and protocol with no real staff or organization to administer and enforce its provisions. The Canadian proposal also would place dispute settlement within this new organization.

Many GATT members were not enamored with the Canadian proposal. The United States in particular voiced its opposition. The United States feared that the Canadian proposal would create a WTO too much like the UN. The United States questioned whether one country, one vote was the best form of representation for such a body, as it feared the development of voting blocs that would not be supportive of a liberal trade environment. It believed that weighted voting based on economic size would keep this from occurring. U.S. negotiators also feared a loss of sovereignty would accompany any new organization. This would make it especially difficult to sell to the Congress as well as the public. Finally, the United States feared that creating a world trade organization would overshadow other substantive issues, keeping them from being resolved.

Agriculture, of course, continued to plague the round as well. No progress was made in negotiations between the United States and EC between April 1989 and May 1990. The deadlock was so severe that the parties asked the head of the agricultural group, Aart de Zeeuw, to prepare by the end of June 1990 a compromise draft. De Zeeuw's draft agreement called for reductions in agricultural supports in three areas: internal farm supports, import barriers, and export subsidies. Export subsidies were to be reduced more than the other areas because, as de Zeeuw said, "Everybody apart from the EC and Austria want it that way."[48] The EC was not pleased with the report, but in mid-July 1990 it released a statement saying that it was a good basis to continue negotiations. All countries agreed that they would submit final agricultural proposals by October 15, 1990.

Monday, December 3, 1990, trade ministers met in Brussels in hopes of concluding the Uruguay Round. Pressures to finish were immense. Fast-track negotiating authority for the U.S. president was set to expire in February 1991. The world had also changed considerably since the opening of the round. With the fall of the Berlin Wall, the Cold War had ended. The United States and Canada had also created a free trade area and were negotiating to expand it to Mexico. Many other countries around the world were joining regional free trade areas of their own. Many believed that failure of the Uruguay Round would lead to a trade system that was Balkanized among different groups. The system created by the GATT would collapse.

However, no amount of pressure could end the deadlock on agriculture. The EC came to the December meeting with a new proposal. It offered to reduce internal farm supports by 30 percent, with 1986 as the base year for determining these reductions. That year was the high point of EC internal supports, so this offer meant only a 15 percent reduction in supports from 1990 levels. The EC offered nothing in the area of export subsidy reductions. The United States and the Cairns Group objected to these proposals. The EC responded at Brussels that this was a place to begin negotiations, not end them. However, as the week of December 3 approached, it became clear that the EC was not going to move from its position. By the end of the week, U.S. and Cairns Group representatives were trading epithets with EC trade representatives. On Friday, December 7, 1990, the Brussels meeting was adjourned. No final agreement was passed. The round was suspended again. Director General Arthur Dunkel was charged with getting the round back on track by the beginning of the new year.

1991–94

Placing the Uruguay Round back on track required solving the agricultural impasse. No official Uruguay Round meetings took place in the three months after Brussels.

Instead, Arthur Dunkel spent time mediating the dispute between the EC and the United States/Cairns Group. In late February 1991, these efforts paid some dividends. The EC was brought to the realization that the only way that the round could go forward was if it agreed to negotiate not only on internal farm support levels, but also on export support levels and barriers to imports into the community. At a GATT meeting on February 20, 1991, the EC signaled its changing position by holding silent on a vote that negotiations on agriculture would be resumed with the goal of "specific binding commitments to reduce farm supports in each of the three areas: internal assistance, border protection and export assistance."[49]

One factor helping to break the deadlock on negotiations was that pressures had developed within the EC to reform the CAP.[50] The CAP had led to unprecedented surpluses in European agriculture, and disposing of these was proving costly and difficult for the community. Moreover, the CAP was becoming ever more expensive. The more farmers produced, the more aid they received. If this continued, the CAP might place the EC in serious fiscal difficulty. After the Uruguay Round fell apart in December 1990, Ray McSharry, EC Agriculture Commissioner, presented a "green paper" to the commission detailing these problems with the CAP and potential reforms. Many of the ideas presented were adopted in 1992 by the EC. The nature of these reforms gave the EC more bargaining room in Uruguay Round negotiations.

The change in the EC position in February 1991 did not bear immediate fruit. Fast-track authority for the U.S. president expired at the end of February 1991, and no country was willing to bargain with the United States until the president achieved an extension. In March 1991 the U.S. president requested a two-year addition to his negotiating authority from the Congress. Under the law, Congress had sixty days to approve or decline the request for fast-track authority. The extension proved quite controversial, and GATT negotiations became tied to negotiations over fast-track authority for the North American Free Trade Agreement (NAFTA). Many in Congress feared that allowing Mexico into NAFTA would lead to the loss of U.S. industrial jobs. Environmental groups opposed extending fast-track authority, fearing that lax regulations in Mexico would be exploited by firms in the United States wanting to save money on pollution abatement measures. In a tight vote after fierce pressures were applied, fast-track authority passed the House on May 23, 1991, and the Senate on May 24.

Talks on agriculture stalled throughout the summer of 1991 and into the fall. The only progress made on this issue was calculating how to measure agricultural supports across the three main areas. These calculations led to agreement on what types of policies would be exempt from coverage under a new agreement and on what was termed an "aggregate measure of support." This was important because using the aggregate measure of support, it was possible to measure the overall level of support a state was giving agriculture through subsidies, tariffs, and other policies. It also allowed a blending of policies by each country to reach an overall level of reduction in support for agriculture. No progress was made, however, on what levels of reduction should be made.

In December, President Bush met directly with EU[51] ministers. Bush lowered the level of reduction in agricultural support required by the United States in any agreement. This led to similar concessions from the EU, making it seem like the agricultural impasse had been broken. But again, this was not the case. By December 20, talks had once again broken down. Progress had been made, but a sizable gap in the levels of reduction acceptable to each side still existed and could not be bridged.

Arthur Dunkel earlier in the year had taken the rare step of warning that if the impasse was not ended by the end of 1991, he would issue a complete draft treaty on his own. He followed through on this ultimatum after talks fell apart in late December of 1991. His draft was submitted on a take it or leave it basis, as any significant changes to the draft, he thought, would risk its unraveling. A country could either accept what he had wrought, or it would have to publicly state its opposition. This would allow others to lay the blame for failure of the round on those who opposed the draft. Most of the draft merely codified agreements that had already been made within the negotiating groups anyway. However in some areas, like agriculture, Dunkel laid out on his own what he thought was a fair or proper compromise agreement.

Reactions by GATT members to the Dunkel Draft were mixed. The French, along with the EC, South Korea, and Japan, stated that it was unacceptable. The French foreign minister Edith Cresson stated that the draft had been circulated "without any regard for European interests, whether in agriculture or other fields."[52] The United States gave weak support to the draft while making clear that nothing was decided until everything was decided. Still, the United States saw the draft as a good starting point for bringing closure to the round. Most of the Cairns Group was supportive of the draft, as were most developing countries.

Dunkel's initiative, not surprisingly, proved unable to break the deadlock over agriculture. Negotiations on this issue were to continue into the summer of 1992 until, at the G-7 summit in Munich, U.S. Secretary of State Baker asked the French foreign minister whether they were ready to move on the issue. The response was no. Baker then asked whether the French would be willing to move if they were to receive everything they wanted; the answer was still no.

After the G-7 summit in 1992, the Uruguay Round appeared to be dead until 1993. The United States was in the midst of a presidential race, and countries were leery of negotiating with an administration that might be gone after the beginning of the year. Clinton's victory in November of 1992 seemed to insure that no progress on the agricultural issue would be made until after his inauguration. Surprisingly, however, events in international trade worked to jump-start negotiations between the United States and EU. In November 1992 two GATT dispute panels found that the EU was in violation of the treaty in regards to oil seed policies. The United States reacted to these decisions by announcing trade sanctions on the EU amounting to almost one billion dollars with the EU threatening retaliation. However, pressures were building in the EU to settle the dispute by crafting a compromise within the Uruguay Round. Negotiators from the United States and EU met at the Blair House in Washington DC on November 18, 1992. Over two days, a settlement was crafted solving the oil seed dispute and reinitiating the Uruguay Round agricultural talks. The EU agreed to cut the quantity of agricultural products receiving an export subsidy by 21 percent—three percent less than the Dunkel Draft had proposed, but three percent more than the EU's previous position. The EU also agreed to a less favorable base year for measuring these cuts.

The accord opened the floodgates to negotiations. The round began again in earnest as the Bush administration pushed for its conclusion before its term in office ended. Throughout the end of November and into December 1992, representatives met and negotiated at a frenetic pace. Haste did not work, however, and sadly, a conclusion to the round was not yet to be. There were still too many issues and too many deals to make in too short of a time. Bush left office on January 20, 1993, with no deal completed and fast-track authority for the U.S. president once again running out.

During the transition from the Bush to Clinton administrations, negotiations languished. The Clinton administration did not turn its attention to the Uruguay Round until March 1993 as fast-track authority ended. It was another month before Clinton requested a one-year extension from Congress. This time the extension was given with little opposition and debate.

In June 1993 Dunkel retired as director general of the GATT and was replaced by Peter Sutherland. Unlike Dunkel, Sutherland was far more vocal and used his position more as a bully pulpit to obtain completion of the round. In July 1993 at a meeting in Tokyo, GATT members successfully negotiated a general tariff agreement on industrial goods. The meeting initially looked like it would end in deadlock; however, Sutherland made it clear to the participants that failure to reach agreement on other issues would probably lead to the failure of the complete round. After several days of negotiations, Japan initiated a series of compromises by agreeing to drop tariffs to zero on alcoholic beverages. This concession led Canada to reciprocate with zero tariffs on beer and furniture, and the EC followed suit on farm equipment. Before long GATT members had agreed to zero tariffs on eight industrial sectors and huge cuts in five others. This agreement led many world leaders to believe that success once again seemed possible for the round as a whole.

After the July meeting, Sutherland began visiting the capitals of the various GATT members. He reminded them that the last date for finishing the round was December 15, 1993. He also made clear that failure to complete the round would be devastating. It would affect the credibility and image of all of those participating. Progress continued in the round through the end of November when, ominously, the French vocalized their objections to the Blair House Accord from the fall of 1992. In November the French complained that they had achieved nothing within the round to date, and they threatened to scuttle the round by refusing to vote for it at its finish. The French government was under strong domestic pressure to reject Blair House. These pressures came from within the governing party as well as from the strong farm lobby.[53]

At the beginning of December, the United States agreed to restructure the Blair House Accord in order to placate the French. The base year for determining the level of support reductions was changed to one more favorable to French farmers, and the United States agreed to allow the reductions to be spread evenly over a six-year period, which would ease the pain. The United States also agreed to allow the EU to first dispose of its twenty-five million tons of grain surpluses. Finally, the United States agreed to a so-called "peace clause." This was a pledge that the United States would not challenge any EU support policy for the first eight years under the agreement. The French made some concessions as well. The United States received greater access to the EU for a variety of agricultural products, and the earlier agreement concerning U.S. grain exports to Spain and Portugal was extended.[54]

With the immediate agriculture issue settled, the round was set to conclude by December 15. Working into the evening of December 14, final agreements in all areas laid out by the Punta del Este Declaration were completed. The concluding area of agreement was on the creation of a WTO. U.S. opposition to the organization had been overcome by a series of compromises. The United States demanded that all sections of the GATT should apply to all members. Up to this time, one could be a member of the GATT but opt out of some provisions at will. The United States believed this should be prohibited; accession to the WTO would require a country to abide by all portions of the treaty. The rest of the GATT members eventually agreed to this. The United States also won regarding rules for voting. Some members of the GATT wanted the one country, one vote standard with majority rule on most issues. The United States wanted either consensus decision making for the most important issues or votes to be weighted by the wealth of the country. Developing countries opposed the idea of weighted voting since it would greatly reduce their power in the new organization. However, they were willing to go along with the idea of consensus voting, which requires that all members agree to any changes in the treaty. In this way, theoretically at least, all countries could protect themselves from significant decisions they opposed.

It should be noted that, in the end, the Dunkel Draft proved to be the basis of the final agreement. Dunkel's gamble had succeeded. In creating a package that could tolerate little change, he forced GATT members to negotiate on the basis of what he had wrought, or to watch the round unravel.

On April 15, 1994, countries involved in the round came together to officially sign the agreement at Marrakech, Morocco. The finished product contained more than twenty-six thousand detailed pages; it was a complex agreement. At an elaborate ceremony that spring day, 109 countries took the plunge and signed the treaty. The Uruguay Round had officially ended. (Appendix 3.1 gives a brief synopsis of the key aspects of the agreement.)

U.S. RATIFICATION

The United States signed the treaty, but this signing meant nothing until ratified by Congress. Under the U.S. Constitution, the president negotiates treaties, while the Senate must approve them. This procedure, in practice, was adjusted for economic agreements by the granting of fast-track authority to the president. Under fast-track procedures, the full Congress approves a treaty through the adoption of implementing legislation. Usually the president submits a draft of the implementing legislation to Congress. Next, Congress discusses the draft and makes amendments to it. The legislation is then passed back to the president who makes any changes needed to keep it in compliance with the treaty he negotiated. Finally, the president passes the implementing legislation back to the Congress for an up or down vote; at this stage, amendments to the implementing legislation are prohibited.

The Clinton administration was slow in sending the implementing legislation for the Uruguay Round to Congress. This was mainly due to President Clinton devoting his attention to the development of a universal health care program and because of federal budget constraints. The Uruguay Round required the United States to lower tariffs with an expected twelve-billion-dollar decrease in government revenues. A 1990 budget deal between the Congress and president required that any reduction in tax revenues be offset with either program cuts or increases in revenues from other sources. The Clinton administration had significant problems in finding politically palatable cuts or tax increases to cover the revenue losses from the treaty. The result of these delays was that the implementing legislation was not submitted to Congress until September 27, 1994.[55]

Congress was scheduled to adjourn for the year on October 8, 1994, allowing members to return home to their districts to campaign for the upcoming election in November. This left just over a week for Congress to act on the implementing legislation. President Clinton believed a week was all that was needed since he had lined up supporting majorities in both houses of Congress. His belief was quickly shattered.

On September 28, 1994, Senator Ernest Hollings (Democrat from South Carolina) declared that he would use his power as chair of the Senate Commerce Committee to delay a vote on the implementing legislation for forty-five days. The Uruguay Round eliminated the Multi-Fibre Arrangement (that had limited textile imports) and was expected to cost more than five hundred thousand jobs in the U.S. textile industry, much of which was centered in South Carolina.[56]

Hollings did not need to obtain a majority to derail the treaty in the Senate. Senate rules required that any new spending or taxes be shown to be budget neutral for ten years, and Clinton's implementing legislation made these projections for only five. In order to pass the Senate, a special waiver of Senate rules was required. Sixty votes were needed for passage. If Hollings could round up forty-one votes, he could block the waiver and thus block passage of the Uruguay Round implementing legislation. Moreover, if the waiver failed, the legislation would have to be resubmitted to

Congress, and this would void fast-track procedures, thereby opening the treaty to amendments.

Hollings's delay led to the unraveling of support in the House for a vote on the treaty before Congress adjourned. House members did not want the GATT to become an issue in the election, and the delay allowed them to walk away from a vote on it. As a consequence, Clinton immediately obtained support from House and Senate leaders to hold a special session after the election specifically for a vote on the Uruguay Round implementing legislation. The session was to be called at the end of November and beginning of December.[57]

During the rest of October, environmental and labor groups began organizing opposition to the treaty. These groups believed that the Uruguay Round would lead to the undermining of U.S. environmental and labor laws and to the exporting of jobs to developing countries. Opposition also formed over the creation of the WTO. Ralph Nader, Pat Buchanan, and Ross Perot (a strange alliance at best) were quite vocal in arguing that the WTO would challenge U.S. sovereignty and American democratic values.

The 1994 election threw yet another wrench into the U.S. president's efforts to obtain ratification of the Uruguay Round. For the first time in fifty years, the Republican Party obtained majorities in both houses of Congress. Clinton, the Democrat, was now forced politically to bargain with the incoming Republican leadership in Congress in order to obtain passage of the treaty.

The largest stumbling block was Bob Dole (Republican from Kansas), the new majority leader of the Senate. Dole linked three issues to ratification:[58] First, he wanted the president to agree to support a cut in the capital gains tax in the United States. Second, he demanded that one of the methods for raising revenues to pay for the tariff reductions in the agreement, an increase in some telecommunications license fees, be changed. Finally, Dole refused to allow the treaty to come to a floor vote unless he was given assurances that the United States could pull out of the WTO if it harmed American interests.

Clinton and Dole negotiated throughout the middle of November. Dole was unable to move the president on his first two requests. However, on the issue of the WTO, Dole succeeded in obtaining support for the creation of a special panel of judges. These judges would examine WTO decisions, and if they believed that three of the decisions within a five-year period had been arbitrary, the U.S. Congress would have the opportunity to pull out of the organization.[59] This compromise allowed the special session of Congress, called for November 29 to December 1, to move forward.

Clinton next turned his efforts to obtaining enough senatorial support to obtain the sixty votes needed for the waiver on Senate rules. Clinton made at least six deals with various senators to obtain their support for the waiver. For example, Clinton agreed to support a change in U.S. dumping laws to help a German company with operations in Missouri, thus obtaining Senator Kit Bond's (Republican) support for the waiver.

On November 29, the House passed the Uruguay Round implementing legislation 288 to 146. On December 1, the Senate passed the waiver on funding for the Uruguay Round, 68 to 32, and then the implementing legislation 76 to 24.[60] U.S. ratification of the round led to a flood of ratifications by other signatories. By January 1, 1995, eighty-eight countries had ratified the round results, thereby joining the newly created WTO and assuring its centrality in the international political economy.

CONCLUSION

The Uruguay Round was the lengthiest set of negotiations in the GATT's history, but considering the fundamental changes created by the round, we should not be surprised by the length and effort that went into it. With the creation of the WTO, the GATT was for the first time in its history placed on a sound organizational footing. The WTO was given jurisdiction to arbitrate disputes, administer the GATT, and monitor its implementation by member states. A formal secretariat and method for funding the new organization was also created. No longer would the GATT be administered by a temporary expedient that existed in the gray areas of international law and politics.

Interestingly, the formal organization was almost an afterthought. It was not until late in the round that Canada proposed the idea of a WTO, and it was not until the final days of negotiation that all countries assented to its creation. This afterthought has now grown into the most important consequence of the round. Its significance can be seen by the opposition to it that developed during the ratification debate in the United States and its continuance ever since. In 1999 for example, opposition to the organization led to riots during the WTO ministerial conference in Seattle, Washington, an event chronicled in Chapter 9 of this book.

The Uruguay Round showed clearly the problems that states have in defining and assuring the benefits of comparative advantage brought by free trade. For instance, most economists argued that freeing agriculture completely from trade barriers would lead to higher farm incomes and lower food prices for all. These arguments were not enough to convince the countries involved in negotiations. Governments feared the adverse political effects created by the transition costs to a free trade agricultural system. Each country fell back on old mercantilist arguments—for each gain someone else received, each country had to receive a similar one.

The EU and France were particularly concerned with winning as much as they gave in regards to agriculture. The Common Agricultural Policy created an agricultural constituency within Europe, and especially France, that saw its futures tied to the CAP and the trade protections that came with it. Fear of this constituency led the EU and France to resist most any bargain that required reductions in agricultural protections, and this resistance almost led to the failure of the round. In the end, the round resulted in freer trade for agriculture, but not free trade in the area.

Agriculture remains a sticking point within the WTO and has been responsible for the delay in completing the Doha Round that began at the turn of the millennium.

We can also see the importance of formally encoding rules and procedures of operation in this round of negotiations. For example, the United States argued that the WTO would become like the UN General Assembly unless consensus voting was continued or weighted voting was used. By holding out on this issue, the United States insured that it could protect itself from changes in the WTO that might harm its interests, which it cannot do within the General Assembly of the UN. We can also see the importance of rules as the developing countries pushed hard for ways to limit unilateral action by the rich states within the WTO. Developing countries feared the use of weapons like the United States' Super and Special 301 Trade Laws. These laws were designed to allow countries to act on their own to pry open the domestic markets of other countries. Developing countries believed these laws were used more often against them than others and that they did not have the economic weight to counter them. In the end, the developing countries succeeded in getting some protection from these types of actions written into the Uruguay Round agreements.

Many also say that for a free trade system to work, it must be based on the rule of law, not the individual caprice of powerful states. The Uruguay Round, by creating the WTO and a new dispute settlement process, moved the GATT/WTO closer to the ideal of rule of law, and hopefully this will increase the legitimacy of the organization and therefore member compliance with it.

This chapter demonstrates the complexity of international negotiations. The number of countries involved as well as the number of outside interests and groups (nongovernmental organizations) all make agreement difficult. Farmers in Europe and the United States pressured their governments, making compromise difficult. For instance, the United States stuck with its zero option in agriculture because farm lobbies in the United States supported it heavily, making it more difficult for the United States to compromise with the EU on the issue. This almost led to the scuttling of the complete Uruguay Round.

Context also affects success. Changes in the world and international economy at different times both spurred negotiation and hindered it. When the round began, the international economy was in crisis; the developed countries were suffering from inflation, high unemployment, and low growth, while many developing countries were in the midst of a serious debt crisis. By the early 1990s, economic conditions had changed dramatically, allowing countries to take positions on issues that earlier would have been impossible.

Finally, this chapter illustrates that negotiations between countries can lead to completely unexpected outcomes. No one at the time expected that the WTO would evolve the way it has. If many knew then what they do today, the WTO might well be very different if, indeed, it existed at all. This can be seen most dramatically in the area of dispute settlement. The Uruguay Round gave the WTO formal dispute settlement authority and made it very difficult for members to block decisions that go against them. Since 1995 many states have brought complaints to the WTO, and many have seen decisions go against them. Many outside commentators believe this has made the world trade system more fair and transparent. Still others believe that the WTO has become a form of world government overturning the laws of its members and instituting in their place rules that may help trade but that hurt other fundamental interests dealing with the environment, consumer protection, and labor practices. They believe that the organization should be more representative of the various domestic interests of members represented by nongovernmental organizations (NGOs). They also believe that citizens of the world should have more of a direct say, through some substantive mechanisms, in how the WTO operates and the decisions it makes.

While the WTO may not be what it was expected to be, it is difficult for its members to change or to leave it just because they are displeased. Too much now rides on their involvement with the treaty. Anyone that leaves may find export markets closed off and mercantilist rules applying to it alone. Thus, no one wants to reopen negotiations over the WTO's organizational structure for fear that this will lead to the unraveling of the whole GATT/WTO series of agreements.

CHAPTER 4

THE WTO

STRUCTURES, ISSUES, AND CHALLENGES

For almost fifty years, the GATT had no formal institutional foundation. The failure of the United States to ratify the treaty creating the International Trade Organization in the late 1940s led to the GATT being implemented provisionally. A consequence of this was that the agreement was served by only a small secretariat that was on tenuous legal and financial grounds. Other GATT mechanisms were on a similar unstable footing.

As we saw in the last chapter, major participants in the Uruguay Round did not intend to create a new institutional structure for the GATT when negotiations began. When the round was completed, however, the GATT institutional structure had been revolutionized with the creation of the WTO. No longer was the agreement or its supporting organizations provisional in nature. The GATT moved from essentially a gentlemen's agreement among states to a binding treaty under the WTO. The GATT secretariat was transformed from a necessary expedient to an organization capable of administering GATT/WTO affairs in addition to other new duties.

Today, the WTO is seen as the most important outcome of the Uruguay Round. As a result, it has become a center of controversy around the world. Chapter 8 describes in some detail the controversy surrounding the WTO and the protests that resulted at the 1999 Ministerial Conference in Seattle. Before we can begin examining and developing an understanding of why the WTO has become so controversial, we need to understand what the organization is and how it functions. That is the focus of this chapter. It will explain the organizational structure of the WTO, how it is funded, its decision-making processes, and its major functions and activities. Finally, it will discuss some institutional issues and concerns that have arisen in the last several years.

THE WTO'S STRUCTURE

The WTO has been given six primary functions: (1) to administer the WTO trade agreements, (2) to act as a forum for trade negotiations, (3) to handle trade disputes among members, (4) to monitor the trade policies of its members, (5) to provide technical assistance and training for developing countries, and (6) to cooperate with other international organizations. These functions are performed by a variety of conferences, councils, and committees that are in turn supported by a permanent secretariat located in Geneva, Switzerland.[1]

The highest governing body in the WTO is the Ministerial Conference. It is a representative body composed of all member states. Under the WTO agreement, the Ministerial Conference is required to meet at least once every two years. The

Figure 4.1

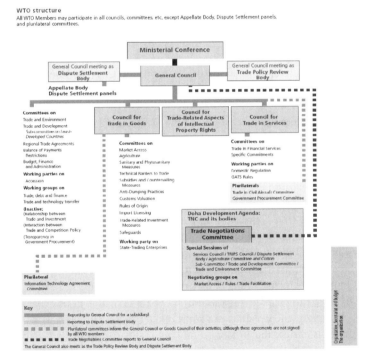

Ministerial Conference sets the WTO agenda and is fundamentally responsible for major decisions regarding changes to the GATT, the operation of the WTO, and the addition of new members. Importantly, the Ministerial Conference is responsible for interpreting the GATT, which was wholly incorporated into the WTO treaty. Though striving for consensus, these interpretations require support from at least three-fourths of members present at the conference. The Ministerial Conference can also waive member obligations under any of the agreements within the WTO's jurisdiction; this requires the same three-fourth support as a treaty interpretation. A two-thirds vote of representatives within the Ministerial Conference is required to accept a new member into the organization. Finally, the Ministerial Conference can amend provisions of the various agreements administered by the WTO if two-thirds of members support the amendment. Interestingly, however, amendments without unanimous support affect only those voting in support. This protects members from being forced to accede to something that is against their interests. This logic is what leads to the heavy pressures to conduct all of the business of the organization under a rule or at least an assumption of consensus. Given the growth in size and complexity of the WTO, this may not remain possible.

Though voting percentages are established within the rules, actual votes are rarely taken in the Ministerial Conference. A norm of consensus seeking was a long-time component of GATT decision making, and this has continued under the WTO.[2] Member governments work to eliminate opposition to any plan or proposal within the organization through negotiation and consultation. As part of the norm of consensus, members of the WTO without a large stake in a decision agree not to oppose it even if they are unhappy with it. They are expected to remain silent on the issue or, at worst, to express their opposition through quiet diplomacy.

The next level beneath the Ministerial Conference is the General Council of the WTO. This body consists of a representative from each member country. The General Council is responsible for the day-to-day oversight of WTO operations. It meets at least once per month to act as a continuous forum for discussion among members. Most importantly, the General Council serves as the WTO's Dispute Settlement Body and the WTOs Trade Review Mechanism. As the Dispute Settlement Body, the General Council establishes dispute panels and decides whether to support a dispute panel's decision.

As the Trade Review Mechanism, the General Council periodically performs reviews of member trade policies and points out in published reviews where members have fallen short of their trade obligations.[3] The Trade Review Mechanism was designed specifically to bring more transparency to GATT/WTO member relations and to make it easier for members to monitor each other's behavior. Trade policy reviews are performed every two years on the four countries with the largest shares of world trade; the next sixteen countries are reviewed every four years, and all others are reviewed every six years. The General Council oversees this function, though the secretariat carries it out, writes, and publishes the reports.

Underneath the General Council are three other major bodies: the Council for Trade in Goods, the Council for Trade Related Aspects of Intellectual Property Rights, and the Council for Trade in Services. All WTO members are represented on these councils as well. The councils administer major sections of the GATT and Uruguay Round agreements. For instance, the Council for Trade in Goods helps administer the original GATT agreement, while the Council for Trade in Services administers the new GATS. Besides helping to administer and monitor compliance with the various sections of the GATT, these councils perform research on trade issues related to their areas of jurisdiction and develop proposals for future negotiations within the WTO. In order to expedite the work of these councils, each has created specialized committees. WTO members have the right to participate in any or all of these committees; however, few countries participate regularly in all of them.[4] Instead, most states focus their efforts on the committees that are dealing with issues that touch their interests the most.

There are many other committees and working groups that fall under the General Council. These deal with everything from the connections between trade and the environment to budget, finance, and administration of the WTO. These committees are also open to all WTO member representatives.

The primary movers within the WTO are the member countries. The organization is theirs; it is not independent from its members, nor can it act outside the collective interests and desires of its members. Coalition and power politics, as we show in the case studies (Chapters 5–9), play a major role in this organization as in all of international relations, but opportunities are present here more than in most arenas for less powerful states to have an impact.

The secretariat supports the conferences and councils of the WTO. The secretariat's primary function is to provide technical and professional support to the various WTO bodies. This support ranges from collecting information requested by the councils and committees to providing legal assistance and technical support. As part of this, the secretariat handles the logistics of the ministerial conferences and the conferences of the negotiation rounds.[5]

The secretariat also has the task of providing special support for the developing countries that are members of the organization.[6] As part of this, the secretariat runs training courses to help countries with little international trade expertise. Perhaps more importantly, it also has begun to help the developing countries, especially the poorest, with the dispute settlement process. Many WTO members have no experience in formulating a legal case within the dispute settlement process, nor do they have the expertise among their bureaucrats. The secretariat mentors these countries as they gather evidence, develop a case brief, prepare for oral arguments, and go about fulfilling the various steps of the process.

A third function performed by the secretariat is monitoring and chronicling developments in international trade.[7] Recently the secretariat has begun to not only monitor, but also ask outside experts to analyze important trade issues. This has created some controversy because it may place the secretariat in the position of advocate for specific policies or programs instead of merely a reporter of what is occurring. It also may give the secretariat the ability to influence and change member behavior. Through the framing of issues, one inevitably has some control over how they are handled. Finally, the secretariat is charged with the task of representing the WTO to the media and public. As the organization has become more visible and opposition more active, particularly after Seattle and Cancun, this task has become more important and demanding.

The secretariat is headed by a director general who serves a six-year term and manages the day-to-day affairs of the secretariat. Starting in 2006, he was Pascal Lamy, the organization's face, its representative to the world. By 2006 the secretariat was composed of 594 staffers from 62 member states, growing by about 120 staffers since 1994. Much of this increase has resulted from the heavy member use of the dispute settlement process.

The director general must also manage WTO finances. In 2006 the secretariat budget totaled 173.7 million Swiss francs—about $140 million.[8] Compared to other major international organizations, this is quite a small sum. For instance, the OECD has a budget twice the size of the WTO, even though it has only about one-third the membership. The WTO budget is barely 1 percent of the total for the seventeen other major international economic organizations combined.[9]

Most of the secretariat budget comes from the dues of members. Each country is assessed a percent of the total budget based on its contribution to world trade. The United States, accounting for the largest share of world trade, contributes about 16 percent of the WTO budget, while Niger accounts for one of the smallest shares, contributing 0.015 percent, the minimum possible (Graph 4.1 gives a sample of countries and their WTO dues). Countries failing to pay dues are supposed to be placed on inactive status and are denied access to technical assistance, the chairing of

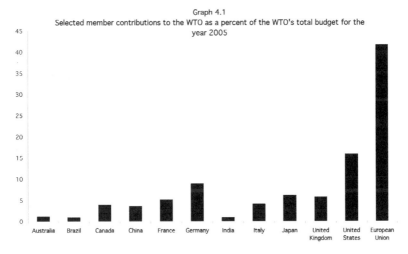

Graph 4.1
Selected member contributions to the WTO as a percent of the WTO's total budget for the year 2005

Source: World Trade Organization Annual Report - 2005

committees or councils, and documents produced by the WTO.[10] The vast majority of countries suffering from this problem, as you might imagine, are the least economically developed. In 1997 one-third of members defined as least developed were considered inactive because they had failed to pay their dues, but they continue to participate in the decision making of the organization. The WTO also has some independent sources of revenue through the sale of publications and other services totaling over one million Swiss francs in 2006.

Neither the secretariat nor its director general can initiate a dispute settlement case, nor can they interpret any provisions of the WTO charter or other agreements covered by the WTO.[11] They are staff bodies. This means they are to support members in their activities and nothing more. But this does not mean that they are without influence since they are an important source of information and expertise as well as being the visible arm of the organization. The director general has often assumed the role of chief mediator in WTO negotiations, which gives him some influence over events, as seen in the last chapter. Most issues are brought to a consensus through what are termed "Green Room" meetings, as we also saw in the diplomacy of the Uruguay Round. These are chaired by the director general and include, in theory, countries that have the most at stake in a particular issue. The director general usually attempts to insure that a range of countries are represented in these meetings, though controversy has surrounded these meetings since less developed members claim, with some merit, that the major trading states tend to dominate them. While the director general has no decision-making power in these meetings, our case studies show that he has been instrumental in bringing sides together in attempting to help them to compromise differences. However, this too is not uncontroversial. One study that interviewed many participants in and around the negotiations at the Doha and Cancun meetings contained a chapter on Director-General Mike Moore and the secretariat titled, "Wolves in Sheep's Clothing."[12] For the secretariat and director–general, mediation meant betrayal and pro-Western stances.

THE DISPUTE SETTLEMENT PROCESS

The Uruguay Round created a new dispute settlement process for the GATT. The old system suffered from a major weakness: it required that all members of the GATT accept the decisions of any dispute panel before being implemented.[13] This meant that a country losing its case before a dispute panel could stop implementation of the decision, which allowed countries to violate the terms of the GATT agreements without fear of penalty or sanction. Another problem was that there were no official timetables regulating the dispute process.[14] Disputes would enter the settlement process and remain within it for years. Both of these helped undermine support for the GATT and its principles. The Dispute Settlement Understanding created by the Uruguay Round was designed to solve those problems by establishing timelines for cases and changing the way dispute panel decisions were accepted by the Dispute Settlement Body and the WTO membership.

The WTO handles two major types of disputes between members. The first type is termed a violation dispute.[15] This consists of claims by one member that the actions of another have violated the terms of the GATT or one of its associated agreements (see Chapters 5 and 6 for examples of these). For example, the United States has been cited for several violations of trade rules under the GATT. It lost cases dealing with cotton and steel subsides and an antidumping law that took fines from dumping countries and gave them to U.S. companies.[16] The second type is termed a nonviolation dispute. This is a claim by one member that the actions of another have led to nullification or impairment of trade benefits expected to accrue from membership in the GATT, but the actions are not violations of the treaty. An example of this would be when country A lowers its tariffs on oranges, while country B reciprocates with lowering tariffs on beef. Country A expects that this will allow it to export more beef to country B; however, country B then takes an action ostensibly allowed under the GATT, perhaps labeling the beef as an import, that makes country A's beef as expensive, or less desirable, as it had been before the lowered tariffs. In this way, country B nullifies the benefits A expected while complying with all aspects of the GATT. Nonviolation disputes are difficult to adjudicate. They also comprise few of the formal complaints made to the Dispute Settlement Body.

The intent of the WTO's dispute settlement process is not to find members guilty of violating the treaty. It is designed to allow the "positive solution to a

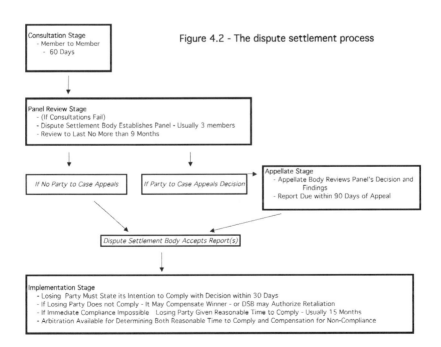

Figure 4.2 - The dispute settlement process

Consultation Stage
- Member to Member
- 60 Days

Panel Review Stage
- (If Consultations Fail)
- Dispute Settlement Body Establishes Panel - Usually 3 members
- Review to Last No More than 9 Months

If No Party to Case Appeals

If Party to Case Appeals Decision

Appellate Stage
- Appellate Body Reviews Panel's Decision and Findings
- Report Due within 90 Days of Appeal

Dispute Settlement Body Accepts Report(s)

Implementation Stage
- Losing Party Must State its Intention to Comply with Decision within 30 Days
- If Losing Party Does not Comply - It May Compensate Winner - or DSB may Authorize Retaliation
- If Immediate Compliance Impossible Losing Party Given Reasonable Time to Comply - Usually 15 Months
- Arbitration Available for Determining Both Reasonable Time to Comply and Compensation for Non-Compliance

Source - The United States General Accounting Office -
2000

dispute."[17] This means that the process is designed to allow a mutually satisfactory solution between parties involved in a dispute that is GATT/WTO consistent. It is hoped that if all parties are happy with a settlement, the WTO and GATT process will be seen as more legitimate, and thus parties will be more willing to comply with it. As such, consultation between members involved in a dispute is allowed throughout the process. An agreement stemming from these consultations is allowed and even encouraged at any time even up to General Council action on a dispute panel's report. Indeed, often even after a case is settled, the two sides come to some agreement that mitigates or eliminates the "penalties" allowed by the WTO ruling. This is illustrated in the next chapter dealing with a trade dispute involving bananas. The United States and EU eventually crafted a solution that both found satisfactory several years after the case was heard by the WTO.

The dispute settlement process has four major steps.[18] Figure 4.2 gives a brief outline of these steps. The first is a formal period of consultations. Members are required to consult with each other for sixty days before any other action can be taken. If these consultations fail, the director general of the WTO may step in to mediate the conflict if both parties to the dispute agree. If mediation fails or if one party refuses to agree to mediation, the parties move to the next stage of settlement—the creation of a dispute panel.

The General Council of the WTO acting as the Dispute Settlement Body creates dispute panels. A member wishing a panel to be formed makes a formal request to the Dispute Settlement Body. A party to the dispute can block the initial request for a panel; however, the Dispute Settlement Body must approve a second request. Why would one side block a request? Blocking a request allows a party to force consultations until the next meeting of the Dispute Settlement Body (meetings usually occur only once a month). Panels consist of three to five members. The WTO secretariat recommends panelists from a list of trade experts, and both parties must agree to each candidate proposed. If members cannot come to agreement on the panelists, the director general will choose them. This process takes between thirty to sixty days on average to be completed.

Once a panel has been created, it begins to review the dispute. The parties to the dispute present oral and written arguments. Other member states that feel affected by the dispute have the right to present oral and written arguments to the panel as well. In complex cases, panels may call on outside experts to help them in adjudicating the case. Interestingly, groups (NGOs) separate from the dispute have won the ability to participate in the review through the submission of amicus briefs (friendly briefs from outside interests). Their influence is limited, since panels are not required to examine or use these as part of their proceedings.[19] At the end of the review process, the panel submits a preliminary report to the parties involved who then have two weeks to submit comments on the report. A final report is issued to the parties involved, and three weeks later the report is given to all members of the WTO.

Once the final report has been made, parties to a dispute have the right to appeal the panel's decision. If no appeal is made, the report is passed to the Dispute Settlement Body that then has sixty days to consider and approve the report. Reverse consensus is required to block acceptance of a report since all members must disapprove of a panel report in order for it not to be accepted. This is a significant reform of the old dispute process where any GATT member could veto a dispute panel ruling that went against it. Note the specific time restrictions imposed by the process as well. No longer can cases drag out for years without resolution. This initial review process is supposed to take nine months—long enough to be sure, but not too long for a judicial process.

Unlike dispute panels, the WTO's Appellate Body is not ad hoc, but a standing body within the WTO containing seven permanent members who serve four-year terms.[20] Members are chosen to be broadly representative of member interests as well as for their expertise; they are expected to act in the interests of the WTO, not for any particular member interest. Three members of the Appellate Body are assigned to hear each appeal. Reviews of a panel decision are expected to take place within sixty days after receipt of the case and not more than ninety days after. The Appellate Body may affirm, reverse, or modify any panel decision. The only requirement for the decision is that it remains within the confines of the issues laid out in the original panel report. The decision of the Appellate Body is forwarded in a report to all WTO members and to the Dispute Settlement Body, which must approve the report within thirty days after receiving it. Again, only a unanimous vote against the report can block its acceptance.

The final stage of the dispute settlement process is, of course, the implementation of dispute panel decisions.[21] Parties losing a dispute panel decision have thirty days after the Dispute Settlement Body's acceptance of the report to detail how they will come into compliance. If the party cannot come into immediate compliance, it must either enter negotiations with the other parties to the dispute or accept arbitration to determine the amount of time that will be allowed for implementation. In some cases, states can change their practices overnight; in others it takes a legislative change, and that takes time. The general rule allows fifteen months for compliance. If a party has not come into compliance by the end of the time allotted, it must enter into negotiations with the parties involved to determine compensation. If negotiations fail, then parties may petition the Dispute Settlement Body to approve a suspension of concessions. Suspension of concessions means that a GATT member may raise tariffs against a country refusing to comply with a decision. The monetary value of the increase in tariffs is to be commensurate with the harm done by the member's failure to comply with the panel decision. For instance, if country A's failure to comply has cost country B $250 million in exports of fish, country B will be allowed to increase tariffs on country A's products so that it will lose $250 million in exports to country B. These sanctions need not be in the categories of goods under dispute; look to case studies in Chapters 5 and 6 for insights into these points.

The Dispute Settlement Body handles all disputes within the WTO. This includes disputes under the GATT, GATS, Trade Related Investment Measures Agreement (TRIMS), Trade Related Intellectual Property Rights Agreement (TRIPS), and the Sanitary and Phytosanitary Agreement (SPS). Before 1995 there were separate dispute settlement bodies for each of these within the GATT process, and naturally this created uncertainty among members and often led to problems of consistency in determining the obligations of GATT members.[22] The single dispute settlement process has proven to be a very important reform of the GATT.

The Dispute Settlement Body itself has no means to force a member to comply with its decisions. This situation was intentionally created to keep enforcement in the hands of member states.[23] Sometimes politics within a member state make it impossible for the state to meet its GATT obligations. Forcing it into compliance would only lead to the member leaving the organization or finding ways to cheat. Instead, dispute settlement allows for compensation for members that are harmed by another member that does not meet its obligations. If compensation, on the other hand, cannot be agreed on, then concessions can be suspended indefinitely. For domestic political reasons, a member may find suspension of some concessions, though harmful to its interests, more palatable than changing its offending policy. We will see this in Chapter 6 where the EU has been willing to accept trade sanctions in order to preserve its regulation concerning the use of hormones in the production of beef.

It is important to note that the dispute settlement process has been deemed a success by most commentators on the subject.[24] During the first five years of the new process, members filed 185 requests for consultations. Consultations either succeeded or led to the withdrawal of the complaint in 105 cases. In the other 80 cases, a panel was established to solve the dispute. However, panels were forced to report in only 62 of the cases. In the other 18, the parties involved were able to resolve the dispute before the panel released its decision. Finally, of the 62 decisions made by panels, 44 were appealed to the Appellate Body.[25]

These numbers suggest that the process has functioned the way the founders intended. Consultations have resolved the majority of disputes, leaving dispute panels as a last resort, not a first resort. Members have also shown a willingness to comply with decisions made by panels. A U.S. General Accounting Office (GAO) report found that in disputes with the United States, WTO members had complied with panel decisions 75 percent of the time. Overall, compliance rates were 65 percent.[26] This may not sound high, but recall that the WTO Dispute Settlement Body has limited tools for forcing members to obey its decisions.

However, the first six years of operation did uncover some problems with the dispute settlement process. The large number of cases has taxed the ability of the WTO to find suitable panelists. The secretariat has also had trouble providing staff resources needed for each panel. Both of these factors have made it difficult for the panels to stick to the timelines for decision making set out in the Dispute Settlement Understanding.[27] The majority of panel decisions have been circulated to members ten to thirteen months after the panel's establishment. The formal timeline calls for reports to be circulated within nine months of the panel's creation. Meeting the timelines has been a problem, but it must be remembered that the panels have resolved conflicts significantly faster than under the process that existed prior to 1994. Increasing the size of the WTO secretariat would be an easy reform to address this problem. A second fix would be to create a permanent dispute panel body—like the Appellate Body—so panels could be created more efficiently. A permanent body would also allow the development of institutional expertise, which may quicken the decision-making pace. Currently, panelists are drawn from across the world on a case-by-case basis, and for the vast majority of panelists, the case they are assigned is not only their first, but often their last.

A third problem is caused by the fact that the Appellate Body is unable to remand cases back to the original dispute panel.[28] This has become a difficulty for the Appellate Body when a case involves multiple violations of the WTO agreements. The Dispute Settlement Understanding requires dispute panels to resolve disputes efficiently. Many panels have interpreted this to mean that as soon as they find that a member has violated a portion of the agreement, it should end its review and issue its report without looking at the other potential violations. When these types of cases are appealed, the Appellate Body is faced with the dilemma that if it overturns the dispute panel's decision, it cannot ask that the other potential violations be examined. Nor does the Appellate Body have the jurisdiction to examine the issues on its own since the Dispute Settlement Understanding requires the Appellate Body to limit its focus to the issues of law and fact covered in the panel's decision. This can lead to members having to resubmit complaints in order to obtain compliance with the WTO agreements.

To solve this problem, the Appellate Body in some cases has decided that its duty to solve disputes overrides its duty to stick to the facts and issues of law covered in the panel report. Some dispute settlement panels have also begun reviewing all issues presented to them to prevent this problem from occurring in the first place.[29] Neither of these adaptations completely prevents the situation because they have only been utilized in some cases, not all. Giving remand authority to the Appellate Body would be an easy solution. However, it would require the establishment of a permanent dispute panel body or require that panelists can be recalled as needed, unlike the current situation where panelists return to their countries and occupations as soon as their work is completed.

There has also been some confusion over the suspension of concessions for members that fail to comply with a panel decision.[30] This confusion became a major issue in the banana case between the United States and EU.

Another problem is that compliance with a decision is too often connected to the power of WTO members.[31] As we have seen, decisions where the United States is a party to the dispute have a far higher compliance rate than that for all cases. The reason for this is clearly that the United States has the largest single economy in the world, and countries that fail to comply with a panel decision favoring the United

States may find the United States closing its market to some of their products or placing punitive tariffs on their goods. In some cases, this may mean that a country loses a major or even primary market for one of its exports. Small, especially developing countries are usually not primary markets for other countries' exports. The result is that losing these markets is not particularly painful for those refusing to comply with a WTO decision, and thus they have less reason to comply. The disproportionality of power and influence between countries does not go away just because there is a regime of rules and regulations.

ISSUES AND CHALLENGES FOR THE WTO

PROBLEMS FOR DEVELOPING COUNTRIES

Member governments control the WTO, which means that members get out of the organization in proportion to what they put into it. Since the creation of the WTO, its developing country members have had the most difficulty participating in its affairs and making the organization work for them. One reason for this is that developing countries often do not have the resources to insure proper representation on WTO councils and committees.[32] Only 66 percent of developing countries maintain a permanent mission in Geneva for the WTO, while all of the more developed country members have delegations there. Only twelve of the twenty-nine least developed members (these are a subset of the developing countries) have a mission in Geneva. Countries without a permanent mission in Geneva obviously have problems participating in the many meetings held by councils and committees and therefore only have input in the larger, and later, decision arenas. For instance, there were over 1,600 meetings held during 1995, about 30 per week. More importantly, the General Council meets monthly and is the central decision maker of the WTO between ministerial conferences. States without a mission to the WTO may not be represented at these meetings, meaning they have no substantive influence on General Council decisions or the various committees of the WTO.[33] How do poorer states keep up with this level of activity? It would appear they do not.

A second problem is that the developing countries have smaller delegations representing them at the WTO when they are present.[34] In 1997 the average size of missions for all WTO members was 4.1 persons. The average size of developed country missions was 6.7, while the average for the developing countries was 3.6. For the smallest and poorest members, the average was 1.2. Mission size is important; not only does it allow a country to participate in more committees and conferences, but it also allows individuals to get valuable experience and to specialize in certain areas and issues of particular concern to their country. It goes without saying that a larger presence improves the ability of a member to affect outcomes within these committees. Ironically, developed countries have complained about their WTO workload, and if these countries with their large missions are having problems, then the developing countries are surely having serious difficulties.[35]

Third, many of the poorest countries lack the expertise within their country, let alone government, to properly implement the various agreements within the WTO.[36] This lack of expertise obviously makes it difficult for these states to represent themselves effectively. Countries must know where they stand in respect to others and which policies of other members are affecting them before they can begin to negotiate. They must also have a knowledge and appreciation of the complex "rules of the game" of international trade as well as of the processes and procedures used to make GATT/WTO decisions. Without trade expertise and experience, defending their interests is difficult, if not impossible.

Some of the developing country members of the WTO have begun hiring outside consultants to help them bridge the expertise gap.[37] Initially there were questions about whether outside consultants could be used in WTO forums—especially in the dispute settlement process. An Appellate Body report in 1997 ruled that nothing in the Marrakech Agreement establishing the WTO prohibited a member from using outside counsel in disputes. The Appellate Body also ruled that it was up to members to determine the composition of their delegations. Questions continue about whether members may use nongovernmental personnel to represent them on other WTO committees, conferences, and bodies.

The WTO secretariat has also increased its effort, particularly after the Seattle and Cancun ministerial meetings, in providing technical assistance to developing country members. Largely it runs training programs, collects trade data and disseminates it to the countries most affected by it, and provides assistance in interpreting WTO commitments and in meeting WTO reporting requirements.

Finally, many developing countries believe they are inadequately represented in the informal Green Room discussions that have been used to forge consensus in the WTO on major issues.[38] Developing countries believe that the four largest trading members, the United States, Canada, the EU, and Japan (the Quad countries), have too much influence in these meetings. They also believe that the "developing countries" that are often chosen to participate are not representative of the wide variety of interests in the developing world, but tend to be newly industrialized countries, or those industrializing, and have different agendas. The commonly chosen developing countries, China, India, and Brazil, simply see the international political economy in significantly different ways than do smaller, poor countries. At the Seattle Ministerial Conference in 1999 and at Cancun in 2003, efforts were made to bring more developing countries into the process. Still, these efforts ran into the problem that many developing countries did not have the personnel available to participate adequately.

Despite these weaknesses, developing countries are more involved in the WTO than they were under the old GATT and more involved since the early years of the WTO.[39] A very noticeable change has come in the filing of dispute complaints. Developing countries filed 64 percent of complaints in 2005, up from 20 percent in 1997.[40] Developing countries also control more committee chairmanships than they did in the GATT during the 1980s. The most important positions, like heads of the

Council on Trade in Goods, have been carefully balanced between developed and developing country members. If a developed country representative is the council chair, a developing country representative is made vice-chair. Developed and developing countries are then reversed when new chairs are appointed.

Again, there has been a self-conscious move by the WTO since the beginning of the latest negotiations, the Doha Round, to include a more diverse group of developing countries in consultations and negotiations. This is particularly true in the controversial and important areas of agriculture and services. However, many writers representing the developing countries have stated that they still believe that progress has been superficial at best.[41]

TRANSPARENCY

Transparency has become one of the larger concerns of the WTO. The WTO was designed to make trade regulations and policies between members more transparent, more open. Transparency requires that the policies and practices of members are easily seen and understood. Members should not use hidden means to block trade. Transparency also requires that GATT/WTO decision making and negotiations are open to all members and easily understood by them. The expectation is that by opening the organization and the policies of members to scrutiny, uncertainty will be reduced and trade facilitated.

However, since the WTO's creation, there have been calls from some developing as well as developed countries, and vociferous demands from a variety of nongovernmental organizations, for the WTO to become more transparent. For the bulk of its existence, the GATT/WTO has been a relatively closed organization. Decision making has traditionally been carried out by members behind closed doors. The dispute settlement process is for member states only; third parties in disputes, unless members of the WTO, have no rights of participation, and dispute settlement processes are also closed to the public.[42]

The closed nature of the WTO has led many to argue that the organization is undemocratic and unaccountable. These same critics charge that only narrow economic interests are represented in the WTO, while interests like the environment and human rights are ignored. This bias leads to decisions, it is argued, that adversely affect the social and environmental conditions in member states, the very conditions in which individuals live.[43]

Several members, the United States in particular, have called for opening the WTO processes.[44] The United States has proposed that dispute panels be opened to the public and that all briefs by contending parties be made publicly available. The United States has also argued that individuals and groups be allowed to present their arguments to the panels and that panels consider these arguments. Currently, outside interests can file briefs with dispute panels, but it is up to the panel to decide whether it wants to use them in its deliberations. Some members have acted to open the dispute process on their own by disseminating briefs to the public and releasing panel decisions to the public as soon as the member receives them. Many interest groups have also called on the WTO to open its various councils and committees to the public and to provide transcripts from all meetings.[45]

Many members oppose opening the organization. They argue that the WTO is held accountable to the public at large through its members, and that the WTO is a state-based international organization. These members also argue that opening decision-making forums to the public will make it more difficult to negotiate and compromise on issues. Under the glare of public scrutiny, states often find it difficult to make the trade-offs needed to resolve a dispute or come to an agreement. Imagine the interest group pressures that would have been brought to bear on the various governments during the Uruguay Round if the proceedings had been public. Fiona McGillivray in an essay for the Hoover Institute argues that opening the WTO to the public would empower protectionist interests at the expense of those who support free trade.[46] The costs of freeing trade are usually concentrated in a few industries or economic sectors, while the benefits are usually diffused across a country. Consequently, McGillivray argues, losers have a strong incentive to organize and lobby against changes that will hurt them. Those winning do not have the same incentives because the benefits to any individual within the country are rather small. Thus, negotiators in an open environment will be forced to listen mostly to the opponents of free trade. By keeping negotiations secret, the sectors affected can be kept in the dark until the agreement is completed. It is then possible to mobilize those winning from the agreement to stop those who would like to derail it.

Others insist that democratic governments in particular must insure that actions taken by the WTO are aligned with the general interests and principles of their people. Even nondemocratic governments must worry about support from their business communities as well as the activist portion of their public. Labor unions and environmental groups have been the most vocal supporters of opening the WTO and even curtailing its power. Developing countries fear that allowing these groups access to the WTO will lead the WTO to begin supporting efforts to raise member labor and environmental standards.[47] Many developing countries believe that lower standards in these areas reflect the local culture and conditions and are one of the few fundamental trade advantages that they have. If developing countries are forced to adopt the same standards as the developed countries, then many industries will decide to remain in the developed world instead of relocating to the developing world.

The concern with transparency and democracy was a central factor leading to the protests at the Seattle and Cancun Ministerial Conferences (covered in Chapters 8 and 9) both from the inside, by members who felt marginalized, and from outside the meetings, where many NGOs and others claimed to represent the worldwide public interest. Since these meetings, the WTO hierarchy has elevated transparency as an issue on its agenda. Whether the organization will accept more transparency is still an open question.

DECISION MAKING

Since its beginnings, the GATT, and now WTO, have relied on consensus in the making of decisions. This did not create significant problems when the agreement was created since there were only 24 countries as members. As of 2006, the WTO had 149 members. Forming consensus among this many countries is difficult to say the least, and it is possible for any country to stifle change, gridlocking the whole system.

In order to streamline the decision-making process, several WTO members have proposed the creation of an executive committee consisting of representatives from twenty to forty countries.[48] Membership would be designed to reflect both geography and the economic interests of member states. The executive committee would not be able to make decisions on its own; it would be charged with developing proposals for the whole WTO membership to examine both as the General Council and as draft proposals for the biennial ministerial meetings. It is hoped that this would facilitate the development of consensus within the organization by focusing on issues and identifying early potential solutions to problems. Members of the executive committee would be expected to take committee proposals to their client groups and to mobilize support for them, in the end facilitating passage of executive committee decisions by the General Council.

Opponents of this idea argue that any kind of executive committee is likely to make the major trading countries even more powerful within the WTO than they already are.[49] It is almost inconceivable that an executive committee would not contain the Quad countries, for none of them are likely to approve of any proposal that does not give them representation. Furthermore, many argue that transparency could be a problem. The proceedings of the meetings of the committee would have to be open to all other members, and transcripts of its activities would have to be made publicly available. Then again, if the committee is completely open to all members, as a few suggest, then the process is likely to degenerate back into the general model of consensus decision making, and we are back where we started.

Fixing the decision-making process will not be an easy task. This issue is on the agenda of the Doha Round of negotiations, and that means it may remain unresolved for some time. Perhaps the solution to the decision-process problems simply resides in utilization of the voting percentages already embedded in the WTO documents for the broader organs of the organization.

CONCLUSION

Some critics of the WTO have expressed fears that the treaty is the first step toward a world government, that it will strip members of their sovereignty and reign over citizens of the world in an unaccountable and unchecked fashion. If there is one lesson to be learned from this text, however, it is that these fears appear to be unfounded. The WTO is run by sovereign member states on the basis of their own interests. It has no authority independent from what its members have given it. Moreover, the collective membership may take back any power it has given the organization at any time. Members, not the WTO, enforce dispute settlements, taking away any police powers that the organization might have accrued. Moreover, as the ultimate act of sovereignty, a member may leave the WTO at any time with simply a six-month notice. This may not be practical for many members, but it is an option.

This does not mean that the WTO has not established itself as an important international organization, or that its creation has not had fundamental consequences for international trade. We have seen the dramatic growth of international trade in the GATT/WTO period. We have also seen better handling of disputes under the new rules created within the WTO. The result has been a reduction in the amount of uncertainty in trade relationships, which helps to foster economic growth. Trade relationships now hinge more on the rule of law and less on the rule of might, which encourages countries to open their borders to trade. It is no small thing that the GATT/WTO affords all countries the possibility of getting even the most powerful members of the organization to follow and live up to their commitments.

The permanent nature of the WTO's structure has allowed it to facilitate the actions of its members. Today, the WTO provides substantial assistance to its developing country member states, opening access to more opportunities for them. Because of their insistence, there has been an enhanced role for developing countries in the more recent WTO meetings. Members have also benefited from the larger permanent staff that helps run and facilitate more universal participation in the various councils and committees that govern the WTO. Finally, the director general has moved into the role of primary mediator between members and coalitions of members of the WTO.

We have also seen that the WTO faces several issues and challenges. Developing countries are still at a significant disadvantage within the organization. The dispute settlement process, while vastly improved over the system that existed prior to 1994, still has some areas that need improvement or reform. Decision making by consensus has become unwieldy and difficult.

The most glaring problem for many remains the continuing lack of sufficient transparency. One of the reasons that so many organized interests, coalitions, and individuals fear the WTO is that they either do not understand it or they find no viable entrance into decision making in the important arenas in which the WTO operates. It seems legitimate to demand that even if the public is not afforded the opportunity to watch or participate in WTO proceedings, it should at least be given more information about what decisions are made, how it goes about making those decisions, and who is participating in them. Information needs not only to be as comprehensive as possible, but it needs to be presented in a timely manner as well.

There is no inevitability to the continued existence of the GATT/WTO as the visible hand of international trade. Structural reforms are just one of the elements that need careful scrutiny if broad acceptance of the rules, regulations, and processes of the organization is to be achieved. Important decisions are made within the bodies of the GATT/WTO. Eventually, without broad civic support for its legitimacy, states may find it impossible to continue to follow its tenants.

PART II

THE WORLD TRADE ORGANIZATION: CASES AND CONTROVERSIES

CHAPTER 5

THE GREAT BANANA WAR

In the 1990s, the banana was anything but tasty or humorous for the WTO and its two leading members. The fruit was at the center of a very significant trade dispute between the EU and the United States. Resolving this conflict tested the WTO's ability to settle disputes and to enforce its decisions. It all started innocently enough in 1993 with a change in the EU's banana regime, but by March of 1999, the dispute over bananas had grown to such an extent that some commentators feared for the very survival of the WTO. How could the humble banana become the focus of such a nasty conflict?

In answering the above question, our case study will illustrate (1) how the internal politics of a country affect the trade policies the country pursues, (2) the problems the EU has had in developing a single trade policy for its members, (3) how European trade policy is still affected by its colonial past, (4) how the need to set precedents within the WTO can lead to the escalation of trivial disputes into international conflicts, and (5) some of the weaknesses of the WTO dispute settlement process.

THE ORIGINS OF THE DISPUTE

The banana dispute arose from the EU's attempt to balance two international commitments and one internal policy: the Lomé Convention, GATT treaty obligations, and the Single European Act. During negotiations to create the EC[1] in 1957, France obtained special treatment for its former colonies. They were provided with aid and market access in order to help them grow and develop economically. Like France, Britain wanted special treatment for its former colonies when it entered the EC in 1973. This led to the formation of the Lomé Convention.[2]

The convention was ratified in 1975 and has had three subsequent rounds of negotiations. It requires the EC to give special treatment to all former colonies of Britain and France, referred to as the African, Caribbean, and Pacific Countries (ACP). It also requires the EC to help these countries in their efforts to develop. Reconciling the requirements of the Lomé Convention to the GATT has been a significant problem for the EC. GATT principles prohibit members from giving preferential treatment to other members, which Lomé requires.

The Single European Act was adopted by the EC in 1987 and implemented in 1992. It was designed to create a seamless market within the EC by eliminating all obstacles to trade between members. This required the EC to develop uniform trade regimes or sets of rules for a variety of goods and services that until 1992 had been handled by individual members.

Before 1992 there were in essence three different banana regimes for Europe. Germany had a completely open market with no quotas or tariffs.[3] Denmark, Ireland, and all of the Benelux Countries had a 20 percent tariff on bananas. France, Spain, Britain, Italy, Greece, and Portugal had a system of quotas and tariffs that gave preference to various producing countries and firms that imported bananas from them. For instance, Spain's market was completely closed to all bananas not produced in the Canary Islands, while France and Britain gave preferential access to bananas from their former colonies. Britain's system also gave preference to two major importers of bananas: Geest and Fyffes. Together they controlled 85 percent of the banana market in Britain, but had very little market share elsewhere in Europe. Creating one regime from these three was very difficult for the EC.

In the end, a single banana regime—Regulation 404—was created. It was announced in December 1992 and scheduled to be implemented July 1, 1993.[4] The regime was largely the product of the EU Commission's directorate generals for agriculture and external affairs. ACP countries and European importers conducted a well-executed and coordinated lobbying campaign for a managed and protected market, while non-European importers and non-ACP producers of bananas were silent.[5]

The result was a very complicated policy that guaranteed ACP countries a protected share of the European market and that favored European companies like Geest and Fyffes at the expense of non-European companies like Chiquita, Dole, and Del Monte.[6] Germany also lost out on the new regime. Small companies used by Chiquita and Dole in Germany to ripen and distribute their bananas lost market share, and German banana prices rose. Germany reacted by filing an unsuccessful suit against the regime with the European Court of Justice in 1993.

What exactly did Regulation 404 do? The first part of the regime consisted of a system of tariffs and quotas for bananas imported into the EU. An annual quota of 857,700 metric tons was given to ACP countries based on their best previous export year to Europe. Imports within the quota would receive no tariff, and the expectation was that the ACP countries would not reach this quota in the foreseeable future. An annual quota of 2 million metric tons was set for non-ACP countries. Bananas imported within this quota were charged a 75 ECU per ton tariff.[7] Bananas imported over the quota were charged an 822 ECU per ton tariff, essentially limiting banana imports into the EU to 2,857,700 tons.[8]

The banana regime also consisted of a series of import licenses required of anyone wishing to import bananas into the EU. The licenses were distributed to three different categories of importers: Category A licenses went to historical importers of bananas from non-ACP countries, making up 66.5 percent of the total. Category B licenses went to historical importers of ACP bananas, making up 30 percent of the total. Category C licenses went to newcomers to the market, a mere 3.5 percent of the total. Category A and B licenses were further subdivided into primary importers, secondary importers, and ripeners. Primary importers were companies that either produced bananas themselves or bought them directly from banana producers for import into the EU. Secondary importers were companies that bought bananas from primary importers and then imported the bananas or distributed them within Europe. Ripeners were companies that stored bananas until they were ripe for consumption. In the United States, this type of business does not exist since grocery stores ripen bananas themselves.[9]

Finally, a special set of Hurricane licenses were created to help Category B importers. In the event a hurricane damaged the crops of these importers, they could apply for special Hurricane licenses. These licenses could be sold by the Category B importers to others, either other ACP or non-ACP importers wishing to distribute bananas in Europe. In this way, ACP countries and importers of ACP bananas would still be able to generate banana export revenues even if they had no bananas to export.[10]

The GATT prohibits a member country from discriminating against the products of other members. The banana regime clearly violated this principal. First, it discriminated between ACP countries and non-ACP countries, most of which were members of the GATT and now of the WTO. Under the EU's banana regime, non-ACP countries saw their ability to import bananas into Europe curtailed significantly while ACP countries saw their ability to import rise significantly. The Hurricane licenses also were a form of discrimination among banana importing firms. Firms not importing ACP bananas were not eligible to receive Hurricane licenses in the event a natural disaster destroyed the crops.[11]

GATT/WTO rules also prohibit members from treating domestic firms differently than firms from other countries. The license system created under the banana regime violated this principle as firms within Europe were given special access to import licenses that firms outside Europe did not have. This led to European importers gaining market share at the expense of non-European importers. For instance, Chiquita controlled more than 30 percent of the European market for bananas in 1992; this dropped to 19 percent by 1997. Meanwhile, Fyffes, a European firm, saw its market share rise from 5 percent in 1992 to 17 percent in 1997.[12]

The EU's commitment to the Lomé Convention required it to create a banana regime that would help the ex-colonies of France and Britain. The Single European Act, creating a seamless EU market, required the EU to develop a uniform import regime for bananas. Finally, the GATT and WTO agreements prohibited many of the actions the Lomé Convention and Single European Act required the EU to take. If any of these items had been absent, there would have been no banana conflict.

The incompatibility of these items was the tinder. A challenge to these items was required to actually set the tinder on fire. The rest of this case study chronicles who challenged, the motivations behind the challenge, and the consequences of the challenge.

LATIN AMERICAN OPPOSITION

Opposition to the EU banana regime, Regulation 404, arose immediately from the large banana producing countries in Central and South America.[13] Five of these countries, Colombia, Costa Rica, Guatemala, Nicaragua, and Venezuela, challenged the regime's compatibility with the GATT and filed a formal complaint soon after the EU announced the regime in December 1992. The EU's banana regime threatened to cut imports from these countries significantly, leading all of them to fear for their economic health. Some of these countries, like Colombia, also feared that the cuts caused by the regime would lead to political instability and the increased growing of crops like coca and poppies used in the production of illegal drugs.[14]

On May 19, 1993, a GATT dispute panel ruled in favor of the five countries.[15] The EU refused to consent to the panel's report, blocking its adoption and keeping it from being implemented. The five countries filed a second complaint in June 1993 and in February 1994; a GATT dispute panel ruled in their favor. Again, the EU refused to accept the GATT panel report, thereby keeping it from being implemented.[16]

It should be noted that these complaints were filed with the GATT secretariat, not the WTO. The WTO would not be created until the ratification of the Uruguay Round, which was still being negotiated at this time. This is important because the GATT, prior to 1995, required all members to accept the reports of GATT dispute panels. Thus, any member found to have violated the GATT could keep the GATT from taking action against it simply by not accepting the findings. This, of course, was a major weakness of the treaty. Countries under the treaty could be denied justice by the member that had committed an injustice. This is what the EU did to both the 1993 and 1994 GATT reports that found its Regulation 404 in violation of the agreement.

The failure of the GATT dispute process forced four of the five parties to the complaint to make a deal with the EU.[17] In May 1994, Colombia, Costa Rica, Nicaragua, and Venezuela entered a framework agreement with the EU that guaranteed the four countries a specific amount of the non-ACP banana quota. It also created a new set of licenses—export licenses. Anyone wanting to import bananas to Europe from these four countries not only needed to obtain an import license from the EU, but an export license from these countries. This had the benefit of forcing large multinational corporations to buy bananas from the parties to the framework agreement and gave the four countries the leverage to force these companies to pay higher prices for the bananas as well.

The framework agreement solved the major problems between its signatories, but it created a larger banana problem. Non-ACP countries outside this new framework agreement now saw their access to the European market even further reduced. Mexico, Ecuador, Honduras, and Guatemala, in particular, saw their exports of bananas fall an additional 27 percent from when Regulation 404 was first enacted.[18] These cuts hit Ecuador, the world's largest banana exporter, hardest.

U.S. OPPOSITION

The United States has historically produced few bananas and exported none to Europe. Why then would the United States care if the EU created a banana regime that was discriminatory and in violation of the GATT? The United States was drawn into this conflict because two of the largest banana trading companies were based in the United States: the Dole Fruit Company and Chiquita Brands International. Both of these companies were directly affected by EU Regulation 404. Each knew a change in European banana policies was coming well before Regulation 404 was announced or implemented, and each developed a strategy to account for the change.

The Dole Fruit Company's strategy was largely successful.[19] As soon as the EU adopted the regulation, Dole began moving some of its banana production from Latin America to ACP member states, and it bought several ripeners and banana distributors in Europe. Both these actions allowed Dole to obtain the import licenses it needed not only to maintain, but even to expand its market share in Europe from 12 percent in 1992 to 19 percent in 1997. While Dole adapted to the new regime, its leaders were not happy with it. The banana regime was complex and costly. Dole had to buy licenses to import bananas to Europe, and moving banana production from Latin America to Africa was expensive. These additional expenses forced Dole to cut employment and to diversify into other areas.[20] Moreover, the EU banana regime limited banana consumption creating a global surplus of bananas, decreasing their price and making it difficult for Dole to make a profit on banana distribution.

Chiquita was not so lucky or wise. When the EU began developing its new banana regime in 1991 and 1992, Chiquita believed it would open its markets, not close them.[21] This belief led Chiquita to add significantly to its fleet of ships used to deliver bananas to the European market and to divest itself of many of its banana plantations in Latin America. Chiquita believed that it could do better as a distributor of bananas to Europe instead of producing and distributing them. It would use its fleet to purchase and move bananas from the lowest cost producers of bananas. Chiquita could then sell these bananas at a more favorable price in Europe.

Regulation 404 ruined this strategy. Since each producer country had a set quota for exporting to Europe, Chiquita would not necessarily be able to choose from whom to buy bananas. Once a country had used up its quota, it would not be able to export more to Europe. The framework agreement developed between the EU and Venezuela, Colombia, Costa Rica, and Nicaragua made things worse. Chiquita now needed export licenses from these countries if it was to sell their bananas in Europe, which allowed these countries to demand higher prices from Chiquita.

As a result of all of this, Chiquita saw its financial prospects decline significantly. Chiquita's sales to Europe declined 19 percent between 1992 and 1997.[22] The company was also saddled with debt from its purchase of new ships leading to losses of $346 million between 1992 and 1994.[23] Chiquita was only sporadically profitable between 1995 and 2001, and in the spring 2001 Chiquita announced that it would either have to negotiate with its creditors for help or declare bankruptcy. The company also announced that it would sue the EU for damages caused by the banana regime.[24]

Both companies began lobbying the U.S. government shortly after the implementation of Regulation 404, asking the U.S. Trade Representative (USTR) to initiate a Super 301 case against Europe.[25] The Super 301 law, created in a 1974 trade bill, allowed the USTR to investigate complaints of a country or company engaging in unfair trade practices. If these practices were confirmed by the investigation, Super 301 required the USTR to place sanctions on the offender. No exceptions were to be made to this. The USTR initially turned down the companies' request to investigate, believing that the case did not pose enough of an interest to the United States. Few U.S. jobs were at stake, and the United States did not export any bananas to Europe itself.

This did not end Chiquita's pleas for help. Instead, Chiquita and its chairman and CEO, Carl Lindner, changed tactics. Beginning in late 1993, Carl Lindner and his holding company, American Financial Group, began donating large sums of money to both the Democratic and Republican parties. Between 1995 and 1999, Lindner and American Financial Group donated $635,000 to the Democratic Party and $2,374,000 to the Republican Party.[26] Lindner also cultivated close ties with several members of Congress. The most important of these was with Senator Robert Dole (Republican from Kansas) who was majority leader of the Senate. Lindner donated money to Dole's campaigns and allowed Dole access to his private jet for his 1996 presidential campaign.[27]

The cultivation of these ties began to work for Chiquita late in 1994. Senator Dole arranged several meetings between Lindner and the USTR, Mickey Kantor. In September 1994 the USTR expressed a willingness to support a Super 301 complaint if Chiquita filed one. In October 1994 the United States threatened the EU that it would take action against its banana regime. In January 1995 the USTR included in its Super 301 investigation the four Latin American countries that had signed the framework agreement protecting them from the EU's banana regime. However, the Super 301 investigation never bore fruit. One year after beginning the investigation, the USTR ended it without releasing any formal conclusions or final report. But this did not end U.S. action on the banana regime.[28]

During the year the USTR investigated the EU's banana regime, a new method for solving trade disputes was created: the WTO's stronger Dispute Settlement Body. In September 1995 Mickey Kantor announced that the United States, along with Guatemala, Mexico, and Honduras, was filing a complaint against the EU with the WTO. Ecuador joined the complaint in early 1996, shortly after becoming a member of the WTO. Coincidentally, one day after the U.S. announcement was made, Carl Lindner and his holding company began funneling five hundred thousand dollars into Democratic Party coffers.[29]

BANANAS BEFORE THE WTO

In order to bring a case before the WTO, a country must show it has standing (it has suffered direct harm from the actions of a member). There was some question concerning how much harm was done to the United States by the EU's banana regime, and thus whether the United States had standing. The USTR countered this question with two strategies. First, he enlisted the aid of several Central American countries in the complaint: Mexico, Guatemala, Honduras, and Ecuador, as previously noted. Each of these countries exported bananas directly to Europe and each was negatively affected. Second, he filed a broad complaint against the EU. The complaint argued that the banana regime not only violated several sections of the GATT, but also the newly adopted GATS. The U.S. position was that distribution of bananas was a service predominantly provided by U.S. companies in Europe before the regime was created. After the regime emerged, these companies saw a significant share of their business given to European firms. The regime not only kept non-ACP bananas from the European market; it kept American firms from supplying a service within Europe.[30]

The Europeans argued that the regime was consistent with the GATT and WTO. The EU, seeing this conflict brewing, had negotiated a special waiver to the GATT and WTO provisions in the last stages of the Uruguay Round negotiations in 1994. This waiver allowed the EU to continue to discriminate in favor of members of the Lomé Convention and, according to the EU, made the complaint invalid. The EU also argued that the United States did not have standing to bring a complaint before the WTO. The United States exported no bananas of its own; therefore, the EU banana regime did not have an effect on the United States. Finally, the EU argued that the marketing and distribution of bananas was not a service. Thus, the United States could not file a complaint under the new GATS.[31]

The ACP countries also weighed in on the debate. None of these countries were direct parties to the case; although, all of the banana producers among them would feel its effects. The most affected were located in the Windward Islands, located in the southeastern part of the Caribbean. Three Windward Island states, St. Lucia, Dominica, and Saint Vincent, were heavily dependent on bananas for their economic well-being. In 1991 these countries saw 31 percent of their labor forces tied either directly or indirectly to the production and export of bananas. In 1995 bananas accounted for 14.3 percent of Dominica's GDP, 12.3 percent of St. Lucia's GDP, and 11.1 percent of St. Vincent's GDP. Bananas in 1995 also accounted for 51.4 percent of exports in Dominica, 46.5 percent of exports in St. Lucia and 42.5 percent of exports in St. Vincent.[32]

Bananas in the Windward Islands were largely produced on small family farms. These farmers had better living standards than those working on large plantations in Central and South America. The governments in the Windward Islands also believed that the large number of family farms had created a better environment for democratic government. The problem, however, was that bananas produced in this fashion cost twice as much as those produced on large plantations. Without the EU banana regime, these countries would not be able to compete in the international market, resulting in the destruction of their economies and possibly their political systems. The governments of these countries also argued that once bananas were eliminated as their major export, farmers would have an incentive to begin growing plants used in the manufacture of illegal drugs.[33]

The position of these countries hit a responsive chord among many groups within the United States. This forced the USTR to argue that the United States was not opposing preferences to ACP countries, but that it was opposing the method that Europe had used in giving these preferences. A far simpler, less expensive, and less discriminatory regime of preferences could have been developed to help the ACP countries. Also, the USTR pointed out that a study done by the World Bank showed that the EU regime helped European banana distributors far more than it helped any of the ACP countries. The World Bank concluded that a direct subsidy for banana production would have been more beneficial to ACP countries than Regulation 404.[34]

The WTO requires that parties to a dispute consult with each other before turning to a formal WTO dispute settlement panel. The hope is that consultations will lead to an amicable settlement of the conflict. In early 1996, the United States, Mexico, Guatemala, Honduras, and Ecuador filed an official complaint with the WTO over the EU banana regime. However, arranging consultations turned out to be somewhat difficult. The EU wanted to consult with each party separately. Its strategy was to isolate the United States by settling individually with the other parties to the complaint. Barring a settlement, individual consultations would allow the EU to call for a dispute panel to deal with each individual complaint. The EU thought that depending on one panel to make a decision was more risky than depending on several. At first, the United States and its partners refused individual consultations, but eventually all sides agreed to a compromise. The EU could consult with each party separately, but only one dispute panel would be formed to hear the case if the consultations failed. Consultations took place between February and March 1996 but failed to resolve the dispute.[35]

The failure of consultations led to the forming of a WTO Dispute Panel at the end of March 1996. WTO Dispute Panels consist of three members, agreed upon by the parties, who are drawn from a permanent pool of trade experts. In this dispute, the EU and United States, Guatemala, Honduras, Mexico, and Ecuador could not agree on who should be on the panel. The Director General of the WTO, Renato Ruggerrio, was forced to intervene, and in June 1996 he picked the individuals that would hear the case. He chose Stuart Harbinson, Hong Kong's permanent representative to the WTO, Kym Anderson, an economist from Adelaide University in Australia, and Christian Haeberli a trade expert in the Swiss Ministry of Economics.[36]

Formal briefs were filed with the dispute panel on July 30, 1996. Under WTO procedures, once briefs are filed, the dispute panel holds a series of meetings with the parties involved. The first of these meetings was held in September 1996. The meetings are used as a forum for representatives of each country involved to make their cases and to rebut the cases of others. Six months after a panel is formed, it is expected to report its findings, if possible. Keeping with this requirement, the panel released its decision on May 22, 1997.[37]

The panel supported the complainants almost in their entirety. It ruled that the EU banana regime violated both the GATT and GATS. Specifically the panel ruled that the granting of Category B licenses, the setting of quotas for individual non-ACP countries, the requirement that some countries give export licenses to import bananas into Europe, and the giving of Hurricane licenses violated the GATT, the GATS, or both. The only bright spot for the EU was that the portion of the regime granting quotas to ACP countries was upheld as being allowed under the Lomé Convention.

The EU appealed the panel's decision in June 1997. In September, the WTO Appellate Body affirmed most of the lower panel's decision. One significant place where it did not was in the banana regime's creation of quotas for ACP countries. The Appellate Body ruled that the lower panel was incorrect in seeing this as being allowed by the Lomé Convention, dealing the EU yet another blow.

The Appellate Body's report was then sent to WTO members where it was accepted. Unlike the GATT where unanimity was required for acceptance, the WTO only requires unanimity for a report by a dispute panel or the Appellate Body for nonacceptance. This makes it impossible for a member found in violation of WTO, GATT, and GATS rules to block a decision and its implementation. The EU was given fifteen months from the date of the Appellate Body's decision to comply.[38] One thing should be noted: WTO Dispute Panels report what they find in violation of the GATT, but they do not tell violators what they must do to comply with the decision.

A TEST OF WILLS

Remember that in 1992, the creation of the banana regime had been quite contentious. Germany sued the EU to keep the regime from taking effect. The EU feared that changing the regime in response to the WTO decision would create a split among its members. In addition, the regime had already changed banana distribution in Europe. In changing how bananas were distributed, it also changed political support for the regime. There were now firms and groups with a vested interest in Regulation 404, and they would oppose any attempts to change it. Finally, France and Britain were under immense pressure from their ex-colonies to keep in place the system that benefited them.

In late 1997 and the first half of 1998, the EU worked to develop a new banana regime. Two solutions were offered: One was a set of small changes to Regulation 404 supported by the UK and Ireland. The other was to change Regulation 404 from a combination of tariffs and quotas to one consisting only of tariffs supported by Germany, Sweden, Denmark, Belgium, the Netherlands, and Italy. France believed that neither approach did enough for its ex-colonies and Caribbean territories.[39]

Reforming Regulation 404 was eventually tied to the complex process of developing other common agricultural policies within Europe. Over several days of bargaining in June 1998, a compromise was developed. The UK and France agreed to accept changes to the EU's Common Agricultural Policy (CAP) in order to obtain the banana regime they wanted. This new regime continued the tariff and quota system for the import of bananas into Europe, leaving the tariff rate and quotas for non-ACP countries unchanged as well as the quota and tariff exemption for ACP countries. The compromise was formally placed into EU regulations on July 20, 1998.

Negotiations continued among EU members over the licensing system created by Regulation 404. On October 28, 1998, the second half of the banana regime was announced.[40] The reformed regime eliminated the primary importer, secondary importer, and ripener categories in the awarding of licenses.

The WTO had found the use of these categories to be discriminatory because they reallocated business from some banana suppliers to others. A new method for allocating licenses was created that depended on import levels between 1994 and 1996. This time period was chosen to protect businesses that entered the banana market or saw their shares of business increase because of Regulation 404.[41]

The changes to the banana regime were not enough to eliminate the objections of the United States and its partners in the WTO case. The United States argued that the changes were merely window dressing and that the EU was attempting to circumvent the WTO Dispute Panel's decision. The United States believed that using import statistics from 1994 to 1996, a time during which the old EU regime was in place, to determine quota shares and the allocation of export licenses insured that firms benefiting under the old regime would still benefit. Europe was using the state of the world during the regime to determine what the state of the world after the regime would look like. This guaranteed that no change in outcome would occur.

The United States also pointed to the fact that the regime still discriminated in regards to allocating banana quotas. The quotas themselves had not changed; they had merely been increased a bit to allow more nontraditional exporters of bananas to enter the EU market.[42] Otherwise, the quotas were the same ones that the WTO had found in 1997 to be in violation of GATT and GATS treaty obligations.

The United States began taking action against the EU reforms before they were even complete. In July 1998, the USTR asked the EU to agree to reconstitute the WTO banana dispute panel. The representative wanted to obtain a ruling on the changes to the quota and tariff system that the EU announced at the end of June. In late July, the EU rejected the U.S. request to reconvene the panel. In September the USTR again asked the EU if it would agree to have a WTO panel consider the changes the EU had made to its banana regime. Again the EU refused to allow the panel to be reconvened.[43]

During this same time frame, the United States also began to take action outside of the WTO system in response to the EU's reforms. Charlene Barshefsky, the new USTR, warned the EU in July of 1997 that if it did not come into compliance with the WTO ruling on bananas, the United States would place punitive tariffs on various European goods that would be equal to the damage caused by the EU banana regime to U.S. companies.

In October 1998 the U.S. Congress weighed into the conflict. It demanded that the USTR begin taking action against the EU by publishing the EU products that would be the focus of retaliation. This request from Congress came after Carl Lindner, chairman and CEO of Chiquita, met with both the Speaker of the House, Newt Gingrich, and the Majority Leader of the Senate, Trent Lott.[44]

The USTR responded with a preliminary list of products totaling $1.5 billion by the end of October 1998. This was a rather high estimate of the damage caused by the EU banana regime and was eventually reduced to $520 million.[45] A 100 percent tariff would be placed on listed products, essentially eliminating them from the U.S. market.

In making the list, the USTR attempted to punish the countries within Europe that were most responsible for the regime (Britain, France, and Italy) while doing as little damage as possible to EU members who had not supported the regime (Denmark, Germany, and the Netherlands). Also, the USTR attempted to find products that would harm U.S. consumers the least. The list was not finalized until December 21, 1998.[46]

The EU's reaction to this list was immediate. EU Commission Vice-President, Sir Leon Brittan, charged the United States with stepping outside WTO rules by acting unilaterally. He argued that only the WTO could authorize trade sanctions in response to noncompliance with its rulings. No WTO body had ruled on whether the EU's reforms were in compliance or not. The United States had decided on its own to act as judge, jury, and enforcer of WTO transgressions. Sir Leon Brittan stated that Article 21.5 of the WTO Charter required the formation of a new dispute panel to determine whether the reformed banana regime was in compliance with WTO rules. Only after a new panel had ruled on the reformed regime could the United States act.[47]

The United States responded that to publish a list of products for retaliation was within its rights. The United States maintained that Article 22 of the WTO Charter gives members the right to place sanctions for noncompliance with WTO decisions. The U.S. position was that the WTO Charter requires a party to announce sanctions within twenty days of the end of the compliance period. The WTO must then vote on the sanctions within thirty days of the end of the compliance period. Acceptance of sanctions follows a rule of negative consensus. This means that only unanimity against sanctions can keep them from going into effect. Since the member announcing sanctions will not vote against them, sanctions are automatic. If a party to a dispute fails to announce sanctions within twenty days of the end of the compliance period, sanctions can only be used if members of the WTO are unanimous in their support of them. Members being retaliated against have the right to ask for arbitration on the level of sanctions, but not whether the sanctions are allowable. Arbitration must be completed within sixty days of the end of the compliance period.[48] With this understanding, the United States believed that it had to act by January 21, 1999, in order to place sanctions on the EU.

The United States believed that following the EU interpretation of the WTO Charter would weaken the organization significantly. If a new dispute panel had to be created to determine whether a member was in compliance with a previous panel's decision, it would allow violators of WTO rules to avoid ever having to comply with a decision. A constant series of panels would be created to judge a member's compliance with previous panels. No resolution would ever occur.[49] The EU disagreed with this position. It argued that a new panel could rule on whether the EU was in compliance. If it was not, the United States could then impose the sanctions allowed members under Article 22 of the WTO Charter.[50] The WTO Charter does not give much help in ending this dispute over interpretation, as it is not as explicit as it might be.

In November 1998, the United States again asked the EU to agree to reconvene the original banana dispute panel. The EU conditioned its acceptance on the United States agreeing not to announce its intentions to place sanctions on the EU within twenty days of the end of the compliance period. In return for this, the EU would agree to reconstitute the panel and would sign a separate agreement with the United States allowing it to place sanctions if no agreement could be reached once the panel had examined the issue. This offer was unacceptable to the United States, as it believed the EU was attempting to get the United States to waive its right to place sanctions. Besides, WTO rules do not allow members to make side agreements in enforcing its rules. If the United States failed to announce sanctions within twenty days, the United States believed (side agreement or not) that sanctions could then only be put in place if all WTO members agreed to them. This would allow the EU or one of its allies to stop the United States from punishing the EU for noncompliance.[51]

During this period, the banana conflict began to grow much larger in importance for both the United States and EU. In the case of the United States, winning on bananas was important because of its effect on other important cases that were currently before the WTO. The United States was at odds with the EU over hormone-treated beef and with Canada over beer and magazines. The United States believed that by showing strength on bananas, it would be more likely that these other issues would be resolved in its favor. The United States also felt that the banana case was setting a precedent for the resolution of future WTO cases. If the EU was allowed to "get away" with reforms to its banana regime that did not meet the spirit of the WTO's decision, then countries in future cases would be able to do the same. In the end, the WTO would become a weak regulator of international trade much as the GATT had been.[52]

The EU saw U.S. actions as setting a precedent that undermined the rule of law within the WTO. If the United States could determine whether the EU was in compliance with a WTO decision and place sanctions on the EU without WTO permission, then in future conflicts other members could do this as well. This would lead to the unraveling of the WTO as a world trade arbiter. Members would be able to do as they please. The WTO had been formed to insure that a neutral party was arbitrating disputes and determining punishments for violators of world trade rules. The U.S. position challenged this. The EU was also worried that the banana case was eliminating a policy choice, tariff quotas, that states had regularly used to meet their world trade needs.[53] For both parties, reputation was also at stake. So much had been committed to the dispute that both sides saw losing now as a significant blow to their credibility.

The EU and United States traded rhetorical cannonballs through November and December 1998. Neither side was willing to compromise or negotiate on the issue. The United States remained firm in its commitment to announce sanctions after January 1, 1999, unless the EU made significant changes to its reformed banana regime. The EU remained firm that it would not change its regime unless the WTO found it in noncompliance. In mid-December, the EU took the unprecedented step of requesting the WTO to form a new dispute panel to consider whether its reformed banana regime now complied with WTO rules. Against U.S. wishes, Ecuador joined the EU in this request. A new panel was formed on January 12, 1999. Two days later, the United States formally announced its intentions to place sanctions on the EU for noncompliance with the WTO.[54]

The conflict came to a head at the end of January 1999. For the United States to begin sanctions, the WTO had to formally act on them. This required a vote by WTO members on the issue. If the members were not unanimous in their opposition to U.S. sanctions, then the sanctions would be allowed. The United States had placed the issue on the agenda for the WTO's meeting on January 25, 1999. St. Lucia and Dominica, two Windward Island countries that were helped by the EU banana regime, and the Ivory Coast stopped the meeting from occurring by refusing to approve the agenda.[55] This raised questions about whether countries had the right to vote on the WTO agenda. The EU and Windward Islands argued that unanimous consent was required for developing the agenda. The United States and its allies in the banana fight argued that if this were the case, then it would be possible for any member to keep the WTO from acting. Clearly, members had control over decisions of the WTO, but they should not be able to keep issues from being considered.[56]

The head of the WTO, Renato Rugerrio, immediately began to craft a compromise that would end the impasse. Negotiations between the EU and United States began January 25 and ended with an agreement on January 29. The United States agreed to allow a WTO panel to determine whether the EU was in compliance with the 1997 decision. The same panel would also consider whether the United States could levy sanctions on the EU and whether the level of sanctions proposed by the United States was appropriate. The EU agreed to allow the chairman of the WTO to pick the panel. He chose the same individuals who had heard the original case. The EU also agreed that the panel should expedite its activities with a decision to come in late March or early April.[57]

In March 1999, the dispute heated up again as the United States placed duties on EU goods for noncompliance with the WTO before the WTO panel had reported its conclusions. The EU and many other WTO members excoriated the United States in an emergency meeting that was held on March 7, 1999. The Canadian representative to the WTO said that the WTO "was not a house that belonged only to the EU and US but all 134 members."[58] No member supported the U.S. action, and most were vocal in their opposition to it

The United States responded that it had acted on the belief that the panel that was formed in late January 1999 (and had failed to meet its March 3 deadline) would rule in its favor. The United States also commented that while duties on $520 million in EU goods were being placed, they would not be collected until a formal WTO decision permitted them. Instead, EU firms hit by the tariffs would have to place bonds with the U.S. government showing they could pay the tariffs. The bond requirement, in effect, created a tariff on these European firms excluding them from the U.S. market.[59]

Negative rhetoric between the EU and United States remained high until April 7, 1999, when the reconvened panel finally released its decision. The panel ruled that the EU was in noncompliance with its previous decision and demanded that the EU come into compliance.[60] It also allowed the United States to place punitive sanctions on the EU, although it reduced them from $520 million to $191 million since the panel felt that the United States had grossly inflated the damages done to it and its companies by the banana regime. U.S. sanctions would be allowed to continue until the EU banana regime met WTO guidelines. The EU decided not to appeal the decision.

Changing the banana regime was quite difficult for the EU. As we saw earlier, there were many political interests in and outside of Europe that had to be accommodated in any arrangement. In November 1999, the EU Commission announced a new banana regime that it thought would be WTO compliant.[61] Opposition from the United States and others was immediate. This led to further delays.

The slowness of EU action on this issue led Ecuador to ask the WTO to allow it to levy $450 million in trade sanctions on the EU. Ecuador's permanent mission to the WTO stated that "the illegal restrictions imposed by the EU have done considerable damage to the Ecuadorian economy."[62] It also stated that it believed that the EU was engaged in "stalling tactics" in making the changes required by the WTO.

The conflict was finally settled for the United States and EU in April 2001 when a negotiated settlement was reached. The EU agreed to scrap the regime it proposed in 1999. Instead, it adjusted the quotas under the old regime to allow exporters harmed by it to regain their lost market share. The United States agreed as part of this to support a waiver before the WTO that would guarantee the ACP countries seven hundred thousand tons of banana exports into Europe each year at the lowest level of tariffs. The EU also agreed that the tariff quota system it had created in 1992 would be phased out completely by 2006. The new system is one based on tariffs only. Sanctions were removed in July 2001.[63]

However, in 2005 Honduras, Panama, and Guatemala asked for consultations with the EU concerning its new banana regime, arguing that it was still discriminatory.[64] Arbitration over the level of tariffs set by the new regime also began in 2005. Thus, while the conflict appears to be settled between the United States and EU, it continues to go on for the developing countries that were involved.

CONCLUSION

What does this case show us about trade policies between states and the activities of the WTO? At a minimum, it shows us that domestic politics within states are an important factor in determining their trade policies. We can see these effects in both the United States and countries of the EU. Carl Lindner's political contributions persuaded the U.S. government to pick up the banana issue first through a Super 301 investigation by the USTR and again in the form of an official complaint to the WTO. It is doubtful whether these actions would have occurred in the absence of Lindner's contributions and his influence on policy makers. Remember that in 1993, the USTR turned down Lindner's and Chiquita's appeals for help because the he thought that bananas were too trivial an issue to use the Super 301 process. After large amounts of money had been given to politicians in both political parties, the USTR reversed his position and began an investigation.

Domestic politics affected the actions of the EU as well. We see this most clearly in the EU's attempts to reform the banana regime after losing its WTO case in 1997. The EU eliminated the various categories of licenses for importing bananas into the EU. However, the distinctions made by these categories were maintained when the EU decided to use the banana import figures for 1994–96 in deciding who would be eligible for the new licenses under the reformed banana regime. This insured that European firms that benefited under the original Regulation 404 would still benefit under the reformed version. Eliminating these benefits would have opened a Pandora's box of opposition within Europe, a box the EU wanted to keep closed.

In part, the EU's difficulty in creating a common banana regime for its members caused the origin of this dispute. Different members had different goals and preferences concerning the importation of bananas. Compromising these different views was quite difficult and led to the creation of a complex regime. Moreover, once the banana regime was challenged, the EU resisted suggestions for change because it knew the difficulty of creating the regime in the first place. The EU is one of the world's largest markets and a leader in world trade. It is not a state, but a supranational organization. This makes it more difficult for the EU to develop uniform policies for interacting with other countries. It also makes it more difficult for non-EU members to interact with the EU.

We can also see the effect of the past in this case. The former colonies of Europe played a large role in this conflict. Britain and France have maintained strong ties with their former colonies and have brought these ties into the EU in the form of special preferences, access, and aid. These ties had a great deal to do with the banana conflict. The EU banana regime not only had to meet the domestic needs of EU members, but it had to meet the needs of Britain's and France's former colonies as well.

Complicating things, Britain and France had both encouraged the development of banana production in their former colonies, and then gave bananas from these countries special access to their markets before the EU created a single banana regime. If the EU had refused to discriminate between ACP and non-ACP bananas, many of the ACP countries would have been harmed significantly due to the dependence that British and French encouragement had created on the banana for their economic well-being. The ghost of Europe's colonial past continues to haunt the present and will be haunting its future as well.

This case also shows us that treating developing countries as a unit with shared interests is not always accurate. Developing countries lined up on both sides of this trade dispute. The ACP countries supported the EU banana regime, while Central and South American banana producing states lined up with the United States. Their interests were clearly at odds.

Bananas seem such trivial things for a dispute as large as the one we have chronicled. Yet, the banana dispute must be seen in the larger context of trade issues before the WTO. All sides to this dispute began to see bananas as a symbol of something larger. The United States thought that losing on bananas could affect the resolution of disputes on beer and magazines in Canada and hormone-treated meat in the EU. On the other hand, the EU thought losing on bananas would similarly affect the trade disputes it was having with other members of the WTO. The more that became invested in the banana dispute, the more important the dispute became, and the less any participant wanted to risk losing it. Thus, all states were extremely reluctant to compromise or to negotiate. The only solution was to push the issue to the bitter end—as it was.

In pushing the dispute to the bitter end, the EU and United States also pushed the WTO and its dispute settlement procedures to their limits and in the process almost broke them. Normally, a dispute like this would be resolved by negotiations between the parties involved. All would give something, and all would gain something. In this dispute, negotiations came to naught. None of the parties were willing to compromise, and the WTO had to resolve the dispute. Once it did, parties either attempted not to comply with the decision (the EU), or decided to enforce the decision outside of WTO procedures (the United States). Both of these approaches could have weakened the WTO dispute settlement process. If members of the WTO can succeed in defying WTO judgments and the treaty underlying them, then the WTO is irrelevant. If members of the treaty, especially the United States, can take it upon themselves to act as judge, jury, and enforcer of the treaty, it creates questions about the legitimacy and fairness of the WTO, which, in the end, will lead members to withdraw from its auspices or simply ignore it.

The result of both approaches is the same: there would be no WTO and no neutral body that can intervene to settle trade disputes between countries. Thus, countries would find it more and more difficult to maintain a free trade rule of law. The WTO was created to facilitate unfettered trade by making it more difficult for countries to attempt to exploit other countries or obtain unfair trade advantages. Without the WTO, supporters argue, countries might be more suspicious of each other and thus more likely to erect trade barriers to protect themselves from the actions of others. The result would be less trade and lower standards of living for all.

In pursuing the banana dispute, the EU and United States also illuminated weaknesses in the WTO that otherwise would have remained in the dark. One reason the EU could fail to comply with the WTO's 1997 decision on the banana regime is that the WTO's Dispute Settlement Body fails to describe how countries should come into compliance with their treaty obligations. Its decisions merely tell members that they are not in compliance. This forces members of the WTO to interpret for themselves what they should do to come into compliance and opens up the door to unauthorized retaliations. This weakness could be easily fixed by having dispute panels simply add to their reports recommendations of what countries should do to come into compliance with international trade laws instead of leaving it up to members to decide on their own.

We also saw that there was a difference of opinion on the process that should be followed before one member could place sanctions on another for failing to comply with a WTO decision. The WTO Charter is unclear on whether a country can act unilaterally, as the United States did in January 1999, or whether a country must first ask for a WTO panel to approve sanctions, as the EU believed. A positive outcome from this case, however, is that it set a precedent for dealing with this issue. The original dispute settlement panel was used to determine whether a state has complied with its decision, and it also judged the level of sanctions used against a noncomplying member. However, this precedent merely covers the incompatibilities or contradictions in the WTO Charter, not solve them. It is possible that a future dispute will once again occur between member interpretations of Articles 21.5 and 22, once again stressing the organization.

Finally, this case shows that any good or service can become the center of a major international trade conflict. Trade disputes can arise over even the most obscure of products, and once they arise, they can be hard to settle.

The banana may be tasty and humorous, but in this case it was poisonous as well. The banana dispute left some scars on both the United States and EU, and these are likely to affect their trade relationships for some time to come.

CHAPTER 6

THE BEEF OVER BEEF

FOOD SAFETY STANDARDS AND THE WTO

In the last few years, the WTO has come under increasing attack by individuals and groups who believe that its decisions will lead to a race to the bottom among member states in regards to health, safety, environmental, and labor standards. Critics argue that members will be forced to standardize the types of protections they offer their citizens and consumers and that the lowest common denominator among WTO members will be chosen. The reason for this is that those with low standards will refuse to agree to raise their standards, and countries with high standards will be pressured by businesses and others to lower theirs.

Ironically, these criticisms are an outgrowth of the success of the GATT process and the WTO. As tariffs have fallen to negligible levels among GATT members, other barriers to trade have become visible. National leaders can now see how the regulations passed by others to protect the health and environments of their citizens can also be used to distort trade and to protect markets. For instance, a state requiring the installation of air bags in automobiles sold in its market excludes all imports that do not have air bags. Clearly, air bags improve the safety of automobiles. But the standard could also be used to protect domestic manufacturers. If all domestic producers included air bags in their automobiles before the standard was created, but none of the importing companies did, then the standard becomes a method of raising the costs of imports by forcing foreign firms to include air bags. Thus, domestic manufacturers gain an edge from the new air bag standard. The problem is determining whether the standard was legitimately created to protect a state's citizens or whether it was created to protect a state's market. If the latter, it violates the spirit of the GATT since the GATT is about freeing trade among members. If lower tariffs can be offset by regulations and other nontariff barriers to trade, then nothing has been gained by the agreement.

The WTO has increasingly been called on to arbitrate conflicts over whether a state's policies have been legitimately created to protect the health of citizens or whether they have actually been created to protect the state's market from outside competition. Concerns over standard setting has also led to GATT members adding supplements to the agreement laying out specific rules for members to follow when developing regulations to protect their citizens. These supplements, in essence, clarify the types of processes and information that members must use for their regulations to be considered legitimate under the GATT. Finally, these supplements are enforceable under the WTO.

Despite the supplements added to the GATT, the WTO has had difficulty in making determinations concerning the legitimacy of members' regulations. These determinations require the WTO to judge not only the effects of a rule but the intent behind the rule and often the science used to support the rule. They raise questions about the competence of the WTO to determine whether a rule legitimately protects human health and safety and whether states even want the WTO to make these types of judgments.

These questions and others will be examined by looking at the conflict over the use of hormones to produce beef exported from Canada and the United States to the EU. This has been one of the more vituperative trade conflicts between Europe and North America. In the mid-1990s, Canada and the United States filed complaints with the WTO over the EU's ban on hormones in cattle. A dispute panel formed to arbitrate the conflict ruled in favor of Canada and the United States in 1997, and the EU lost a subsequent appeal of the decision. However, the EU has refused to come into compliance with the WTO decision saying that it has the right to protect itself from what it considers the potential harmful effects to humans eating meat containing hormone residues. As a result, since 1999, Canada and the United States have levied approximately $125 million annually in additional tariffs on EU goods in retaliation for its ban on beef from hormone-treated cattle.

Examining this conflict will allow us to see the difficulties the WTO has had in dealing with challenges to specific regulations and standards by its members. It will allow us to see how the WTO attempts to determine whether or not a standard is legitimate and the types of evidence and information the WTO draws on in making this determination. We will also see, as we did in the banana dispute, the weaknesses that still exist in the WTO dispute settlement process, as well as the effects that domestic politics of WTO members have on the positions and stances they take on issues. Finally, the case will show how the desire to create favorable precedents within the WTO dispute settlement processes affects the actions of GATT members.

THE SANITARY AND PHYTOSANITARY AGREEMENT

Before examining the conflict between the EU and the United States and Canada over hormones in meat, we need to examine the Sanitary and Phytosanitary Agreement (SPS). This is a supplement to the GATT created as part of the Uruguay Round in 1994. It was intended to clarify an exception to GATT rules that allows members to create measures necessary to protect human, animal, or plant life from certain specified risks, but it also distorts trade.[1]

The agreement creates several important principles for members to follow in using this exception. First, sanitary and phytosanitary protections (regulations that protect human, animal, and plant health and safety) must be based on scientific evidence and scientific principles.[2] The agreement assumes that any regulations not fulfilling this principle are illegitimate and were actually created to protect a country's market, not human, animal, or plant health. The second principle of the agreement is that any measure used should be the least restrictive in regard to trade. If an alternative regulation could create the same level of protection for a GATT member while distorting or restricting trade less, it should be chosen. Along with this, members must be willing to accept standards from other members that lead to the same level of protection. The third principle of the agreement is that members should attempt to harmonize their standards. The agreement encourages members to adopt standards that have been created by relevant international bodies. Any standards of GATT members that are consistent with these international bodies are considered GATT compliant; no member can challenge their legitimacy. As part of the goal to harmonize, the agreement demands that members of the GATT join the various international standard-setting bodies and comply with their rules.

Members of the GATT may set sanitary and phytosanitary standards that are higher than international standards.[3] However, the SPS agreement requires that these standards be supported by a risk assessment. A risk assessment is a study outlining the various harms and the likelihood of each harm to human, animal, and plant health generated by the product or process. Each country must provide the procedures it used in performing the risk assessment. Evidence must also be provided to show that risk tolerance is the reason for the difference in standards, not a country's desire to protect its market. Risk tolerance is a country's willingness to accept any harm and its probability of occurring from any product or process. Finally, members may set standards to protect themselves from unknown harms, but these standards can only be created provisionally and must be reevaluated as more evidence concerning the activity or product becomes available.

All challenges to the SPS agreement go before the WTO, and it is the WTO's responsibility to determine whether a member's standards comply with the agreement. In doing so, the agreement allows the WTO to draw on independent experts in the area of dispute. The WTO uses these experts to judge not only the trade effects of a standard, but whether proper risk assessments were performed by the member creating the standard and whether there is scientific evidence supporting that standard. Otherwise, the WTO handles disputes over the sanitary and phytosanitary standards in the same manner that it handles other disputes between or among GATT members.

THE EU BAN ON HORMONES

The EU ban on hormones predates the creation of the SPS agreement in the GATT.[4] The EC banned the administering of hormones to cattle by its members in 1985, and it extended this ban to meat imported into the EC in 1989.[5] The ban was a reaction by the EC to several internal developments.

In the late 1970s and early 1980s, there were several reports of European infants suffering from developmental problems due to high hormone residues found in baby food.[6] For example, it was reported in Italy that infants were developing the physical characteristics of the opposite sex. Studies also showed a connection between the hormone diethylstilbestrol (DES) and cancer in both children and adults. European farmers were injecting DES directly into cattle and veal to increase their weight by 15–25 percent before slaughter. These injections left behind high hormone residues in the portion of the cattle where the injections occurred, resulting in the consumption of DES by EU citizens. Babies were particularly susceptible to the residues since the cuts of meat used in baby food were often the ones where the injections were given.

Europeans in the summer of 1980 reacted to the reports of harmful residues by boycotting beef and veal.[7] This resulted in huge surpluses of meat throughout Europe and placed a burden on the EC's Common Agricultural Policy (CAP). In order to relieve consumer fears, the EC Commission proposed a ban on the administering of all hormones to cattle except for therapeutic use. This meant that farmers would no longer be able to use hormones to fatten cattle before slaughter. They would be able to use hormones only if they were a part of the prescribed treatment for an illness or injury.

In 1981 the EC banned the use of DES in cattle.[8] This was after several studies showed that residues from this hormone were carcinogenic. The EC was not the only member of the GATT to ban DES; the United States had banned it as well in 1979.[9] However, the EC was the only GATT member to consider banning the use of all hormones in the fattening process of cattle. Cattle producers have regularly used three other natural hormones and three synthetic hormones that mimic the natural ones, besides DES, in the fattening process.[10] The EC commissioned a panel in 1982 to examine these natural and synthetic hormones.[11] In 1983 the panel reported that meat produced with the natural hormones posed no threat to humans, but it did not have enough information to conclude whether the synthetic versions posed a threat. The same panel examined the hormones again in 1987 and ruled that meat produced with any of the six hormones posed no threat to humans, if used as directed.

Despite the rulings of its own commission, the EC decided to ban the use of the six hormones.[12] It argued that proving a link between cancer or other ailments and the use of a hormone was quite difficult and that erring on the side of caution was the best choice. European consumers also continued to lack confidence in community-produced beef and veal as there were reports in the mid-1980s of a "hormone mafia" in Europe supplying farmers through the black market. Adding credibility to these reports were several studies that found high levels of hormone residues in European beef despite the EC ban on their use.[13]

Consumers were the most concerned in Germany. A Politbarometer survey performed in Germany in 1988 found that almost 25 percent of Germans believed their health had been damaged by eating illegally treated veal; 95 percent of Germans believed that the problems with veal were emblematic of problems in the entire food system, and 41 percent said that they would not eat veal again even if the government said it was safe.[14]

These kinds of attitudes resulted in even larger community surpluses that had to be dealt with under the CAP. If one recalls from Chapter 3 on the Uruguay Round, by the mid-1980s the CAP was becoming an immense burden on the EC, and finding relief was essential if the CAP was not to break the EC budget. By banning all use of hormones the EC hoped to raise consumer confidence, thus sparking demand for beef and veal, thereby ending the problem of surpluses.[15]

Connected to these issues was the development of a movement within Europe during the mid-1980s that supported green agricultural policies. These are policies that support farm practices that protect the environment and also create humane living conditions for livestock. Many European consumers, especially those in Germany, believed that ethics should be a part of farming. In the same poll quoted above, 95 percent of Germans opposed factory-farming methods, and 88 percent of Germans said they would pay more for meat that came from non-factory farms. This movement pushed for the EC to ban hormones in order to better the living conditions of livestock and create healthier meat for consumers.

All of this can be seen in the conclusions of a report to the EC Parliament in 1988 that stated that the ban must be continued and expanded because "this was the only way to restore consumer confidence in the meat sector. . . . that use of the natural/nature-identical hormones carries the risk of inexperienced application, incorrect dosage and unsupervised injection which could pose a risk to the animal and the consumer. . . . that the Commission should promote the concept of *animal welfare* in agricultural production."[16]

However, two EC members opposed the ban on hormones.[17] Both Ireland and the UK relied on natural hormones for fattening their cattle because they had more steers in their herds than other European countries (steers are castrated male cattle). Since steers produce too little natural male hormones, it takes far longer for them to develop than other cattle. By giving them hormone supplements, steers can be made to develop as quickly as noncastrated cattle. Ireland and the UK also were opposed because of the lack of scientific evidence supporting the ban.

Still, the ban went into effect for EC farmers in 1985.[18] No hormones, natural or otherwise, could be administered to cattle for fattening after December 1985. The EC extended this ban to imports in January of 1988, but complaints from a variety of beef-exporting countries led the EC to delay implementation of the ban until January 1, 1989. The import ban continues to this day. Thus, no meat may be imported into the EU that comes from animals administered hormones as part of their fattening or growth process. Importing countries are also required to develop an inspection and certification system for meat to insure that none of it was produced with hormones. Countries failing to do so are prohibited from importing meat to the EU.[19]

CANADIAN AND U.S. OPPOSITION TO THE BAN

Canada and the United States are two of the largest beef producers in the world. Unlike many European producers of beef, U.S. and Canadian herds are composed almost entirely of steer. The use of large feedlots requires that steers be used since noncastrated males do not mix easily and would cause feedlot operators significant problems.[20] However, as we saw above, steers do not develop as quickly. The result is that 90 percent of cattle used for beef in Canada and the United States are given hormones to speed their growth. This decreases significantly the time needed to fatten and can be the difference between a feedlot turning a profit or not.

The EU ban resulted in the elimination of almost all Canadian and U.S. beef imports. Canada lost about twenty-five million dollars and the United States one hundred million dollars in annual sales to Europe. In comparison to the total trade between them and Europe, these values are quite small. Yet, Canadian and U.S. opposition to the ban has been fierce.

There are several reasons for this.[21] One of the most important reasons is that Canada and the United States believe that the EU's action opens the door for any GATT member to use the guise of health and safety standards to protect their market from competition. Connected to this, the United States and Canada believe that there is no scientific justification for the EU hormone ban. They argue that hormone use is strictly regulated. Hormones for fattening must be implanted in the ears of cattle, not injected into them, and the ears containing the implants are discarded at slaughter. Also, cattle are inspected at the time of slaughter to insure that hormone levels are not above what is found naturally in untreated cattle. This insures that any hormone residues from implants are no more harmful to consumers than those in cattle without hormone implants. Additionally, they argue that hormones have been used in beef production for almost fifty years, and no study during this period has shown any adverse health consequences from their use when administered according to the procedures mandated by the United States and Canada. Hormones have also been approved for use by all major international standard-setting organizations.[22] Finally, the UN World Health Organization and Food and Agricultural Organization created a joint committee in 1987 to study the use of hormones in meat, and it concluded that they were safe.[23]

Canada and the United States also fear that the EU ban could cause other countries to perceive Canadian and U.S. beef as unsafe, leading them to enact similar bans. The economic consequences of additional bans would be far more severe, perhaps even crippling, for Canadian and U.S. beef producers. For instance, in 1989 the United States exported about $670 million in beef to Japan and more than $1 billion in beef worldwide.[24] By fighting the ban, the United States and Canada hoped to prove that their beef is safe, preventing others from closing their markets.[25]

The United States and Canada filed their first complaint against the hormone ban in September 1986.[26] Consultations between U.S. and Canadian representatives and EC leaders failed to settle the dispute. In 1987 the United States invoked the

GATT's dispute settlement procedures to solve the conflict, but the EC was able to block its use because the GATT at the time required that all members agree to invoke a decision. This allowed the EC ban on hormone-treated meat to take effect in 1989. The United States responded with one hundred million dollars of new tariffs on European goods. These were subsequently suspended to allow for continued negotiations.

In May 1989, the United States and Canada came to an interim agreement with the EC.[27] The EC agreed to develop a list of meat producers in Canada and the United States that would be certified as having no hormones in their meat. All cattle taken to slaughter by these producers would be accompanied by affidavits stating that no hormones had been used in their development, and the U.S. Department of Agriculture agreed to inspect these producers to insure that the affidavits were truthful. The interim agreement, while not satisfactory to meat producers in Canada or the United States, did allow for the avoidance of a trade war. Europe had threatened to retaliate if any sanctions were placed on it for its ban. This could well have led to more sanctions by the United States and Canada and another reaction by the EC and so on. Once a snowball of retaliations begins, it is hard to stop. It was possible that a dispute over one hundred million dollars of beef imports could lead to billions in lost trade revenue among all parties involved.

The interim agreement stopped a trade war; it did not end the dispute. Canada and the United States continued to push for a change in the EC policy to no avail. The EC adamantly refused to change it. However, the successful completion of the Uruguay Round and the creation of the WTO in 1995 gave the United States and Canada a new weapon to use in this dispute. The EU would no longer be able to use GATT procedures to keep a dispute panel from examining the issue, and the SPS agreement insured that the WTO would have jurisdiction over the issue if a complaint were filed. An additional weapon was given to the United States and Canada in 1995 when the Codex Alimentarius decided that there was no need for setting any standards for the three natural hormones used in the fattening of cattle.[28] These hormones could be used without fear in regards to human health. The Codex Alimentarius at the same time set maximum residue standards for two of the most widely used synthetic hormones in the world. Thus, five of the six hormones used in the production of beef by Canada and the United States were deemed safe by an international standard-setting body. This meant that the EU would have to justify why its standards were significantly higher if a complaint was filed with the WTO.

The EU reacted to these developments by holding a conference on growth promotion in meat production in late 1995 in the expectation that it would give some support for the EU ban. The six hormones used in meat production by the United States and Canada were examined. Unfortunately for the EU, the conference concluded the following for five of the six hormones: "At present, there is no evidence for possible health risks to the consumer due to the use of natural sex hormones for growth promotion, since: Residue levels of these substances measured in meat of treated animals fall within the physiological range observed in meat of comparable untreated animals. The daily production of sex hormones by humans is much higher than the amounts possibly consumed from meat, even in the most sensitive humans (prepubertal children and menopausal women)."[29] No conclusions were given on the safety of the sixth hormone, melengestrol, due to a lack of evidence on its effects on human health. Under domestic pressure, the EU decided to ignore the conference's conclusions. In January 1996, the EU Parliament voted 366 to 0 to maintain the hormone ban. The EU Council of Ministers followed by reaffirming the ban as well.[30]

HORMONES REACH THE WTO

In reaction to the EU's refusal to remove its ban, the United States and Canada requested the formation of a WTO dispute panel to hear the issue. This led to the formation of two panels, one in July 1996 to hear the U.S. complaint and one in October 1996 to hear the Canadian complaint. New Zealand and Australia then joined the U.S. complaint because they had also seen imports to Europe decline because of the ban. Both panels were composed of the same three members since the core issues were the same in each.[31]

The United States and EU presented arguments to the panel on October 10, and November 11, 1996. Canada and the EU presented arguments on January 7, and February 18, 1997. The arguments made by the United States and Canada were similar. The EU's stance remained the same throughout both sets of hearings.

THE U.S. AND CANADIAN POSITION

The United States and Canada attacked the EU ban across a wide front. They argued that the ban violated six sections of the SPS in the GATT and one major section of the GATT itself.[32] Most of these attacks revolved around the idea that the EU had not scientifically justified the need for a ban, nor had it scientifically justified that the ban would meet its food safety goals. Here the United States and Canada pointed to the fact that several EU panels and commissions had examined the safety of hormones for the fattening of cattle, and none had concluded that they were unsafe when used properly.

They also argued that the EU was unable to meet its goal of zero risk from hormone residues in meat from its current policy. They used as evidence the fact that untreated meat contained hormone residues, and in many cases these were higher than the residues from treated meat. For instance, the residues of testosterone in meat from a bull are fifty times higher than the residues found in a treated steer. Along with this, the EU continued to allow the use of hormones for herd management and therapeutic purposes. Thus, if the EU was truly seeking zero risk from hormone residues, it would have to ban all meat, or test all meat and ban any of it, treated or untreated, containing hormone residues. It did not do this.

Another argument made by the United States and Canada was that the EU had failed to perform a proper risk assessment before instituting the ban, as required by the SPS agreement. The EU never stated the risk it was attempting to minimize with the ban. Instead, it said that it wanted no residues from hormone-treated meat to reach its consumers. Clearly this is not sufficient grounds for banning a product. A risk assessment requires a country to explicitly lay out the risks to human, animal, or plant health from which it is attempting to protect itself. In this case, according to the United States and Canada, this meant that the EU needed to state what potential harms could come from hormones used in meat production. Once the potential harms were listed, one could then assess the various probabilities that each would occur if treated meat were allowed to be sold. The United States and Canada believed that the EU could not in fact list these potential harms because various studies would have shown that treated meat would not cause them; thus, there was no reason to institute a ban.

Additionally, the United States and Canada argued that the EU had failed to justify why it had failed to use the aforementioned international standards regarding the use of hormones for the fattening of cattle. The SPS treaty allows any member to set standards that are different from those created by international bodies. However, for these standards to be valid, they must be justified using scientific principals and methods, and the country must show that the risk it is willing to accept is less than what the international standard allows. The Codex Alimentarius had determined that three of the hormones used in meat production did not need a maximum residue level standard because they were safe when used properly. Two others had maximum residue levels set, but when used properly the resulting meat would fall beneath these maximums. Thus, five hormones were deemed safe when used properly by the Codex Alimentarius. It was up to the EU to show why it believed there was a potential for harm and the need for a standard different from the Codex's. The EU failed to do this.

Another argument was that the ban violated the principle of nondiscrimination set by the GATT. Here the two countries argued that hormone-treated meat did not have higher hormone residue levels than untreated meat produced in Europe. Since the meat at time of import was comparable to European meat, banning it from the market was a form of discrimination. The GATT requires that like products, no matter their origins or how they were produced, be treated the same by all members.

Finally, the United States and Canada argued that the real reason the ban was created was to protect the European market from meat imports. They noted that the ban was challenged shortly after its creation in the European Court of Justice and that the Court had stated in its ruling that one of the primary reasons for the ban was the reduction of large meat surpluses in the EU. Furthermore, a report to the European Parliament stated that "the Inquiry Committee believes that only a total ban on the use of growth-promoters is concordant with the strategic aims now adopted for the Common Agricultural Policy, in particular the reduction of surpluses and the safeguarding of a viable regionally-diversified farming community."[33] Meat surpluses had become a huge problem under the CAP by the mid- to late 1980s. Between 1981 and 1987, CAP spending on beef had risen 56 percent, and it rose an additional 25 percent between 1987 and 1988. Beef stocks also more than doubled between 1981 and 1987.[34] In 1988 alone, 123,000 tons of beef were added to the surplus, and by the end of 1989, 723,000 metric tons of beef were being stored in the EC.[35] At the same time, European exports of beef were declining, making it impossible for the EC to export its way out of the surplus problem.[36]

THE EU'S POSITION

The EU, of course, had a response for each argument made by Canada and the United States. First, the EU argued that scientific support for a sanitary or phytosanitary measure did not have to be supported by the majority or even a large portion of the scientific community. The EU argued that requiring a majority of the scientific community to support a measure would leave a state open to dangers it may not want to tolerate. Evidence from scientific studies is constantly changing, and a chemical or process deemed safe today may not be thought safe in the future. The majority is not always right, and countries must have the latitude to ignore the majority opinion to protect themselves. A good example of this would be the United States refusing to allow the sale of the drug thalidomide in the 1960s, even though most studies had found it to be safe, and many countries certified it for sale. It was only after the drug was in widespread use that its dangers to humans became truly known. The United States' ban on the drug protected Americans from the birth defects that plagued the countries that had approved it.

For the EU, the SPS agreement merely required a state to show that it had adopted a measure after examining an issue scientifically, and that at least some or even a few of these results supported the need for the measure. EU leaders asked, were there any studies that supported a ban? They said the answer was yes and cited several of them. The fact that several of its own commissions and panels had found hormones to be safe was moot.

Second, the EU argued that it had performed a proper risk assessment. It had examined the risks that could result from hormone residues that were not produced naturally in cattle, and it had decided that the risks associated with these unnatural residues were intolerable. This led directly to the measure it had adopted—banning the use of hormones for fattening cattle. There was no other method for managing the risk according to the EU, and therefore, the hormone ban was also the least restrictive measure that it could adopt.

Moreover, the EU argued that determining risks was different than managing them. A risk assessment could tell you only the possible dangers that a product may create. It is up to each country to determine whether these dangers are tolerable. Some countries may decide that a one-in-a-million chance of cancer is too much of a risk, while another may believe it is not. Here the EU pointedly quoted the United States' Delaney Rule that requires the Food and Drug Administration to ban any product that could cause cancer, no matter how small the risk. This, according to the EU, was unchallengeable; only the United States could determine what it would tolerate. The only thing that could be challenged was whether the United States had followed scientific standards in determining whether a product might cause cancer. The EU argued that its ban was in the same class as the Delaney Rule. It was unwilling to tolerate any level of risk from hormones administered for fattening, and it had some scientifically performed studies to justify this ban.

Third, the EU argued that the ban clearly did not discriminate against Canada and the United States. If EU farmers could not use hormones, why should the community allow imports of meat treated with hormones? The ban merely insured that all producers of meat would play on the same field. European farmers could not use hormones; nor could Canadian and U.S. farmers. Fourth, while the EU did agree that the ban helped with management of the CAP, it was a secondary reason for the ban, not the primary reason. A measure, according to the EU, should not be found invalid just because one of its unintended or secondary outcomes may give an advantage to its user. The EU pointed to several previous WTO decisions supporting this view. Moreover, the EU ban was first discussed in the early 1980s, before meat surpluses developed, and the EU reaffirmed the ban in 1995 and 1996 when beef surpluses had disappeared. This substantiated that the policy had not been used to protect its market from imports, but to safeguard the health of citizens.

THE WTO DECISION

After hearing oral arguments, the dispute panel convened, for the first time in WTO history, a panel of six experts to help it consider the issue. A precedent was being set. Over a two-day period, the experts fielded questions from the dispute panel and helped it to determine whose arguments were the most legitimate.[37]

On June 30, 1997, the dispute panel released its report. It found that the EU was in violation of the SPS agreement because it had failed to perform proper risk assessments and had not properly justified why its standard was higher than that set by the Codex Alimentarius. The panel also concluded that the ban created different levels of protection leading to discrimination and an unfair burden on trade. The fact that the EU was willing to accept products with naturally high hormone residues meant that it could not ban meat that had been administered hormones with the same or lower levels of hormone residue.

On September 24, 1997, the EU appealed the panel's decision.[38] The Appellate Body, after due deliberation, released its report on January 16, 1998. Its report affirmed most of the lower panel's decisions.[39] It agreed that proper risk assessments had not been performed. The EU had produced studies that hormone residues could cause health problems; however, it had performed no studies to assess whether eating meat with low levels of hormone residues was harmful to humans. A proper risk assessment required one to actually examine the outcomes to be prevented or managed by a measure. If one wanted to ban treated meat, one must show that eating it could cause harm.

The Appellate Body also ruled that while a state may use a minority view to back a standard, it must have sufficient evidence to back the view to make it legitimate. This means that no country could find just any scientist to perform a study to rationalize a standard. There had to be some real doubt in the broader scientific community over the safety of something for a standard to be set. In this case, the Appellate Body ruled that the EU had not provided sufficient evidence to support its standard.

The Appellate Body went even further by stating that the EU could not use the precautionary principal as a justification for its ban.[40] The precautionary principal is a long-standing piece of international law that allows countries to take actions to protect themselves from unknown harms or dangers. For instance, when a new technology is developed, no one knows whether its long-term effects may be dangerous or harmful. The precautionary principal allows a state to ban the technology until more is known about its effects.

The Appellate Body ruled that the SPS agreement allows provisional standards to protect members, but provisional standards must be constantly evaluated as information develops. In this case, enough information was then known on the safety of hormones, according to the panel, that the EU could not justify a provisional rule to protect itself from "unknown" harms.

Under WTO guidelines, members are expected to come into compliance with a decision promptly. However, if time is needed to come into compliance, a member must negotiate with the other parties to the case over the time that will be allowed. If negotiation fails, an arbitrator decides how much time should be given. In this case, the EU argued that it needed at least two years to come into compliance since it wanted to perform new risk assessments and studies of the six hormones. EU negotiations with Canada and the United States over this demand failed to produce agreement. On May 29, 1998, a WTO arbitrator ruled that the EU would have until May 13, 1999, to come into compliance.[41]

AFTERMATH OF THE WTO DECISION

Consumer reaction in Europe to the WTO decision has been fierce. Europeans have consistently supported measures that keep additives and chemicals out of the food they eat. A Eurobarometer poll in 1998 found that half of the respondents considered food to be safe "when it contains neither pesticides nor hormones and when it is controlled by competent bodies."[42] The same poll found that 80 percent of Europeans wanted more and stricter controls on food, particularly at the production stage, to insure that it was safe. In 2001 more than 50 percent of Europeans believed that food safety should be a priority for the EU.[43]

Popular pressures to keep hormones out of meat have made it difficult for the EU to comply with the WTO decision. Instead of dropping the ban on Canadian and U.S. imports, the EU commissioned seventeen new studies on the effects of hormones in meat.[44] The EU hoped that these studies would be completed by the end of the twelve months it had been granted to comply, and that the studies would support a continuance of the ban. The EU argued that the WTO decision allowed this course of action. In its view, the panel had ruled against the EU because it had not performed the proper kind of risk assessments, and the seventeen studies would resolve this problem.

In February 1999, the EU Commission warned both the European Parliament and the Council of Ministers that the risk assessments were not likely to be completed by the WTO's deadline.[45] This communication presented four options for the EU. First, the EU could negotiate with the United States and Canada for additional time, requiring the EU to offer compensation in the form of reduced tariffs on other goods imported into the EU. A second option was to adopt a new ban provisionally. Under SPS rules, provisional standards or regulations can be adopted when a country does not have full information on the risks of an activity. Third, the EU could lift the ban. Finally, the EU could refuse to comply and suffer sanctions from the United States and Canada.

In April 1999, the EU Scientific Committee of Veterinary measures relating to Public Health (SCVPH), after receiving some of the results from the seventeen studies commissioned by the EU, concluded that all six hormones were a danger to human health. Consumer Policy Commissioner, Emma Bonino, stated in a press release that "the scientific evidence [provided by the SCVPH] is of enormous importance to European consumers as it demonstrates that the Commission was right to strenuously defend the ban on hormones. We now have a scientific basis to defend our position."[46] In order to win international support on the issue and possibly affect Canadian and U.S. reactions, the press release went on to say that the EU "was deeply concerned about the United States' attempt to belittle the risk which scientists have identified. The Commission cannot understand that the United States has not reacted in a more responsible way to the conclusive findings of the scientific committee." Not surprisingly, the EU Commission used these conclusions as the basis of a decision in May 1999 to continue the hormone ban, the fourth option discussed above.[47]

Equally predictably, the United States and Canada followed the EU's action with a warning that they would raise tariffs on European goods for failure to comply with the WTO decision.[48] On June 3, 1999, the United States and Canada formally requested permission from the WTO to place $202 million and $51 million respectively in trade sanctions on the EU.[49] The EU responded by arguing that it was in compliance with the WTO decision and that the U.S. and Canadian monetary estimates for the damage to meat imports were too high. A three-judge panel was convened by the WTO to decide the matter. On July 12, 1999, it found the EU to be in noncompliance with the earlier decisions, but it lowered the level of sanctions. The United States was authorized to place 100 percent tariffs on $116.8 million, and Canada was authorized to place 100 percent tariffs on $8.2 million of European goods, as these were the levels of harm it deemed the EU ban had caused.[50] U.S. sanctions were focused on the countries it felt were most responsible for the hormone ban: Germany, Denmark, France, and Italy. Lists of products to receive tariffs were composed to inflict maximum damage on others while doing the least damage to Americans. No tariffs were raised on products from the UK due to its consistent opposition to the ban.[51]

Undeterred, in May 2000, the EU once again extended its ban on meat from hormone-treated cattle.[52] This extension was accompanied by a new review of studies on hormone safety that found that one hormone was directly linked to cancer and that the others were probably linked to cancer. The United States responded that the science still did not back the EU policy. The review merely reiterated previous EU conclusions; it did not add anything new to the issue. U.S. and Canadian sanctions continue to be applied as of 2007, and in order to increase the pain, the United States developed a carousel approach to them. This means that the United States rotates about every six months the products that receive the 100 percent tariffs, spreading pain across a variety of economic sectors in Europe. The hope is that this will lead to diverse political pressures on the EU to change policies.

Compliance by the EU is unlikely to come anytime soon. Mad cow disease moved from England to the European continent in the fall of 2000. Europe in 2001 also faced an epidemic of foot and mouth disease. While this posed no harm to humans, it did raise new concerns about the reliability of the continent's food system. In recent years, Europe has also seen a scandal concerning dioxin in chicken, and Coca Cola was implicated in the poisoning and illness of several hundred people in Belgium, France, and Poland. All of these have led to even more consumer concern that the EU food supply is not safe. The EU reacted to these concerns by creating a food safety plan and a special authority with the responsibilities to advise on food safety issues, disseminate food safety information, and give alerts when a food safety crisis develops or is imminent.[53] Under these circumstances, it would be political suicide for the EU countries to allow the import of meat produced from hormone-treated cattle.

IMPLICATIONS OF THE CASE

The WTO hormone decision has created some important issues and precedents. First, this decision places in the hands of the WTO the power to rule on the science used by a country in justifying and creating its sanitary and phytosanitary standards. In 1998, Public Citizen, with four other U.S. interest groups, challenged this concept in a written comment to the WTO Appellate Body considering the hormone case.[54] The groups argued that WTO dispute panels do not have the expertise to make judgments on science.[55] Panels are composed of economists, trade experts, international lawyers, and others with expertise in trade issues—who are they to judge the legitimacy of scientific evidence on the effects of hormones in meat or the effects of any product for that matter? Public Citizen also argued that input from experts is not enough to close the expertise gap because most issues cross disciplines, and closing the gap would require the use of scientists from all disciplines involved. This would mean that the advisory body would become quite large and unwieldy.

Some believe that the WTO should only judge whether the evidence obtained to support a rule was collected in a scientific fashion, which is much easier to do. Science has distinct norms of behavior that must be followed for any study to be seen as legitimate. A WTO panel could easily determine if a study followed these norms or not.

However, if the WTO is not given the power to make some judgments on the legitimacy of evidence supporting SPS rules or any standards used by a member, it could allow countries to find pet scientists to create studies that will support any action the member wishes. The result would be an SPS agreement that is worthless. Countries could protect themselves with standards supported with the slimmest of evidence. The EU claimed that minority views in science should be legitimate support for establishing a standard. But how large of a minority must the view be? If the WTO cannot judge the actual science behind a standard, a minority of one might be enough to ban anything.

A related concern is that the WTO's decision undermines the precautionary principal in international law.[56] The precautionary principal, as mentioned earlier, allows countries to take actions with little or no scientific or other justification for protection from harm. These actions are only to be taken when the harms from something are unknown. In this way, an unknown harm can be prevented. Why should any country have to wait until people are maimed or killed before action is taken? The precautionary principal, in essence, allows a country to demand that a product be proven safe, rather than presumed to be, before accepting it into its market.

The EU claimed that hormones have not been adequately studied. We really do not know the long-term effects of their use for fattening cattle; fifty years may not be enough time to judge since the effects of something may take a lifetime to discover. Should not the EU be allowed to use the precautionary principal to ban the use of hormones until the long-term use of them has been proven safe? The WTO concluded that this was not the case. The SPS agreement includes the precautionary principal through its allowance of provisional measures and standards. However, these provisional methods and standards must be constantly reassessed as new evidence presents itself. At some point, there will be enough evidence that the standard is validated or not. In our case, the WTO took upon itself the role of determining whether there was enough science to validate the EU standard, and it decided there was not.

The problem is that science never guarantees truth. What is seen as healthy today may be unhealthy tomorrow. If the WTO is allowed to judge whether a provisional rule is supported by current evidence, it creates a possibility that a country's protections will be eliminated even though they are needed. Again, we have an outside organization determining the standards a country may use. But if we did not have this, the section of the SPS agreement allowing provisional standards would become the loophole that the elephant of protectionism could walk through.

Critics of the WTO decision point out that the only values represented were those of scientists and trade specialists.[57] Consumer and citizen values were largely ignored. Consumers in Europe are very concerned about the safety and health of their food supply. Many citizens argue that these fears should be accommodated even if there is little or no scientific support behind them. For these critics, an unfair standard is one solely created with the intent to protect a market. Standards created with the intent to eliminate fears or concerns should also be legitimate.

The problem with this line of reasoning is that intent can be difficult to discern. All countries wishing to protect their markets with a standard would say they were doing it not to protect, but because of citizen fears. Moreover, the SPS agreement specifically states that science must be the basis of standards. Members of the WTO agreed to this language and so are bound by it. The WTO institutions are also bound by it. They must make decisions based on the language of the agreement. This does not mean citizen fears are completely ignored by the SPS agreement or the WTO. Countries can set standards that are higher than international norms as long as there is some legitimate evidence supporting them. Countries must perform risk assessments, but in the end each must determine the level of risk it wishes to allow on its own. This means that one country may be willing to risk a low probability of human cancer from a product or process while another does not. Science merely tells us what the risks are; societies must determine to what degree they will tolerate them.

Concerns over who determines the legitimacy of a country's standards are only one set of implications from this case. The case also shows, once again, that enforcement of WTO decisions is difficult. The EU has been able to shrug off for as long as it has wanted the trade sanctions imposed by Canada and the United States over the hormone ban. Trade between the United States and Europe at the close of the twentieth century amounted to about $400 billion annually; $121 million in sanctions is about 0.03 percent of the total.[58] Weak sanctions allow members of the GATT to think instrumentally. Each member can examine the costs of sanctions versus the benefits of protection. When benefits are high, they may well violate the treaty. Each time members do this, they are in essence weakening the agreement. The more violations that occur and the more members see that sanctions are not particularly painful, the more likely members will choose to violate the treaty in the future. The result of this is a gutted treaty. Or just as dangerous, the large state can defy the treaty knowing that sanctions will harm them little, while more vulnerable small states dare not.

One thing that does help enforcement is that members of the WTO can be expected to be on both the winning and losing sides of various cases. If a member fails to comply with a decision when it loses, it can expect others to not comply with decisions when it wins. We can see this in the attitude of U.S. Trade Ambassador Peter Scher in a 1999 briefing for the Foreign News Service when he said that "the effect will be that the EU will now have a big scarlet 'F' for their failure to comply with the WTO."[59] The EU's reputation, like Hester Prynn's, may be ruined, and it may now expect to be treated differently by other WTO members, especially the rich ones.

This case, like the one dealing with bananas, shows that a high level of conflict can occur despite the fact that the monetary value of the dispute is low. The United States has lost only one hundred million dollars annually in beef exports to Europe, a small amount compared to its total trade with Europe. It is also a small amount compared to the total beef exports of the United States. The same is true for Canada. Why then have these two countries opposed the European ban so vociferously? One reason is that they want to influence the setting of early precedents within the WTO. Both Canada and the United States also want to insure that other states do not block imports of their meat treated with hormones, which would be far more costly to U.S. and Canadian farmers. By demanding that science be used to justify a sanitary and phytosanitary standard, the United States and Canada are insuring access for their meat products into other countries. More generally, the United States and Canada are helping the WTO set a precedent for standards dealing with all products. By opposing the EU's ban so adamantly, they have forced the WTO to determine, in an early case, what the SPS requires for justification. Both Canada and the United States will benefit, as will other members, from the requirement that science be the basis of all protective measures.

The danger is that the push for science to be the basis for all measures may come back to haunt the United States and Canada. Measures they themselves have taken to protect consumers or assuage consumer fears may be challenged by other GATT members as not being based on proper risk assessments or enough scientific evidence. Precedent, after all, works for all. This may someday force the United States and Canada into the same bind that the EU has found itself. Should they comply with a WTO decision that invalidates their measures, or should they listen to citizen and consumer interests by keeping the measures in place?

The EU was also hoping to set a precedent within the WTO. So far, other members have not supported its views. However, The EU's refusal to comply with the WTO panels may lead to some compromise among members that is far closer to the EU's views. Members may see the merits of the EU's arguments and decide that the SPS agreement, or the WTO's interpretation of it, should be changed. On the other hand, the EU has won recent cases against the United States and Japan before WTO dispute panels. Perhaps it will want to sustain the dispute panels' legitimacy by finally accepting the hormone decision and eliminating its ban.

CONCLUSION

Most people think of free trade merely as a tariff issue. As we have seen with this case, free trade has become much more than the lowering of tariffs by countries. As tariffs have dropped to negligible levels among GATT members, other barriers to trade become more visible, and these barriers could be far from amenable to easy negotiation. Continued deepening of the GATT/WTO process could lead to ever more pressures on members to create uniform standards for products, services, and the methods of manufacturing. One country's practices could always be seen by others as a barrier to trade. One solution is for all countries to have the same standards.

Creating uniform standards would be difficult to say the least. States cherish the concept of sovereignty, and the drive for uniformity would challenge that concept. Moreover, uniform standards are not likely to meet the needs of all countries. As this case shows, Europeans have different views of what constitutes safe food than do Americans and Canadians. Leaders of countries, especially democratically elected ones, would have to deal with the pressures from other countries to comply with uniform standards while also catering to the values and desires of their citizens. For leaders of WTO members, this may place them, as the EU states found, between the proverbial rock and a hard place.

CHAPTER 7

ENTER THE DRAGON

CHINA'S ACCESSION INTO THE WTO

The WTO is an organization committed to the expansion of trade through the promotion of liberal tenants. Maximizing competition within an open worldwide marketplace is the goal. The problem with China joining this free marketplace has historically been, of course, the centrally planned, state directed nature of its communist system.

To join the WTO, China would have to transform its economy into one compatible with competitive free market economies. In short, it would have to abandon its central control by allowing not only free competition among its domestic economic enterprises, but also free access to its internal markets by foreign enterprises. Significant elements of privatization of state-owned enterprises (SOEs) would have to be accepted. Market forces would have to replace the state-planning agency directives as the key to economic movement in everything from resource allocation to the establishing of prices on goods.

All the while, China's leadership has been determined to maintain political control of the country through the mechanism of the Communist Party. If this were to mean maintaining the Maoist view of complete socialist ownership of all means of production under central control of the entire system, then our story would end right here. But post-Mao leadership, particularly since Deng Xiaoping (1978–97), gradually faced the reality of China's international environment, its need to face the challenges presented by a world trade regime dominated by free market economies.

While struggling to maintain the supremacy of the Communist Party, China has reluctantly turned to what it likes to call a policy of creating a "socialist market economy." With 1.4 billion people, 800 million living in rural poverty and a per capita GNP at the level of developing countries, China has had to consider the absolute necessity of expanding its economy or face increased internal dissatisfaction, even rebellion. This case study will trace the movement of China toward membership in the WTO as the central fixture in its policy to move from isolationism to engagement with the international political economy.

For a millennium, China has seen itself as the center of the civilized world. It has often, during these centuries and with good reason, seen itself as a superior culture of advanced administration and development, reveling in its isolation from most of the rest of the world. In the last century or more, however, it has perceived itself as the victim of barbarian Western interference to its autonomy and unity. In the nineteenth century, Western imperialism took advantage of internal weakness to force an opening of China's markets and reorient its economic culture.

The twentieth century brought increased internal chaos to China. Revolution, invasion from Japan, civil war, and Cold War isolation all made it difficult for China to join the mainstream of the international political economy. In 1948 the Nationalist (Kuomintang) government of China was one of the twenty-three founding members of GATT. But the 1949 victory of the communist forces in the civil war initiated a period of internal consolidation under the strict centralized control of Mao's Communist Party hierarchy. Feeling hemmed in by the Soviet Union, its archrival, and the containment policy of the United States, China returned to an isolationist foreign policy. Consequently, Beijing withdrew from the GATT as part of a policy antagonistic toward Western institutions.

President Richard Nixon's opening to China, including his dramatic visit in 1972, may have begun the process of Chinese integration back into world affairs, but internal weaknesses and the declining health of Mao Zedong and other revolutionary leaders left China unable to make dramatic changes in its policies. Government rhetoric militantly defied both the United States and the Soviet Union. Then the death of Mao in September 1976 became the catalyst for a decisive struggle for the future of China.

After Mao's death, hard-line Maoists struggled to maintain the Marxist-Leninist-Maoist creed as the foundation of China's policies. Reformers, on the other hand, demanded changes using pragmatism as their fundamental argument. China's economy was not doing well. Its isolation had left it vulnerable. As a consequence, by 1981 the reformists had gained the upper hand, and the pro-Maoist leadership, the so-called "gang of four" that included Mao's wife, was put on trial and imprisoned. The emergent leader of the pragmatic reformers was Deng Xiaoping who said, interestingly enough, that it was okay for some to become richer than others, that there must be some economic modernization.[1]

By the late 1970s and early 1980s, the dominant policy of the leadership had become centered on the Four Modernizations. Deng's mentor and Mao intimate, Zhou Enlai, had endorsed these fundamental doctrines in a quiet 1975 speech, and Deng's short-term predecessor, Hua Guofeng, mentioned them in 1978. It was Deng, however, who at the December 1978 meeting of the Chinese Communist Party (CCP) Central Committee brought them to the forefront of national policy. Dramatically, he "added to them a sweeping reform of the planning and management systems in industry and agriculture."[2] This was the beginning of China's new open policy toward the modern political economy.

The original Four Modernizations, in order of importance, were (1) industry (heavy over light), (2) agriculture, (3) science and technology, and (4) defense. Deng changed the priority of the Four by placing agriculture first, industry second (with light over heavy), and science and defense remaining third and fourth. His reform program aimed at four major objectives:

1. Freeing agriculture by allowing the private sale of portions of farmers' crops
2. Encouraging private sector development in urban areas
3. Giving more responsibility for decisions to SOEs
4. Reforming the pricing system to reflect supply and demand forces[3]

Internal reform, in addition to its domestic benefits, was a prerequisite for joining the international marketplace in any meaningful way. Indeed, "prior to 1980, China pursued an autarkic development strategy. Trade played a very small and passive role in Chinese economic development; foreign capital was not allowed and China did not [belong to] the International Monetary Fund or the World Bank."[4] Foreign trade was only 5 percent of the Chinese GNP. As late as the early 1980s, trade was limited and closely controlled by central government mechanisms.

In 1982 China began observer participation in the GATT in preparation for its 1986 application for full membership. China's hope was that membership would end the annual Most Favored Nation (MFN) vote in the U.S. Congress and facilitate expansion of its business arrangements that had become a spur to growth in international trade. Furthermore, it wanted to join before Taiwan, its erstwhile "province," could. By the time the GATT began serious negotiations in 1988 through the appointment of a membership "working group," China's internal weaknesses began to press against its external ambitions.

Deng's China had to face both daunting problems of internal control of the economic liberalization process as well as decisions on just how to accomplish effective integration into the world economy. Margaret Pearson writes that there were two models available for the Chinese to follow—both championed by differing internal interests. The first she calls the "full-integration" model: "It takes China's integration into the global economy—to a level and depth consistent with the most open industrial economies—as the practical and desirable outcome of China's 'open policy.'"[5] This alternative would commit China to do everything necessary to transform the internal structures of its economy to make them compatible with free market mechanisms—a prerequisite for GATT and later WTO membership.

Half steps, or at least carefully controlled integration, are the foundations of the second alternative: "partial integration." This model wants China to view "its participation in the global economy as practical and desirable yet also as a process that must be controlled carefully."[6] Advocates of this approach are those caught up in a newly invigorated nationalism that perceives a loss of sovereignty in the integrationist process. These forces see China's rightful place as no less than a central actor in world affairs, and they think China should maintain the autonomy to act accordingly. Reinforcing these views have been leaders of the bankrupted aspects of the economy who saw full integration as a threat to their privileged position.

A psychology of partial integration dominated Chinese thought and actions in the years following the 1978 decision by the reform leaders to pursue an open policy. The motivation was purely economic. In the period between 1978 and 1994, China pursued a policy of joining international organizations and participating in a great number of market-based business arrangements. But divisions among the leadership as to how far and how fast to go led to caution when it came to internal reforms. As one author describes it, "the basic idea was to preserve the economy's socialist core—state firms and state banks—by introducing change along the margins. These incremental measures over time saw markets established, state planning effectively eliminated, prices liberalized, and non-state owned industry allowed to prosper, but the underlying logic remained constant. Reforms would be introduced, but always as part of an overriding effort to preserve the traditional core of the economy."[7] Partial reform was a reflection of partial integration since they were dependent on each other.

Economic problems peaked internally in the 1980–82 period as agriculture price reforms (1979–80) and war with Vietnam (1979) led to large budget deficits, inflation, and a credit squeeze. In 1983 these became the impetus for the "first serious financial, fiscal, and enterprise reforms" that, however, helped produce the highest inflation rates in twenty years.[8] Efforts to correct these problems followed, but the boom-and-bust cycle of the economy continued into the late 1980s. Serious economic problems and their potential to produce internal unrest led to the decision to crack down on student protests and the June 1989 Tiananmen Square crisis. The difficulty in balancing reform with the demands of significant constituent groups like farmers and students panicked the leadership into strong repressive measures.

Throughout the late 1980s and early 1990s, administrative reforms and controls were used in an attempt to level the economy's ups and downs. Partial integration was moving the situation forward, but not fast enough, and countries as well as foreign enterprise investment retreated, at least temporarily, from China because of the Tiananmen Square crisis. Still, overall the open policy had produced dramatic results, not the least of which occurred in the arena of foreign trade. Trade growth exceeded gross economic growth in the period from 1978 to 1994 (and beyond) by a considerable margin. In 1978 China's foreign trade stood at $20.6 billion; by 1995 it had ballooned to $180 billion. In 1978 China was the thirty-second largest trader in the world; by 1998 it was the tenth, having grown from a 0.97 percent share of world trade in 1978 to 3.4 percent by 1995. It was 5.1 percent by 2005. In the late 1980s and early 1990s, China's overall economy achieved a remarkable rate of growth, 8–12 percent a year, a rate that continued into the first decade of the new century.[9]

Foreign direct investment (FDI) played a large role in these dramatic figures. Before 1978 there was hardly any foreign investment allowed in China; by 1994 foreign investment reached nearly $100 billion. FDI declined significantly between 1994 and 1999 but has climbed steadily since, topping $150 billion in 2004. The country's annual investment from foreign trade was less than 1 percent of total investment in 1978 but was 18 percent by 1994. In addition, exports skyrocketed; they "rose 19 percent a year during 1981–94. Strong export growth, in turn, appear[ed] to have fueled productivity growth in domestic industries . . . [and] China's strong productivity growth, spurred by the 1987 market-oriented reforms, [was] the leading cause of China's unprecedented economic performance."[10]

Most of this progress came from what Pearson calls "shallow integration," the use of significant tariff reductions and currency reforms for easier foreign exchange. A major breakthrough in access to the U.S. market came with an important agreement with the United States in 1992 that pledged China to lower tariffs and eliminate some nontariff barriers. In 1993 China announced further major tariff reductions on 2,800 goods, agricultural products, and some services.[11] The open policy reformers had gained the upper hand in the decision making within China. They were successful, however, because they did not unduly challenge the internal opposition forces that remained dependent on inefficient government supports—particularly SOEs and the banking system.

Trade continued to expand in the period between 1994 and 2000, though more slowly toward the end of the period. In an attempt to guarantee continued economic growth, the focus of Chinese trade policies began to concentrate on actual membership in the WTO. China participated in the Uruguay Round negotiations as an observer and went so far as to sign the concluding agreements in April 1994. Its attempt to join the GATT before the end of that year in order to be a founding member of WTO was frustrated by its continued inability to meet internal reform standards necessary to join the free market regime.

Progress would come only as new president and party leader Jiang Zemin (1997–2002) consolidated power for the reform group within China's leadership. He placed his protege, Zhu Rongji, into the head of government role as Premier and began a strategic internal and external extension of China's economic reform program. The 1998 government restructuring, for example, reduced the more than forty ministries, commissions, and agencies (more than half had decision roles in foreign trade) to only a handful. The Ministry of Foreign Trade and Economic Cooperation (MoFTEC) took over as the chief negotiating body, though not final decision maker, with the WTO.[12]

By the year 2000, China had become the seventh largest economy in the world and the eighth largest trader. From 1978–2004, its GDP increased from $147.3 billion to $1.65 trillion, an average annual growth rate of 9.4 percent. Foreign trade rose from $20 billion to $1.55 trillion, an average growth of more than 16 percent. China may still be a developing country on many per capita scales, but its size combined with the dynamics of its economy in the 1980s and 1990s created a potential fourth corner to square out the Big Three world economies (the United States, the EU, and Japan). To consolidate these gains, acceptance into the WTO became an essential goal of the Chinese.

WHY DOES CHINA WANT TO JOIN THE WTO?

Here would seem to be a good place to explore more deeply China's motives for joining the WTO: "Chinese behavior in the international system serves five objectives: protecting Chinese sovereignty, maintaining national security, eroding Taiwan's status, cultivating a favorable image, and promoting economic interests."[13] Sovereignty and national security are given goals of every foreign policy. Specific WTO membership has more to do with the other three objectives. Put in simple terms, Chinese political isolation in a post-bipolar world combined with China's volatile economic condition led to its commitment to join the WTO.

Membership provides a variety of benefits. First of all, "China believes in multilateration [*sic*] as a tool to create what it sees as a more viable and attractive world order."[14] A spurt in Chinese membership into international organizations after Mao's death, including the Bretton Woods institutions, reflects this commitment. Its UN membership meant that it displaced Taiwan as China's legitimate government, helping it to fulfill its goal of isolating Taiwan and gaining recognition of it as a province of China, albeit an alienated province. Internationalization of decision making was also seen by China as a way to blunt the hegemonic tendencies of the United States and to bring equality with the EU and Japan.

Secondly, the necessity to maintain economic growth as a means of controlling increased domestic demands and redeem decades of promises by the communist regime became perhaps the paramount goal of post-Mao leadership. Expanded exports were crucial to this goal, and by 1997 exports had soared to $183 billion where they were only $40 billion a mere decade earlier. That decade was marked by 16.5 percent annual rates of expansion, though in the two years following (1998–99), that annual rate had fallen to 3 percent. Foreign investment virtually evaporated in 1998 and 1999. The 1997 bankruptcy of the Guangdong International Trust and Investment Company, the major trading company in China, led to a three-quarter decline in international loans to China. Price deflation accelerated in these years as well, hitting key exports. Inventories began to choke the economy averaging 5.7 percent of GNP.[15] Pragmatic reform seemed to Jiang and the reformists the only way to bring continuous growth. But they did not want to bulldoze the process and by doing so aggravate the many entrenched conservatives still in China. Thus, the "pragmatism of the mid-1990s [and beyond was] a product of bureaucratic bargaining and a consultative, consensual policy process."[16]

The way to bring sustained economic growth, reasoned the post-Mao leadership, was to consolidate the economic liberalization process within China and integrate this with an open policy in foreign trade. Membership in the WTO was a perfect mechanism for fulfilling both goals. Internal liberalization was more easily sold to the competing elite the more it was linked to expansion of foreign trade and investment. It is here that we find Putnam's model of the interrelationship between domestic and international interests most specifically applicable (see Chapter 1). The reform leadership throughout all of China's economic ups and downs depended on the logic of this synergy to maintain the momentum of reform. The WTO gives legitimacy to internal reform, and internal reform opens up opportunities for economic expansion, foreign and domestic.

We can identify two other, more specific, reasons for China's eagerness to join the WTO and to do it early in the twenty-first century. One, the Multi-Fiber Arrangement (MFA), an agreement among textile exporters to regulate trade in this area, was to expire in 2005. China was afraid that if it was not a member of the WTO by then, it might face a shrinking of its export textile market with serious consequences to its textile industry. Some estimated that China would capture 47 percent of the world export market in textiles by 2005 and produce 20 percent of the world's apparels after acceding to the WTO. This estimate proved too optimistic given bilateral agreements with the United States in 2005 and others to limit temporarily (again) China's impact, but growth has been significant in these areas nevertheless. To counterbalance potential Chinese textile dominance, agreements were made stating that until the end of 2008, WTO "members may impose quotas on textiles and clothing imports from China . . . if they are disruptive."[17]

The second specific incentive was that WTO membership would more than likely help the peaceful reunification of Taiwan (in some form at least) into the Chinese state. The reasoning being that as both joined the WTO (and Taiwan's membership date was coupled with China's), mutual trade restrictions that were then in effect would have to be dropped. This was anticipated to increase trade and other intercourse between the two with positive consequences for eventual reunification. Taiwan applied for membership in the WTO as a Separate Customs Territory in 1995, the same basis on which Hong Kong was admitted to GATT in 1986, and thus into WTO as a founding member. But Taiwan had to wait its turn since an agreement was made between the United States, the EU, and Japan that Taiwan membership would come only after China was admitted. Threats in late 2000 by the United States to recommend moving ahead with Taiwanese membership if China did not conclude negotiations soon demonstrated the use of this issue as a bargaining chip. Though Taiwan chafed, it waited on Chinese entry and was rewarded by immediate acceptance (on January 1, 2002) after China's December, 2001 membership.

THE ACCESSION PROCESS

Article XII of the WTO Final Act outlines a specific process by which new states would be admitted into the organization. Since the WTO wholly incorporated the GATT, members of GATT that approved the WTO declaration were automatically members. This produced 129 founding members of the organization. Thirteen more joined by the time of China's accession in late 2001 with several former communist countries, including the Russian Federation, waiting in line to qualify.

The WTO was not only an extension of the GATT commitments to free market policies. The WTO added significant areas missing from the GATT agreement, particularly in the realm of intellectual properties and services. But more importantly, it established an adjudicable rule of law in the area of international trade through its dispute settlement process. These specific enforcement mechanisms of the organization meant that it had the potential to be a true regulator of international trade. To join, each state must accede to the single-package formula of inclusive acceptance of all the GATT agreements, the GATS, and the Trade Related Intellectual Property Rights (TRIPS) agreement.

Even though many states would not see immediate gains from membership, particularly developing countries and some transitional economies, they virtually all believed it would be worse to be out of the regime set up by the WTO than to be in it. Poor countries often lose in the "winner and loser" environment of free trade, but they figure that losses would be greater if they did not join.[18] So membership is becoming nearly universal for all but a few of the former communist states.

The accession process, though simple in outline, is anchored in a negotiation process that can, as the China case shows, extend over a long period of time. The process contains four basic steps:[19]

The first step is a formal one. Using China as our example, it submitted an application to the director general of the WTO in 1995. The director general then established what is called a Working Party to negotiate with China the basis on which it was to substantiate its qualifications for membership. After forty years of GATT and now WTO, it would be unfair to let states join without making sure that they are committed to the precepts of the organization and that they are ready to fulfill the requirements of membership. China had to prove that it had shucked its command economy in favor of free market mechanisms.

Figure 7.1 The accession process

---

1. Application to the director general

2. The Working Party and fact-finding process

3. Bilateral negotiations with interested parties

4. Report, Protocol of Accession, and Entry into Force

Source: World Trade Organization—Secretariat, Technical Note on the Accession Process, Article XII.

As in any contract, member states know that the devil is in the details. Thus, the Working Party was charged with fact finding in an effort to find the condition of China's internal laws, processes, procedures, and policies in relation to the commitments that it must make in order to join the WTO. It would be imperative that all the elements of the Chinese economy were making significant progress toward smoothly integrating with the free trade regime established in the WTO. This meant that China would have to prove to the satisfaction of the Working Party that its economy was sufficiently open and that its internal economic and legal structures were compatible with international practices and adequately transparent. This, of course, would not be easy.

Any WTO member who wishes can join a Working Party. The ones who actually join depend on the nature of each state's trade relations with the applicant and their interest in the place of the applicant in the international economy. Thus, states within the region of the applicant may especially have interests leading them to participate, while others may have a stake in the global extent of the applicant's trade potential. In the case of China, both foundations were operable. China's Asian neighbors were anxious to open up thoroughly the Chinese economy and to do so on the basis of an international rule of law. And the Big Three (the United States, the EU, and Japan) were interested in the conditions of China's entry because of the huge impact they would have on the international political economy—not to mention that they are, and are likely to remain, China's main trading partners (if you exclude the special cases of Hong Kong and Singapore).

In the end, an unusually large Working Party on the Accession of China was formed consisting of forty-three interested states. The EU was allowed to join the Working Party as an organization (its key members were already a part of the forty-three), but not with a vote. The United States and Japan joined, of course, and regional trading countries were well represented. A representative splattering of developing countries rounded out the group. After consultations with the Working Party members, the director general appointed Mr. Pierre-Louis Girard of Switzerland as the chair. He directed and chaired most of the several formal meetings of the group throughout the years of negotiations and monitored the informal ones.

Before the first meeting of a Working Party, position paper memorandums are circulated to members. The most important of these, of course, is the application material submitted by the applicant. Working Party members may then ask questions, receive replies, and begin informal negotiations. When the Working Party first meets, it lays out the strategies for the accession process given the characteristics of the specific applicant. Clearly, the Chinese application was going to take some time and a great deal of negotiation. Separate bilateral negotiations particularly delayed the process, but the Working Party had several formal meetings in the meantime to evaluate progress toward final accession. Questions and answers were exchanged on a continuous basis, information papers were written and submitted, and bilateral negotiations took place throughout the process. It is often the case, as with China, that a working Draft Protocol of Accession is put together in the early stages of negotiation and circulated in order to give the parties something substantive with which to respond. All of this material is strictly confidential and not made public, though aspects inevitably leak. Throughout, the director general's staff provides technical help. Each side has a central negotiating team. The chief negotiator on behalf of the Chinese was Long Yongu (of MoFTEC), for the Working Party, Karl Friedrich Falkenberg. Long was later to help edit a work on the impact of China joining the WTO.[20]

The most important step in the accession process is the third step—the bilateral negotiations. It must be understood that in the end, all members of the WTO have to sign and accept all of the specific pledges and concessions negotiated with the applicant. In practical terms, China, like all applicants, had to negotiate a series of mutual specific trade concessions with a series of states as well as enumerate pledges of internal reforms in order to conform to WTO rules. China had to do this with all the Working Party members interested in bilateral agreements, one at a time (the EU negotiating for its member participants). Most of the interested states did not have large demands to make on the Chinese; they depended on the comprehensive agreements from the Working Party sessions and the bilateral agreements with the United States, EU, and Japan. China was in a more favorable position to placate the interests of small and medium-sized developing economies. The main negotiations, not surprisingly, were with the countries that comprised 70 percent of the world's international trade—the Big Three.

So, China had to negotiate bilateral market accession agreements on goods and services, as well as specific terms of accession, with all interested partners. The process inevitably overlaps with the previous step, fact finding by the Working Party as a whole. In point of fact, the two are intricately intertwined. Obviously, documents establishing the condition of China's economy would have to be part of the decision-making elements in the bilateral negotiations. Bilateral negotiations then form the basis of agreements on specifics that would be packaged for final approval of the Working Party whose report to the full membership must be virtually unanimous. The WTO recognizes that the bilateral negotiations are "the most critical element of the accession process . . . [for] the resulting market-access commitments of acceding governments can be considered to be the payment for the entry ticket into the WTO."[21] Remember that any general agreements between individual members of the WTO are automatically made applicable to all members under the principle of MFN embedded in the WTO charter. Bilateral agreements would echo throughout the membership of the organization and become part of the final Working Party report.

Once all-important bilateral agreements have been made, the Working Group is ready to investigate the resulting package of accession concessions and actions on the part of the applicant. A final report is then made on the package of agreements. This report provides the formal Draft Protocol of Accession: "the terms of accession agreed upon by the Applicant and members of the working party" that is presented to the full membership of the WTO.[22]

Annexed to the Draft Protocol are results of the individual bilateral negotiations. The final report would contain the following:

The Draft Report
The Draft Protocol of Accession
Schedule of Concessions and Commitments on Goods
Schedule of Concessions and Commitments on Services
Annexes: Bilateral Agreements[23]

When these are all finalized by consensus of the Working Party, the full report goes to the Ministerial Conference (all members of the WTO, not merely the Working Party) for approval. While consensus is the preferred method of coming to a decision on approval here as well, the WTO charter indicates that it takes a two-thirds vote of the final decision maker, the Ministerial Conference, to approve membership.

The true final step must be the ratification of the agreement by the legislature of the applicant. In China's case, as with most countries, this was an automatic process. This accomplished, the applicant is to be made a member of the WTO within thirty days.

China is a good example of the principle that the process always takes more time than applicants think or hope. Starting with its GATT membership negotiations, which were unsuccessful, China's acceptance into the international trade regime took fifteen years of negotiations. Bilateral negotiations with the United States and the EU created a variety of costly delays. Each accessing party must, toward the end of the negotiating process, produce a legislative plan for executing their commitments. This includes draft laws and regulations, bureaucratic foundations for implementation, and a specific timetable. This is an important basis for the Working Party's final approval. For China, this was a difficult requirement given its lack of internal legal processes and market economy foundations prior to application.

Even when all arrangements seemed set in December of 2000, delays from both the Chinese, who needed time to legislate and operationalize a whole new legal system, and the WTO postponed the final Working Party agreement. Diplomatic and economic problems with the United States were particularly thorny at this time. As late as March 2001, the new George W. Bush administration's U.S. Trade Representative Robert Zoellick felt it necessary to announce that China had only then "launched a campaign to align domestic laws and regulations with WTO rules."[24] Problems with the United States remained in areas of sanitary standards, quality and inspection procedures, and transparency combined with continuing intellectual properties and agriculture conflicts. Long, China's chief negotiator, reported to the fifteenth session of the Working Party in January of 2001 that agricultural access and subsidies remained the key holdup to a final agreement.[25]

Final acceptance depended on last-minute agreements prior to the crucial opening of a new round of trade expansion talks at the Fourth Ministerial Conference of the WTO in Doha, Qatar, in November of 2001. A flurry of pre-Doha Working Party meetings ironed out agreements between the United States and a recalcitrant

Mexico in time to present a full report from the Working Party ready for consideration for the full ministerial meeting.

That consideration came, and a consensus was reached for Chinese membership on November 13, 2001. Formal acceptance at the Fourth Ministerial Conference of the WTO in Doha, Qatar (and swift Chinese legislative approval) culminated in China's accession into full membership of the WTO on December 4, 2001, after fifteen long years of negotiation.

BILATERAL NEGOTIATIONS

Since the bilateral negotiations are the key to not only accession, but more importantly to conditions for accession, it is necessary to consider the trials and tribulations of China's bilateral negotiations. There were a variety of broad issues that China had to face in approaching bilateral negotiations. The more important of these for the Working Party were outlined in an evaluation of China and the WTO by scholars at the American Enterprise Institute:

> Is the PRC a Developing or Developed Country?
> The Status of China's Transparency and Judicial Review
> China's State-owned Enterprises
> China's Statism and Industrial Policy[26]

Let us briefly consider these.

DEVELOPING OR DEVELOPED?

Since there are different expectations and legal obligations in the WTO assigned to members based on whether they are classified as a developing economy or a developed economy, the way China was perceived and treated in the negotiations had significant consequences. GATT provided concessions for developing countries during the Tokyo Round, and the Uruguay Round agreements maintained many of these.

China's early argument was that it was a developing country under WTO definitions and qualified for concessions in the negotiations. The Chinese argued that they had gross economic shortfalls (in per capita GDP, for example) indicating their developing status. The United States and the EU in particular would not buy this argument given the size of the Chinese economy and its potential for expanding its international trade. They noted that the Chinese Academy of Social Sciences published a report in 1998 with evidence of significant movement in the Chinese economy toward a market economy. And it was hard to hide the high levels of foreign investment in national, regional, and even locally run enterprises, many of them joint ventures with local or regional governments.

Further, though competitive management skills may have been lacking, market activity was significant and increasing. Over one thousand SOEs had been successfully put into operation in the 1990s, and this number continues to mount. Profitable enterprise zones were popping up all over China in the late 1980s and 1990s, even if many were of questionable legality under extant Chinese law. Hong Kong, increasingly integrating with the adjacent Chinese economy, was already a member of the WTO on the basis of developed country status, further undermining the Chinese claim to developing country concessions.

In the end, the Chinese had to accept that their role in the WTO would have to be that equal to a developed economy, based, if on nothing else, on its effect on the international political economy. Final WTO bilateral negotiations came to depend on this mutual recognition.

TRANSPARENCY/JUDICIAL REVIEW

Arguably the most important barrier to China's accession was not external in nature, but internal, both in terms of politics and the legal system. Since China has been emerging from a strictly controlled, one-party-based political system with a set of laws responsive to party individuals and circumstances, the Chinese have had a hard time establishing a transparent rule-of-law system. Transparency in this context refers to the ability for everyone to understand the rules and regulations that determine access to China's markets.

The legal system in China has struggled from the beginning of the basic reform effort to establish a working system of contract law even though foundations were set in the Economic Contract Law passed in 1981.[27] This law opened the door for statutes on property, company management, and bankruptcy; however, fitting all these into a coherent whole proved difficult. The number of new lawyers, a key prerequisite to the operationalization of a new system, has exploded in China from only a handful to 150,000 since a 1997 law allowing lawyers to provide legal services. But older judges find it hard to understand how to interpret and enforce the new economic legal structure.[28] The collectivist mentality fostered by the communist regime has been hard to shake. Developing an independent judiciary may be the greatest challenge in this realm of Chinese advancement. Integrating some 160 promised new basic laws into the old bureaucracy has not been easy, and the confusion and misunderstanding endemic within the bureaucracy leaves ample room for corruption and antiliberalization resistance. Still, the legal framework has developed as necessity has dictated. The late 1990s found the passage of the Administrative Litigation Law, the Administrative Punishment Law, and a bit later, the Administrative Procedure Law. Yet, even after accession, in early 2002, it was estimated that more than 1,000 specific laws and rules still needed to be changed.[29]

Many feel that the courts are less significant for protection of trade, and more trust should be placed in administrative dispute settlement mechanisms. These bureaucratic mechanisms for mediation provide an arena populated by more pragmatic operatives able to make quick and more balanced decisions. On the other hand, it was not until mid-2004 that the People's Republic of China was successfully sued for the first time by a private firm in a Chinese court.

SOEs, Statism, and Industrial Policy

The Ninth National People's Congress held in 2001 passed numerous laws and directives to bring China's overall industrial policy, especially its SOEs, into line with WTO policy. Zeng Peiyan, China's chief planner, in his report to the Congress pledged the restructuring of industries in manufacturing, energy, communication, agriculture, and financial services "to improve their competitive edge."[30] Science, technology, education, and training were stressed. He said that China would establish a strong support system for its "go global" strategy. The Congress changed its joint venture laws to abolish priorities for Chinese goods when purchasing, and it pledged to draft stronger antimonopoly and antidumping legislation. The government clearly wanted to stress its commitment to a rule-based economy.

By the time of accession, China had over 32,000 Chinese enterprises with import/export rights along with 180,000 foreign invested enterprises employing twenty million people. This was the reason Chinese foreign trade minister, Shi Guangsheng, told the Congress that they were faced with a challenge to their way of thinking: "All of our activities must be based on the rule of law, so we must build up our awareness of the rule of law, fair competition and the development of the market economy."[31] To further the goal of maximum transparency, MoFTEC created a new agency specifically to deal with WTO inquiries. Minister Shi announced that all new foreign economic regulations, administrative guidelines, or any local measures must be consistent with national laws and regulations. Further, they must all be reported to MoFTEC.[32]

Premier Zhu Rongji's report to the Congress on the tenth five-year plan for economic and social development (2001–05) emphasized China's entrance into the WTO. Zhu Rongji indicated that the WTO takes precedent. If the economy does not progress, the "new left" in the Chinese political system will be ready to push its argument that the disadvantages to WTO membership are larger than the advantages. These opposition forces, SOE leadership, traditional government officials, agricultural interests, and some academic think tanks have been put in the background, but they have not disappeared. Indeed, they are poised to pounce on any disruptions resulting from WTO membership (unemployment, noncompetitiveness in agriculture, challenges to elite privileges). Internal considerations seriously impact the international position of China, as Putnam predicted and as we will see next in the policies of the United States.

THE SINO-AMERICAN BILATERAL AGREEMENT

Although negotiations with the entire Working Party were necessary, the bilateral agreement with the United States was by far the most difficult and the most important. The

United States, after all, had put limits on trading with nonmarket economies in an amendment to the Trade Act of 1974—the so-called Jackson-Vanik Amendment that set criteria to be met or waived by the president in order to obtain MFN status. MFN negotiations with China continued until 1979 when the United States and China reached a ten-page framework agreement. China was consequently granted MFN status under the bilateral accord of February 1, 1980, but the kicker was that this had to be extended annually by Congress because of the Jackson-Vanik Amendment. Congress did grant this status to China annually through 2001 when China finally joined the WTO, thus receiving permanent MFN status. But each year the debate allowed the anti-China lobby to emphasize the undeniable shortcomings of China's policies toward human rights, the environment, the rights of workers, and the political monopoly of the Communist Party. And each year China had to rally its allies in business to forestall this opposition.

For China, MFN resulted in an increase in the value of exports to the United States from $1.2 billion in 1980, to $100 billion in 2000, and to $200 billion by 2005. The United States had become a major market for Chinese goods; it had also become the major investor in China, with the exception of Hong Kong, Singapore, and overseas Chinese. However, a complaint is that Chinese tariff and nontrade barriers have come down slower than those of the United States, resulting in a trade deficit with China that has grown every year since 1983 to a record $201.6 billion in 2005.

Frustrated with China's unwillingness to open its markets, the United States threatened in 1992 to impose prohibitive tariffs on $3.9 billion of Chinese imports. This resulted in hectic negotiations that led to the 1992 Market Access Memorandum of Agreement and an Intellectual Property Memorandum of Agreement. China agreed to lower tariffs, eliminate nontariff trade barriers, protect copyrights and patents, and eliminate some specific impediments to imports. Nevertheless, China added new barriers in the form of complex regulations, particularly on agricultural imports and in the form of local content legislation. The United States' trade deficit continued to grow. So did calls for sanctions against China (e.g., from CD manufacturers). The piracy of music had become a particular bilateral issue resulting in the United States threatening from $1 billion to $2 billion in retaliation in 1995 and again in 1996. The Chinese relented, closing piracy factories and increasing surveillance, but in the process they demonstrated a tendency toward brinkmanship in the diplomatic process.[33]

A breakthrough on fundamental issues was needed, but things were not going well with Sino-American relations. A decline in economic growth combined with this impasse seemed to the Chinese to produce an opportunity for a turning point in their approach to international integration. This came in the form of a surprise announcement by Jiang at the Osaka meeting of the Asia Pacific Economic Cooperation (APEC) forum in 1995. China announced that it would cut tariffs by 30 percent on some four thousand additional import items, and for the first time, it would allow joint ventures (mostly between SOEs and large foreign enterprises).

This amounted to the first significant wide-reaching liberalization offer since GATT negotiations began. Then, in October of 1997, import duties were cut to an average of 17 percent, down from 23 percent. Although significant differences remained in tariff rates with different trading partners, these were dramatic steps. Within the complex politics of China's bureaucracy, MoFTEC was able to get the crucial support from the highest ranks of leadership, Jiang and Premier Zhu Rongji, and this made the difference.[34] Jiang was clearly trying to not only move along WTO negotiations with the United States and the EU, but he was committing Chinese reform to the point of no return in an attempt to solidify internally the position of the reform leadership.

At the beginning of 1999, Premier Zhu Rongji's government made further extraordinary concessions to the United States—concessions it had steadfastly resisted because they would undermine the remaining elements of state socialism, that core economy the "partial-integration" policy labored to protect. It was time to tear down the shield protecting state banks, state firms (SOEs), and state monopolies in key manufacturing and service sectors. Zhu offered to open to competition agriculture, industrial markets, service industries (banking and insurance), and even the much contested telecommunications industries—some immediately, some within three to five years of WTO membership. Tariffs were to be lowered to roughly the level of most developed trading countries.

This new logic reflected the complete adoption of the "full-integration" model: "Instead of reform serving to sustain the core, the core itself would be destroyed to save reform, along with the growth, prosperity, and stability that reform brought China."[35] China had made the final psychological step needed in order to mobilize its policies through a rapid transformation of its laws, procedures, and administrative rules to conform to its free market trading partners.

American leadership was slow in recognizing this significant shift in Chinese policy. It resisted concluding an agreement citing specifics, particularly in the areas of agriculture and service industries. American leaders did not believe the extent to which the Chinese were willing to go to produce internal reforms to meet the requirements of WTO free trade rules. High-level trade representatives from the United States visited Beijing in the spring of 1999, but there remained significant differences between the two countries. Then in April of that year, Premier Zhu Rongji met with President Clinton to finally bring closure to negotiations for U.S. approval of China's entry into the WTO.

At the last minute, however, Clinton inexplicably balked at the arrangements. Zhu went home embarrassed and upset. He had to face SOE leaders and conservatives who felt that too much was being given up anyway. In May, when a stray U.S. bomb hit the Chinese embassy in Belgrade during the Serbian campaign, China's lingering suspicions about American motives toward China seemed to be confirmed. All bilateral negotiations were suspended. Late in May 1999, the U.S. Congress released a report accusing China of extensive military espionage, worsening bilateral relations but perhaps counterbalancing the effects of the embassy bombing.

In the long run, trade issues were largely unaffected by these collateral political issues. Still, it took a high-level meeting between Presidents Clinton and Jiang at the September 1999 meeting of APEC to jumpstart the WTO negotiations. Jiang spent months repairing the damage, as did Clinton, who belatedly recognized his mistake in turning down the April Chinese package. China came to believe that if it were to complete negotiations for entry into the WTO, it had to stop piecemeal agreements with the United States and come to a comprehensive agreement that would set the model for the final Working Party settlement.

After nearly thirteen years of negotiations, six days of grueling meetings concluded a groundbreaking agreement between the United States and China on November 15, 1999. When the agreement was announced, everyone assumed that the foundations of a final accession accord were in place for the entire Working Party to approve. The comprehensive bilateral agreement covered the entire array of extant trade issues. In the glow of this accomplishment, membership was predicted for the Seattle Ministerial Conference of the WTO in 2000. Seattle, of course, turned out to be a disaster and another story told in Chapter 8. Suffice it to say that it provided yet another excuse for delay in the accession process for China.

The November 1999 pact remained the foundation for the final accession agreement. It was, as U.S. Trade Representative Charlene Barshefsky explained, "a comprehensive agreement which covers industrial goods, services, farm products, unfair trade practices, and all the barriers to American exports; and which in consequence will develop legal norms and rules in an absolutely vast set of fields."[36] In addition, the United States won protection for its industry against import surges for twelve years.

It would appear that this concluded the bilateral negotiations between China and the United States. But the whole deal depended on the United States passing legislation that would give Permanent Normal Trade Relations (PNTR), the new term for MFN, status to China so that U.S. law would not contradict WTO rules. This was easier said than done.[37] The Clinton administration needed an all-out lobbying campaign to convince Congress and the American people that PNTR status for China was in America's best interest. All through the first two-thirds of 2000, the full array of pro and con organizations and interests mounted propaganda and lobbying campaigns. The Office of the U.S. Trade Representative and its chair, Charlene Barshefsky, poured out information to the public and to Congress with help from business and international think tanks.[38] Attacks came from labor, industries impacted from trade, and a variety of public interest groups.

In the end, economics won over concerns about human rights, labor abuses, the status of Taiwan, and nationalists afraid of loss of sovereignty, but only after bitter debates and complex legislative maneuvering. However, further delays meant that China would not actually enter the WTO until late 2001 and after the Clinton administration had left office.

SINO-EU AGREEMENTS ON ACCESSION

The agreements made with the United States made it easier for the EU to negotiate with China. Trade growth and balances for the EU echoed those of the United States, although with a somewhat smaller volume, and the EU was anxious to expand its impact on the Chinese economy. For China, the EU was an important trade partner; in 1998 it accounted for 15 percent of imports and 20 percent of exports. Since MFN rules within the WTO mean that any bilateral agreement extends the same concessions to all WTO members, the EU had only to fine-tune the United States' agreements to meet the needs of its members. The EU hoped to obtain additional benefits in some specific areas and China was, in the end, prepared to concede to them.

EU negotiators wanted to augment the American agreements to fit particular problems European states were having in trading with China. The key items dealt with the stake allowed to foreign investors in China's enterprises and a push for even lower tariffs on some goods. The EU asked for (1) majority foreign ownership in specified telecommunications joint ventures, (2) lower tariff rates on alcoholic beverages, (3) majority ownership in life insurance ventures, (4) automobile tariffs below the 25 percent negotiated by the United States, and (5) majority foreign ownership in manufacturing firms.[39] They did not get all of this. Majority ownership was still too much for China, but it did improve the market access timetable for mobile telephony. Foreign investment in telecommunications ventures would be allowed at 25 percent after one year of accession, 35 percent after the second year, and 49 percent after three years. Finally, "in internet and other value-added services, including paging, foreign firms will immediately be allowed 30 percent stakes in Chinese companies . . . [which will] increase to 50 percent in two years."[40]

Insurance was a particular interest of the EU because it is an area where European firms have had a head start on U.S. rivals in China. Indeed, a side agreement allowed seven additional licenses that allowed German and English firms to enter the market even before WTO entry. In addition, tariff reductions were negotiated on 150 products. EU oil and railroad companies also benefited from the deal.

Since the EU had been the second largest seller of goods to China behind Japan, membership for China was an important goal. EU trade commissioner, Pascal Lamy, put it this way: "China's accession is good for the EU because we have secured a high standard of commitments by China to open its economy to foreign imports, investors and businesses."[41]

Both the U.S. and EU negotiations resulted in significant Chinese concessions. The final Working Party agreement contains these concessions, though China tried mightily at the last minute to mute some of them, in particular on agriculture subsidies.

JAPAN AND CHINA'S ACCESSION

Japan, as was its habit in these matters, kept a low profile during the accession diplomacy with China. It is rather ironic that Japan was the first to complete its bilateral negotiations with China. Japan, as it turns out, did have significant reasons to support Chinese accession.

China had been one of Japan's biggest markets since its opening up in 1987. Japan's bilateral trade had skyrocketed from U.S. $220 million in 1984 to U.S. $3.16 billion in 1998, a 20 percent annual growth. China in 1999 imported more goods from Japan than from any other country—20 percent to 12.1 percent and 14.8 percent respectively for the United States and the EU.[42] Through the late 1990s, Asian economic slowdown produced a decline in the trade and investment opportunities for Japan in China. Membership of China into the WTO, it was hoped, would bring stability to their trade relationship and stimulate Japanese growth.

Japan preferred to take a back seat to the United States and the EU for at least two reasons. First, Japan is a reluctant free trader. While it has lowered tariff rates to equal levels with WTO signatories, has few quantitative restrictions save for the contentious agricultural areas, and while there are few formal regulations limiting foreign investment, Japan has not dealt with a business culture that makes it difficult for foreign companies to actually do business with Japan. Much of its processes remain nontransparent, and discriminatory business standards and practices continue. It has remained very difficult to break into much of the Japanese marketplace.[43] Evidence of this can be seen in Japan's overwhelmingly favorable balance of payments record.

Secondly, Japan still suffers from its reputation for harsh actions during World War II. This is particularly true for Japan's Asian neighbors, China prominent among them. Relationships have been touchy with China even as trade and investment interactions grew in the 1990s. Still, Japan was anxious to see China with a stable rule of law and a transparent system.

Given these drawbacks, Japan waited in the wings as the United States and the EU negotiated their bilateral agreements with China, fully expecting to be the last of the Big Three to conclude a bilateral agreement. However, the breaking of trade talks between the United States and China due to the bombing of the Chinese Embassy in Serbia, along with Clinton's failure to end negotiations in April 1999 and the EU support of the NATO war against Serbia, opened the door for Japan to negotiate a bilateral accord. Suddenly, Japan moved to a leadership role in the accession process and out of its wings. During a state visit to China on July 9, 1999, Japanese Prime Minister Keizo Obuchi announced a bilateral agreement. The key issues for Japan centered around the service areas of insurance and investment plus additions to the goods agreements negotiated with China in the trade protocol of 1997. In addition, Japan had concerns about wholesale distribution practices in China and access to telecommunications and construction contracts.[44] Specifics were held so closely by the two countries that no news of the agreement's particulars appeared in any major international news source or in either government's press releases. In announcing the joint agreement, Japan pledged continuing support for and cooperation with the Working Party to conclude WTO accession in the continuing Geneva talks.

By the end of 2001, Mexico was the only state in the Working Party that had not signed off on a bilateral agreement for China to join the WTO. It had waited for the late 2000 election of President Fox to conclude an agreement that would guarantee that China would not dump its goods on Mexico upon accession to the organization. Mexico had antidumping levies on 1,400 goods imported from China, and before eliminating or reducing these, Mexico needed specific assurances from China.[45] These being given, bilaterals were concluded in October of 2001. The stage was set for final approval of Chinese accession, first by the Working Party and then by the full Doha Ministerial Council.

CONCLUSIONS

China's long and winding road to WTO membership illustrates some of the key concerns of this text. The first lesson learned is that the accession process is extensive and complex given the necessity to please not only the foundation principles of the GATT/WTO, but also the specific interests of member states. China had to demonstrate that its internal structures as well as their operation met the guidelines of free trade outlined in the WTO protocols. It was not easy for a command economy to transform itself sufficiently in a short period of time to operate effectively in a market environment. It took significant bilateral as well as multilateral diplomacy to seal the deal. There are obvious lessons here for the former command economies of Eastern Europe, Vietnam, and Russia as they prepare domestic institutions and international connections for WTO entry.

Our continuing theme of the influence of the powerful economies can be seen in this case by the centrality of the United States and the EU in molding Chinese acceptance. These countries, along with Japan, would receive the greatest impact of Chinese international trade expansion.[46] For example, within five years of Chinese membership, bilateral trade with the United States had tripled, and by 2007 that bilateral trade was at an annual rate of $328 billion—ten times that of 1992. China had become in a very short period of time the fourth largest international trading state with the power of a $1 trillion balance of trade reserve.

To accomplish all this, China's experience demonstrates once again the salience of Putnam's insights into the two-level game of domestic politics coupled with international diplomacy—the win set. Pragmatic domestic open policy champions had to constantly deal with conservative factions and a democracy movement wary of such dramatic transformations. Chinese leaders had to sell the benefits of WTO entrance to these groups; they also could use the needs of these groups to force concessions from the EU, the United States, and other WTO members. Meanwhile, U.S. policy makers had to find a way of bringing China into the WTO while dealing with domestic groups opposed to China's entrance on human rights, labor, and environmental grounds. The growing size and importance of China has made it almost impossible to leave outside of the international liberal trading regime; while at the same time, actors within the United States need the certainty provided by the WTO in order to better insure that their trade relations with China will be stable and secure.

Obviously, the battle between the liberal principles of free trade and the mercantilist thrusts of political and economic protectionism find a fertile battle ground in the history and continuing development of the Chinese opening to the world of trade.

The Battle in Seattle

The nearly unanimous view among scholars and participants alike was that the Third Ministerial Conference under the WTO held in Seattle, its regularly scheduled meeting, was a disaster. The trade ministers from 134 member states had come with a loose agenda to set the foundations for a new round of negotiations that would expand the substantive areas covered by the WTO agreements and fine-tune them. Because of the increased visibility of the organization and because it was venturing into more publicly sensitive areas, literally hundreds of nongovernmental organizations (NGOs) flocked to Seattle to try and influence the direction in which the WTO agreements were headed.

Accompanying this array of NGOs were thousands of people prepared to demonstrate in the streets to raise public awareness and to make demands on the delegates to the conference. Indeed, some of the demonstrators were there in an attempt to close down the meeting as a preliminary step to closing down the organization itself. The WTO had become a symbol of negative globalization and a target for those opposed to what they perceived to be untoward concentration of economic and political powers in an embodiment of the evils of globalization.

Was the conference a bust, a bungled opportunity, a precursor of things to come, a warning shot, or all four? This chapter investigates the Seattle conference in the context of the WTO's attempts to respond to continuing challenges. In doing so, we will look at the environment in Seattle created by the first two Ministerial Conferences of the WTO, the preparations for the meeting, inside the meeting itself, happenings outside the meeting, and an evaluation of the meeting's failures. In the process, this chapter will identify the antagonists and protagonists and the issues in the struggle for control of the future of the WTO.

SINGAPORE PREPARATIONS AND GENEVA

As we have seen in an earlier chapter, the Uruguay Round of negotiations successfully built on and incorporated GATT agreements into a more substantive organization. The Uruguay Round was able to solidify the long-term trend toward low tariff rates and the elimination of a great many nontariff barriers while beginning a rule-based system to settle disputes. There were, however, several areas of trade concern and conflict that the round was unable to address successfully, and it designated some to be reviewed in consequent years. Three areas that continued to press on the organization were specifically mandated for negotiations beginning no later than 2000—sometimes called the *first generation of new issues*: agriculture, services, and intellectual property. Some other new areas were simply delayed until further negotiations could deal with them (perhaps in a new round), often called the *second generation of new issues*: competition policies, electronic commerce, direct foreign investment, labor and trade, and the environment and trade.[1]

The three problem areas of the first generation came to be the primary areas referred to as the *built-in agenda*, meaning that even without any newly formed round, negotiations would have to get underway. These negotiations, informal and formal, began as early as 1998 and were targeted for conclusion at the Seattle conference.[2] Agreements were, in fact, not concluded by late 1999, and therefore these issues became an automatic part of the Seattle agenda, though still independent of any further agenda items. They were to be negotiated regardless, and indeed have proven so resistant to basic agreement that they have found continuing life in negotiations throughout the early part of the new century.

These issues provided a discomforting aura of conflict for the discussions surrounding the Seattle meeting. They are issues that contain significant differences of perspective between the major trading states as well as developing countries. The built-in agenda created a minefield for the Seattle meeting since significant progress had not been made in addressing these issues before the opening in November of 1999. And as we have seen with bananas and beef, conflict tended to mark the period leading to Seattle. Let us briefly follow the progress of the negotiations beginning with the WTO in 1995.

The First Ministerial Conference of the new WTO was held in Singapore on December 9–13, 1996. The meeting marked the beginnings of a rebellion among, particularly, developing countries on the processes of decision making within the GATT and now the WTO. As in most of the GATT rounds, the process of negotiations toward building the necessary consensus (remember that decisions had been made by consensus from the beginning) was centered on a few states. Here is how it worked. Preliminary meetings in the Geneva headquarters with secretariat staff and representatives of major trading states and a splattering of others with interests in the prime agenda items were held to settle on a draft resolution for each coming conference. Then a similar group would meet at the conference itself to negotiate final agreements on a consensus declaration. The full membership was expected to go along with the draft. As the GATT membership increased, the number of members in this inner circle expanded but was still kept at a discrete level (usually around twenty-five to thirty-five).

By the time of the Singapore meeting, there were 120 members of the GATT/WTO; most were developing countries. These countries had been on the margins of the GATT and had seen little benefit from tariff reductions. Since the Tokyo Round, though, they had significant exceptions built into the agreements for them. However, the WTO agreements brought binding rules that awakened the developing countries' interests in the proceedings of WTO conferences. They were now bound to all of the GATT/WTO agreements if they joined and thus could suffer under dispute settlement rulings if their policies were challenged. They also believed that Uruguay Round concessions were not being implemented; they were losing confidence in the agreements. While a few well-placed developing states (e.g., Brazil, Egypt, and India) were a part of many of the inner circle meetings, others began to chafe at being excluded from the inner circle.

Singapore continued the traditional process of limited member agenda building and agreement drafting. Meetings at the Geneva headquarters pounded out a draft declaration, and thirty-four inner circle states met during the conference to pound out compromises that became the final declaration. This has been referred to as the "Green Room" process and was explained in Chapter 4. At the concluding meetings of the Singapore conference, key non–Green Room states took the floor to make three points: (1) they thanked the thirty-four for their hard work; (2) they accepted the draft report; but (3) they would no longer put up with the "undemocratic, unfair and disgraceful" backroom process.[3] They demanded that a high priority be given to a revision of the process that excluded most from direct input into these key negotiations. The conference chair and the WTO director general assured them that reform was on the way. Needless to say, the WTO bureaucracy and those states with a seat in the inner circle dragged their feet on any substantive changes. This was a fatal mistake that would echo through to the Seattle conference.

Suspicious of a proposed Millennium Round to begin with, developing countries were to see Seattle as a testing ground for defining their role in the WTO. The Second Ministerial Conference was held in Geneva in May of 1998. It was largely a ceremonial occasion to commemorate the fiftieth anniversary of the GATT/WTO. It made little progress on substantive issues but encouraged the continuation of talks on issues of the built-in agenda. The only area of real work was the establishment of Working Groups (committees of sorts) under the General Council to prepare for the next Ministerial Conference to be held in Seattle. It was assumed that since the so called Quad members (the EU, the United States, Japan, and Canada—the four largest international trading members) along with several other states were calling for a full new round of negotiations that Seattle would be the launching pad for such a round.

Meanwhile, developing countries pushed their concerns over the implementation of agreements arising from the Uruguay Round: "The widespread perception in the developing world (parliaments, governments, business sectors, academics and NGOs) [was] that the Uruguay Round and its agreements enshrined in the WTO are asymmetric, imbalanced and iniquitous to the developing countries."[4] How these agreements were implemented, then, was and remains a major concern of most developing countries. They believed that the developed countries promised expanded market access on favorable grounds, particularly for key agricultural products and apparel, in exchange for their signing onto the WTO, and they believed that access had not materialized. They were not interested in a new round if implementation of the old round had not progressed significantly. Quotas and tariff levels remained obstacles, as did the lack of promised favorable negotiated access to developed markets for specific developing country goods and services.

President Clinton had taken the occasion of his Geneva speech commemorating the fiftieth anniversary of the GATT to call for a new round of world trade negotiations, and he invited the WTO to meet in the United States for that purpose. So successful was his talk that new round speculation nearly became known as the Clinton Round.[5] Instead, a former EU trade commissioner, Sir Leon Brittan, christened the round the Millennium Round. The round was to address a variety of first- and second-generation new issues, plus the Quad states' recommendation for further talks on reductions of tariffs on industrial goods.

Seattle successfully lobbied for the meeting, as it seemed a good place to downplay the eastern seaboard power centers of the United States, and it represented an opening to the countries of the Pacific. It seemed a symbolically apt choice. Ironically, it also had the supposed advantage of not being so accessible to entrenched interest groups that tended to focus on Washington DC. The stage was set for planning to proceed on the Seattle meeting scheduled for November 1999. The General Council had envisioned a schedule of agenda preparations in three stages: "informal explorations of issues (October 1998 to February 1999), the submission of written proposals for the ministers' agenda (March through July), and the drafting phase (September through November)."[6]

But fate was to intervene and upset this schedule. The WTO Director General Renato Ruggiero announced his resignation effective April 30, 1999. This left a vacuum that proved difficult to fill. The frustrations of the developing states found an outlet in the selection process for a new director general. The major states, the United States especially, were use to picking the leaders of the WTO (and before that, the GATT), and they had someone in mind to fill the post, Mike Moore, trade minister from New Zealand. A second major candidate was put forward by developing states, Dr. Supachai Panitchpakdi, Thailand's deputy prime minister and commerce minister. When the decision came before the General Council, its chair declared that Moore had support of sixty-two members from a wide geographical area and should be the one around which consensus should be built. Panitchpakdi had support of fifty-nine mostly non-Western (with the UK and the Netherlands as major exceptions) and developing states (Japan and Korea gave support as well).

The concept of consensus decision making was put to the test. Clearly, there was no consensus on the choice; indeed there was bitter conflict. Panitchpakdi supporters were certain that the United States was trying to use its power to manipulate a victory for Moore; the United States accused opposition forces of violating the consensus format of the organization. Weeks of squabbling ensued. Finally, Bangladesh and Australia brought forth a compromise "that achieved grudging consensus."[7] The two candidates would share the six-year term, each serving for three years. No one wanted this as a precedent, but there seemed no alternative if Seattle negotiations were to go forward.

By now it was August of 1999, and preparations for Seattle were in a shambles. There were not only substantive issue differences that accumulated between major countries as well as between North and South, but the preliminaries were left without a credible mediator. And draft declarations were needed to facilitate the work of the ministers in Seattle. Mike Moore became the new director general because the United States insisted on him taking the first three-year turn. He was therefore both new in the director general's office with only weeks to go before the meeting and handicapped as a mediator because developing countries greatly suspected his prolabor background (he had been the Labour Party prime minister of New Zealand). Chairman Ali Mchumo of the General Council also had lost credibility because of his ineffective mediation role in the process of choosing the director general. As a consequence, most of the Working Groups were unable to come to agreement on the parameters of major issues to put within a draft declaration to launch a new negotiation round in Seattle.

ON TO SEATTLE: THE PREPARATIONS

The Seattle Ministerial Conference was to be held from November 30 to December 3, 1999, and was to set the foundations of a new round of trade negotiations. These would bring to fruition agreements on the new issues not covered or insufficiently covered by the GATT/WTO so far and fine-tune agreements already in place. The purpose of the meeting was to set a specific negotiation agenda for a new trade round (which was projected to last three years), not to prenegotiate the outcome of that round.

In their report to the British House of Commons, Hillyard and Edmonds quote an official WTO paper on the procedures to be followed for Seattle. This paper indicated that the General Council, as a result of its working groups, was to make recommendations to the ministers so they could make decisions in Seattle. These recommendations were to be pounded out in Geneva before the conference. Then, "based on the General Council's recommendations, ministers will announce the *organization and management* of the WTO's work programme, including the scope, structure and time-frames of *negotiations* to liberalize international trade."[8] The authors quickly added the obvious: "Clearly, high profile conferences of this sort are held only if there is reasonable expectation that it will yield tangible benefits."[9] Seattle was to violate this tenant badly since this process was not completed as it had been for the launch of the Uruguay Round. Refer back to Chapter 3 to understand the importance of careful preparations for new rounds of negotiations.

This is not to say that there was no planning for the Seattle Ministerial Conference. The pre-conference Geneva process of the General Council had tried hard in the six or seven weeks before the conference to build a consensus on a draft declaration. Chair Ali Mchumo circulated drafts; there were Green Room meetings called by the director general late in the process; and informal negotiations proliferated. But developing countries were adamant in their demand that implementation of Uruguay Round agreements be high on the agenda, and developed countries continued to argue issue points, particularly over agriculture. Over 300 proposals were submitted by members for the draft—over half from developing countries. On October 19, with no agreement in sight, the chair simply submitted on his own authority a hodgepodge, overblown draft to the ministerial delegates that was a comparatively hefty 31 pages. It was accompanied by the secretariat's compilation of a digest of the submitted proposals that was 202 pages.[10] Mind you, the Geneva planning sessions were due to end on November 5, but "finally on 23 November Moore and Mchumo threw in the towel. After a year of work, the best they could send to ministers was the 19 November [draft] that no one thought was adequate."[11]

Planning by the secretariat of the WTO had been centered around cooperation with the American hosts and a structure for the meeting revolving around five ministerial working groups—each group attacking a broad issue area and each chaired by a different minister supported by a deputy director general. The deputies were only recently appointed, and the United States did not recruit the ministerial chairs until the day before the conference began. Since the first day of the conference was disrupted by demonstrators making it difficult for ministers even to communicate with each other, time became increasingly short for real negotiation.

In contrast to the WTO and its American hosts, opponents of the WTO were well prepared for the Seattle Ministerial Conference. Some groups had taken a year or more to get ready for the conference. In an attempt to preempt and educate this opposition, the Seattle Host Committee invited several organizations to participate in formal pre-conference and informal in-conference meetings. For example, the prestigious Institute for International Economics sponsored a full-day conference of academics and practitioners to discuss issues surrounding the conference. They were "one of six private-sector meetings that took place to promote public debate and understanding on global trade topics."[12] In addition, many proactive NGOs provided a large number of participants to these forums who were interested in affecting the outcome of the meeting. The International Forum on Globalization, an alliance of nonprofits and individuals from twenty countries, brought together a variety of institutions and others for a two-day "teach in" held on November 26–27. In preparation for this, they widely disseminated a publication called "Invisible Government: The World Trade Organization Global Government for the New Millennium?"[13] Ralph Nader's group, Public Citizen, joined the pre-conference information barrage by publishing *Whose Trade Organization?* in an attempt to give ammunition to the opposition in Seattle and elsewhere.[14]

NGOs and organizations making specific policy demands on the WTO and its members provided the real fireworks in the streets of Seattle during the Ministerial Conference. The most remarkable planning and coordination came from the alliance of labor and environmental groups—elements that often clash in domestic politics. More than six hundred organizations were mobilized to support alliance activities in Seattle. Something called the International Seattle Coalition claimed to have signed on another one thousand civil society groups in support of its campaign called "WTO: Shrink or Sink." Its motto was "WTO: No New Round, Turnaround," which demanded new rules that would put the public interest above those of corporations within the WTO.[15] Groups in this coalition met in Geneva in March 1999 to set their strategies. Individual activist groups planned, even trained, adherents for disruptive tactics during the Ministerial. The Ruckus Society sponsored a boot camp called "Globalize This!" at a farm to train activists in nonviolent disruptive techniques. All these were particularly effective in grabbing headlines and focusing public attention on the demonstrations rather than the meetings themselves.

Needless to say, the planning of the Seattle officials and the U.S. government was completely insufficient to meet the pressures of both the press and the demonstrators. Crowd control and physical access issues dominated the logistics of the meeting, but preparation and training were simply inadequate.

Miscalculation seems to have been the norm for the Seattle Ministerial Conference. From the beginning, participants miscalculated the degree of preparation needed to stimulate a consensus on a new round and its agenda. Most participant members were woefully unprepared to argue the merits of the agenda items; they had not done their homework on the potential contents of the agenda. In particular, they were not adequately briefed on the implications of new issues that were trade related but not trade itself—for example, the WTO's role in the domestic treatment and pay levels of labor and child labor laws, or environmental protection laws that limit emissions or demand manufacturing safeguards. These were, after all, not necessarily "win-win" issues and thus would precipitate hard negotiations.[16]

Organizers of the conference also failed to take into account key variables. The Seattle Host Committee, headed by co-chairs Phil Condit of Boeing and Bill Gates of Microsoft, miscalculated the fury of opposition groups and their high degree of organization. In addition, these planners and their American advisors badly miscalculated the time needed to conclude the negotiations for the meeting. Previous GATT meetings had left time and space open for the end of the meeting in case more negotiation time was needed, as it most often was, to get a consensus. The WTO bureaucracy and United States as host had rented the basic facilities only for the planned four days of the conference. On the following day, the hall had to be emptied to accommodate a convention of optometrists. The irony was that foresight was missing; for many believed that some agreement might well have been reached given an additional day or two. Certainly, the United States, its president, and its trade representative had miscalculated its ability to guide the meeting to a successful conclusion.

Given this history of disparate planning, it is not hard to begin to understand what happened at the Seattle Ministerial Conference. Inside the meetings, when they could occur, conflicts evident since Singapore continued to plague the organization. Outside the meeting, the streets of Seattle were in chaos.

INSIDE THE SEATTLE MINISTERIAL

Over 135 countries sent trade ministers and delegations to the Ministerial Conference, and the WTO officially registered 767 NGOs who sent over 2,000 delegates to participate in official side meetings. On November 29, a day long symposium was officially sanctioned with participation by Mike Moore and several ministers in an attempt to give NGOs a feeling of input into the issues being considered by the WTO. These were little more than panel discussions and speeches, however. Still, these established NGOs were able to lobby the ministers, being given access in the hallways of the meetings. The heart of the inside, however, remained the interplay between and among the ministers and caucuses of ministers on the necessity for a new round of negotiations and on what issues should be on the agenda if there was to be a new round.

Two broad streams of thought dominated the discussions concerning the direction the agenda should take for any new round. First there were, and remained after the conference, those who believe that any new round should have a comprehensive agenda covering a multitude (if not all) of outstanding issues, new and old. These are sometimes called single-undertaking rounds because they have the goal of dealing with a variety of issues in such a way that compromises can be made among several issues. This allows states to link issues, thus easing compromise and bargaining. Alternatively, narrower agenda rounds, referred to as sector-by-sector negotiations, emphasize dealing with separate sectors individually and lead, critics claim, to standoffs.[17]

There is a middle ground where negotiations can center on a few issues within related areas—the so-called cluster approach. The single-undertaking approach to a new Millennium Round was championed by the UK, the EU, the United States, Japan, Canada, and a variety of other states who had an interest in broadening the reach of the WTO into the new issue areas. These countries hoped that the single-undertaking approach would allow them to avoid major changes in their agriculture policies by directing concerns to other issues. They believed that by tackling several issues at once, there is more flexibility to the negotiations with more opportunity for trade-offs. The second, narrower stream championed the idea that the sector-by-sector, or perhaps a limited cluster, approach might be more productive and tended to include those who were reluctant to expand the WTO until issues of implementation of the Uruguay Round were settled. These adherents were largely developing countries who felt, as we have already noted, that they accepted the costs of joining the WTO with its strict codes in exchange for market access from developed states—and that these promises had not been kept. This has meant in practice that they advocated negotiations within only two specific sectors before opening negotiations for a broad new round—namely agriculture and services.[18] Implementation remains the prolog for these states; it was, simply put, the priority issue for this group of negotiators.

Prior to Seattle there seemed to be momentum for the single-undertaking option. The major traders that dominated previous rounds agreed after discussions among themselves that this would be the best tact. They were even able to bring some better-off developing states along with them. But since Singapore, the developing states, aided by continuing conflict over agriculture among and between the Quad states, had become more aggressive. Not only was the process of deferring to the Quad grating, but the dangers of increased costs of further requirements for developing states loomed large and created a great concern.[19]

Both of these perspectives were brought to the table in Seattle because no consensus could be made in pre-conference negotiations. At best, the sector-specific forces wanted to have the conference stick to the built-in agenda and not broaden it to include a blueprint for a new round encompassing the second-generation new issue items. It is hard to know what actually occurred within the conference meetings, for they are closed. The two key players guiding the proceedings, Director General Moore and the chair and host of the meetings, the U.S. Trade Representative Charlene Barshefsky, were, however, both committed to the establishment of the new round on the basis of a single-undertaking agenda. Because of this, many insiders, including developing states, observers, and experts thought that "chances of failure at Seattle were very high."[20] Although, Mike Moore told President Clinton at a luncheon the day before the conference ended, "Mr. President, this conference is doomed, doomed to succeed. Failure is unthinkable."[21] Moore's statement was a supreme act of bravura given the circumstances.

Many believe that one of the structural as well as political problems of the Ministerial Conference was the fact that Charlene Barshefsky insisted on playing not only the host and chair of the meetings, but also acting as the chief representative of U.S. policy positions. She simply did not have enough time and energy to negotiate for the United States and to chair the meetings. Chairs of Ministerial Conferences and meetings of import have always played the role of mediators in the negotiation processes. Certainly this was true of the key role that an imported neutral mediator had in fulfilling the promise of the Punt del Este meeting that began the Uruguay Round. Barshefsky had made that role impossible for herself, leaving the negotiations without a neutral mediator other delegates could trust. From the developing country perspective and others as well, Barshefsky was a disaster. She did not meet with delegates at the Geneva preparations; she arrived only just prior to the meetings on Sunday evening November 28 (while most gathered earlier); and her blunt style seemed to overtly demonstrate the "U.S. arrogance of power."[22]

Street demonstrators had blocked the entrance to the meeting hall so completely on the opening day of the conference, Tuesday, November 30, that Barshefsky and the vice-chairs could not get to their places at the appointed time. Mike Moore took over and opened the meeting, starting official business. Innocent as this seemed, to many it demonstrated the undue influence of the WTO bureaucracy since the rules state that only ministers could chair the proceedings. In order to assuage fears of

WTO bureaucratic influence, the director general decided that he should not be aggressive during the meeting, thus he self-consciously seemed to withdraw from any mediation role. Regardless, active business was curtailed on the first day of the conference because many delegates simply could not get to the convention center.

Disagreements were rife among the Quad at the conference. While the United States wanted cuts in farm subsidies, it was unwilling to give up peak industrial tariffs and did not want to touch U.S. antidumping laws. The EU and Japan resisted farm subsidy cuts and wanted new issues addressed in the areas of investment and competition policy. Canada and the EU wanted special agricultural and other protections that the United States resisted. Without Quad coordination, it was becoming obvious that it would be tough to build any broad consensus.

Still, the conference went forward. The working groups met, and issues were debated. Differences between North and South as well as competing priorities between major trading states meant that nerves were raw. Developing countries did not want to let go of their trade barriers, but they wanted to attack protectionism by developed countries. They continued to demand implementation of existing commitments under the Uruguay Round (especially ending apparel quotas and transfer of technology commitments). The North-South conflicts hardened when suspicions that the United States was trying to bully through its agenda were reinforced by an interview with President Clinton published in a Seattle paper the day he arrived. The president told the paper that core labor standards should be a part of WTO negotiations. He added that "ultimately he would favor a system in which sanctions would come for violating" these provisions.[23] Labor unions were pressing the president for several of their goals, particularly protection for certain goods and for him to champion core labor rights in the international forum. EU commissioner and trade negotiator Pascal Lamy even indicated, as an excuse, that the coming presidential election guided the president's policies at Seattle.[24] Given the economic dependence on cheap labor for their comparative advantage, many developing countries felt the president was throwing down the gauntlet. They were determined to pick it up and throw it back. The president had cut the legs out from under his negotiators.

There was great resistance by most other WTO members to U.S. calls to create a WTO Working Group on Trade and Labor for the new round, and developing countries were intractable on the issue in Seattle: "It [was] hard to conceive of these countries changing course unless the United States respond[ed] more favorably to developing countries' priorities."[25] These concessions were not forthcoming. By the end of Wednesday, December 1, the Committee of the Whole of the conference was in disarray. While some progress was being made in the five working groups, by late Thursday, it was clear that with only twenty-four hours to go, a draft was nowhere near completion. It was at this point that Barshefsky unilaterally decided to call Green Room sessions to pound out a draft. Needless to say, after the commotion of the Singapore Ministerial Conference and the promises of the Geneva Ministerial Conference, developing countries left out of the room were furious. All of a sudden, transparency had become a priority issue. It became clear that whatever the Green

Room came up with would not be able to garner swift consensual agreement from a substantial number of members. The Green Room was hung up on the issues of agriculture and implementation anyway, let alone getting to the full agenda.[26]

Friday was the absolute last day of the conference because of the scheduling snafu by the United States. Charlene Barshefsky chose to handle the situation with a rather heavy hand. She called the president to get clearance for her decision to bring together the plenary session of the conference and simply "to announce the suspension of the meeting [WTO rules do not provide for this] and the freezing of all proposals (formal and informal) on the table."[27] As quickly as that the Ministerial Conference was over, Barshefsky held a press conference and said she called a "time-out." She wanted to indicate that the game was not over, but the conference held no chance for immediate progress. She explained it to a congressional delegation this way: "Our collective judgment was that it would be best to take a time out, consult with one another, and find creative means to finish the job."[28] The director general also held a press conference to talk about the meeting's demise. He said, "We left Seattle disappointed but not dismayed that it was not possible to finish the job we went there to do. . . . [But] a package of results is within reach." He went on to say that Barshefsky, as chair of the Seattle Ministerial, "has directed me to consult with delegations and discuss creative ways in which we might bridge the remaining areas in which consensus does not yet exist [and] develop an improved process."[29] He was putting the best possible face on the failure of the meeting by indicating he would promote almost immediate negotiations for solving the problems that led to the collapse.

Only one success came from the conference. It established the Advisory Center on WTO Law as a means to give legal support to developing countries in dealing with the complexities of WTO agreements. It was to help developing countries defend their legal rights in the WTO. The Center, a new international organization, is independent of the WTO. The EU, the United States, Germany, France, and Japan opposed it, but it was supported and joined by the Scandinavian countries, the UK, Canada, Italy, the Netherlands, and several developing states. Later, financial backing was provided by its developed members to start work. Even this accomplishment was tainted with clashing views on its efficacy. Many saw the organization as an indication of a lack of confidence in the WTO bureaucracy.

The street demonstrators claimed responsibility for the failure of the conference, but few scholars or participants placed the blame at their door. Most observers believe the key damage to the WTO was self-inflicted. It is clear that preparations were inadequate, on the part of the hosts, the WTO bureaucracy, and the members. Some felt that the "reordering [of] North-South interplay was indeed the critical relationship for the failure of Seattle."[30] States outside the circle of influence of the major trading states refused to be pushed around. It may have been that developing states simply came to Seattle with unrealistic expectations, but they had waited a long time for attention to their concerns.

The most popular target for blame has been the United States. The lack of EU-U.S. leadership shares suspicion as well. President Clinton's untimely (for international purposes at least) proclamations on labor, together with Barshefsky's perceived inattentiveness, followed by heavy handedness combined to leave a bad taste in the mouth of many participants and observers. The EU and the Cairns Group clashed over agriculture; Japan wanted competition and antidumping on the table, which the United States opposed; and the United States took an unpopular stance pushing for inclusion of core labor rights on the WTO agenda. One observer put these clashes into a context when he noted, "Successful trade negotiations will require that participants—especially the U.S., EU, and Japan—talk like mercantilists but act like liberalizers."[31]

In the end, most diplomats, ministers, scholars, and neutral observers simply wanted to put the conference behind them and look forward to preparations for what they believed to be the inevitable call for a new round. Many, if not most, believed the conference had accomplished a lot, that the glass was at least half full, and that decent leadership should make possible the launch of a Millennium Round within a short time.[32] Indeed, negotiations for the regularly scheduled Fourth Ministerial Conference began immediately after Seattle and included optimistic planning centered on using the Ministerial Conference in Qatar (in November 2001) as the launching pad for the by now long-delayed Millennium Round.

OUTSIDE: THE BATTLE IN SEATTLE

If disagreements were rife inside the WTO meetings in Seattle, outside there was near chaos at times. The streets were full of the thirty to forty thousand demonstrators who had come to Seattle to make a point. After large-scale marches and targeted violence on Tuesday, November 30, continued demonstrations on Wednesday and Thursday, and relative calm on Friday, the "Battle in Seattle" had captured the imagination of the media and the attention of decision makers everywhere. David had not defeated Goliath, but he slowed him down.[33]

There were large divides between observers of the demonstrations concerning the effectiveness of the protests: "In Seattle, we witnessed an event of historic importance: the first coordinated mass revolt in the United States against global capitalism in the modern era. No less than that," said the Progressive magazine.[34] A former GATT official saw it differently: "This outpouring of misconceived, ill-understood propaganda against a system that has brought vast gains to most nations over the past decades is a threat to the prospects of a better life for millions, perhaps billions, of people."[35] One view proclaiming victory for the people in bringing the voice of democracy to the WTO, the other claiming ignorance of the WTO by large numbers of activists. Both views missed the complexity of the motivations that brought so many people to Seattle.

Activities and events were planned and carried out by a variety of organizations, most of which are entities increasingly referred to as *civil society*, those organizations within society not connected to government but active in trying to affect its decisions and operation. These range from trade organizations in business and labor, to advocacy groups in issue areas, to think tanks. All were well represented in Seattle. As noted, many educational and informational meetings were held to expose issues being contemplated by the conference. Besides those planned events, teach-ins, rallies, symposia, and academic presentations were sponsored by a variety of vastly different groups: the Christian Coalition, the business-oriented Washington Council on International Trade, labor unions from the United States and Canada, the National Farmers Union, the health organization Public Services International, consumer coalitions, and the Biotechnology Action Council. Coalitions and groups challenging the WTO also held concerts. Some of these were groups like the Direct Action Network, the Sierra Club, Ralph Nader's Public Citizen, Jubilee 2000 (attacking third-world debt), and People for Fair Trade. Seattle was a veritable pro/con international trade fair.

Not all of the groups in Seattle were mobilized for direct action in the streets. Many, particularly the think tanks and the trade associations (save for labor unions), had come to make their points by participation in the discussions and to lobby within the halls of the meetings. The EU, for example, boasted of having civil society representatives within its delegation from "business organizations, trade unions and representatives of four sectors of the NGO Community" as advisors.[36] Clearly, there were "insider" NGOs, and there were "outsider" NGOs. It was the latter that dominated the streets with a wide array of purposes and means.

One of the more colorful descriptions of street activity gives some idea of the serious as well as the bazaar-like nature of the demonstrations: "A rumbling Teamster semi-tractor-trailer headed a procession that mixed longshoremen and sheet-metal workers with Earth First!-ers, and bearded rabbis with a contingent of bare-breasted Lesbian Avengers call chanting with one voice: 'This Is What Democracy Looks Like.'"[37] This was an interesting and unexpected contingent of unions, environmentalists, religious and gay demonstrators.

A major theme of the demonstrators was the claimed undemocratic nature of the WTO—that it had become a world government with little accountability. The weekend prior to the Tuesday, November 30 conference opening featured the more cerebral activities, leaving the street demonstrations to start mostly on Monday when environmentalists took to the streets. This was perhaps the most colorful and happy of the street marches; for it featured large puppets, signs, banners, and demonstrators dressed in endangered species outfits—turtles and dolphins. Even some members of Congress joined the parade. Later that night, a Christian ecumenical group, Jubilee 2000, created a human chain around a hotel where a reception was being held for WTO delegates.

The largest demonstrations came on opening day, Tuesday. A Public Citizen field organizer had been in Seattle for nine months getting ready with the announced goal and plan of closing down the meeting. The target was the convention center and the opening ceremonies. In concert with Public Citizen, "during a week of meetings in a Seattle warehouse, Direct Action Network members identified choke points in 12 sectors around the convention center."[38] Sitting in a ring around the convention center, the demonstrators effectively stopped access until the police could clear the streets by use of pepper gas and by firing rubber pellets. At the same time, a massive march of thirty-eight thousand sponsored by the AFL-CIO rallied by the Space Needle and marched downtown. Taking advantage of all this activity, a small group of avowed anarchists used hammers, spray paint, and M-80 firecrackers to attack brand-name retailers like Starbucks and McDonalds. The worst confrontations came when police used concussion grenades and their whole constellation of force to disperse the crowds at the request of the secret service preparing for the arrival of President Clinton.

The consequence of this combination of crowd, tactical placement (small groups would lock arms, chain themselves together, block roads), confrontation, and property damage prompted the mayor to declare a civil emergency. He called out the National Guard and established a forty-six-block "protest-free" zone around the convention center and major hotels.[39] The media had a field day splashing the demonstrator story around the country. It was fed information from protestors by press releases, cell phones, the Internet, and interviews with all sorts of participants, from wacky (Greenpeace, for example, distributed condoms as a metaphor for "safe trade") to substantive.

Countless demonstrations and marches, both large and small, continued through Monday and Tuesday, but Wednesday and Thursday, December 1 and 2, found the police in better control. Their tactics had turned more aggressive; up to six hundred people were arrested, though few were later prosecuted. After Clinton left town on Thursday, things calmed down; volunteers even began to clean up the city and wash graffiti from the buildings. By the time the conference ended late Friday, December 3, the streets were emptying, and demonstrators were joining the delegates in exiting the city. There had been a remarkable amount of coordination and cooperation among a disparate group of organizations.

A common target does not necessarily mean a common objective, however. Some of the groups wanted to close down the WTO. The Globalize This! coalition believed that "the WTO was created to serve corporate interests and should be dismantled before it causes more harm to workers, the environment, and democracy itself."[40] Others wanted to strengthen the WTO; they wanted it to be more effective but more transparent. For example, though many suspected that the labor activists in Seattle represented protectionist unions, most leaders of the union movement wanted the WTO to strengthen its international oversight, even policing, of what the International Labor Organization has called "core labor values."[41] President Clinton's Seattle speech supported this concept of strengthening the WTO in areas of labor and added the environmental area as well. Human rights groups wanted the WTO to be a watchdog for their interests. A coalition of over two hundred organizations, including Greenpeace, the Sierra Club, and European Green parties, sent a petition to WTO members asking them to forbid certain types of agricultural trade with bioengineered foundations. Many of the same groups were part of the beef fight outlined in Chapter 5.

Table 8.1   Anti-WTO platforms

Globalize This! Ten Ways to Democratize the Global Economy	Global Exchange Top Ten Reasons to Oppose the WTO
1. No globalization without representation	1. The WTO only serves the interests of multinational corporations
2. Mandate corporate responsibility	2. The WTO is a stacked court
3. Restructure the global financial architecture	3. The WTO tramples over labor and human rights
4. Cancel all debt, end structural adjustments, and defend economic sovereignty	4. The WTO is destroying the environment
5. Prioritize humans rights—including economic rights—in trade agreements	5. The WTO is killing people [through Intellectual Property Rights—patents, copyrights, trademarks]
6. Promote sustainable development—not consumption—as key to progress	6. The U.S. adoption of the WTO was undemocratic
7. Integrate women's needs in all economic restructuring	7. The WTO undermines local development and penalizes the poor
8. Build free and strong labor unions internationally and domestically	8. The WTO is increasing inequality
9. Develop community control over capital; promote socially responsible investment	9. The WTO undermines national sovereignty
10. Promote fair trade, not free trade	10. The tide is turning against free trade, the WTO!

| (Deborah James) | (Global Exchange) |

For brevity's sake, the program of the more aggressive coalitions of activist groups has been outlined in lists of ten.[42] Globalize This! for example, lists a compilation of its goals in "Ten Ways to Democratize the Global Economy" (Table 8.1). The list outlines much of the program of a variety of organizations from labor to human rights, though not all subscribe to all ten. The program of the "WTO: Shrink or Sink" coalition of civil society groups wants their groups to continue the campaign by targeting the policies of their home governments in these regards. In particular, they want to emphasize human rights, environmental issues, and development issues while stopping the expansion of the WTO into the new issue areas. All these coalitions' goals have a base in a list sponsored by a parallel coalition called Global Exchange that outlines the "Top 10 Reasons to Oppose the World Trade Organization." Yet again, not all agenda items are endorsed by all members of the coalition that created the list of ten (Table 8.1). Global Exchange's last claim of a tide turning against the WTO is proving to be more and more difficult to sustain.

Defenders of the WTO are not without sympathy for many of the problems brought to the fore by the NGOs. They do not, however, buy the argument that the WTO is undemocratic given its country-based representative nature and its consensual decision making. Interest groups simply want a "second bite at the apple," defenders claim, because the NGOs have not met the success they would like within their domestic political systems.[43] Defenders feel that there is broad misunderstanding about the nature of the WTO, whose purpose as an international body is multilateral trade, not solving social issues. By equating the WTO with globalization as a universal concept and process, it is deemed that the opposition focuses too much on the purpose of this one organization. John Dunning outlines three problems with the opposition to the WTO: (1) Those who oppose tend to be myopic concerning their own interests and ignore the broader consequences of globalization and its benefits. (2) They "offer no realistic alternative to global capitalism." And (3) they do not acknowledge the competing goals of other NGOs.[44]

Though frustrated, most trade leaders recognize the need to find a place for civil society to be included in debates on international trade issues and processes. This does not mean a place at the table when the WTO is making decisions, however. Defenders insist on the fact that "the special character of the WTO is both a legally binding instrument and a forum for negotiations [which] requires that it remain strictly intergovernmental."[45] The sheer number and diversity of NGOs make it impractical to find a mechanism for direct participation by civil society. Most members do not even want NGOs participating as observers. Still, as a report to EU Parliament stated, "the WTO must recognize concern over influence of trade on the environment, sustainable development, social issues, and consumer health and safety, means [the WTO] must seek answers that safeguard the trading system [as well as] those societal concerns."[46] President Clinton made this point at the Seattle conference and as early as 1998 at the Geneva Ministerial Conference. Great differences remain as to how to accomplish this task. For neither the WTO members nor the vast array of NGOs agree on what degree of input is needed or on any mechanism to provide that input—thus, the continuing assault by NGOs on international meetings of the WTO, UN bodies, the IMF, and the World Bank, to name a few. The demonstrations in Seattle were not an isolated incident.

CONCLUSION

Seattle was an important watershed for the WTO as well as for its critics. Those four days toward the end of 1999 exposed both the strengths and weaknesses of the WTO and of the NGOs that have formed a movement against globalization and its perceived effects. There were some harsh evaluations of the Ministerial Conference at the time. The *Economist* reflected the general frustration better than most when it editorialized that, "It is hard to say which was worse, watching the militant dunces parade their ignorance through the streets of Seattle, or listening to their lamebrained governments respond to the arguments."[47] Incidentally, the *Economist* came down in favor of the militants because "at least [they] had a good time." Harsh perhaps, but it is this kind of reaction that gave impetus to introspection on the part of WTO members and not a few NGOs.

The key players soon returned to the Geneva base of the WTO to mobilize informal and then formal meetings of the General Council who looked to heal the wounds and looked toward making progress that proved illusive in Seattle. This time there were self-conscious efforts to bring developing countries into the substance of the discussions. In addition, there were pledges of placing procedural reforms at the forefront of the next anticipated round of negotiations. Also projected for the agenda has been consideration of the role of social issues as they are affected by trade and trade regulation. Director General Moore has said that many people in the world "do not want to be looked after; they want to participate. I think we need to accept this and organize ourselves and be prepared to work with them."[48] Discussions even started with the avowed goal of producing a "code of conduct"[49] for NGOs within the international system. Such a code could go a long way in codifying the role of the NGOs within that system.

As a result of the Seattle meeting, the planning for the 2001–02 Fourth Ministerial Conference was to be much more meticulous. The choice of Qatar, for example, was made to minimize the opportunity for mass demonstrations given the small size, limited facilities, and isolation of that highly disciplined principality. The issues to be discussed for inclusion in a new round of trade negotiations was closely articulated, and negotiations toward a draft resolution for the Qatar meeting were extensive. As indicated above, there have been continuing negotiations on the built-in agenda items since Seattle as well. Seattle did not bring an end to trade negotiations toward expanding and fine-tuning the WTO. It seems, at least in general, to have focused the organization and its members on the need to pay attention to its weaknesses and to use its strengths to solve its problems.

NGOs have found that they can mobilize significant numbers of people and organizations to challenge the assumptions and institutionalization of globalization by focusing on formal meetings and conferences. Specific points of activity help to keep a sense of a movement and maintain international visibility. Optimistic euphoria from Seattle brought this evaluation: "We can now envision the formation of a truly global movement capable of challenging the most powerful institutions on the planet."[50] The NGOs continue to suffer from conflicting priorities, if not specific objectives, when it comes to substantive outcomes of their demonstrations. By combining the WTO with all other international organs that promote what NGO's perceive to be negative globalization, the NGOs dilute their influence on any one of those organs. While NGO members may pay attention to the group's objectives, the public at large still has not focused on the meaning and effects of what the more insistent NGOs see as globalized decision making. At the same time, some NGOs find the same institutions, in particular the WTO given its effective dispute settlement system, as potential allies in fulfilling their objectives. It remains easier to find coalitions "against" than it is to find common grounds for positive solutions "for."

For both the WTO and various NGOs, Seattle was a learning experience and just one bump on a very long and arduous road attempting to navigate the challenges of the twenty-first–century international political economy.

PART III

THE LOOK TO THE FUTURE

THE NEW ROUND

DOHA AND CANCUN

The failure of the Seattle conference put pressure on the WTO to find a way to suc-cessfully launch a new round of trade negotiations. It did not help that the 2001 ter-rorist attack on New York and Washington DC enhanced the feeling that security made it difficult to find a venue for the 2001 scheduled Ministerial Conference.

The WTO Director General Mike Moore noted that at the end of the Seattle meeting, Qatar's minister offered to host the next scheduled ministerial meeting in 2003. Subsequently, with the support of the G77 (developing world caucus), Qatar waged a campaign to hold the meeting. World events encouraged the view that Qatar would be the perfect locale. It could be secured with more certainty than most alternative venues, and it had leadership that was perceived to be progressive. Doha, the capital, provided a relatively conducive atmosphere for the meetings, helping to mold their potential success.

As we have seen, there were several reasons for the failure of the Seattle confer-ence, including serious differences among participating states. Not the least of rea-sons was the inability of the WTO staff to prepare substantively for the meeting. Mike Moore had become the director general just before the meeting after a bitter battle for the position that ended in a compromise. He would take the first half of the director general's term, and his rival for the position, Dr. Supachai Panitchpakdi of Thailand, would take over in September 2002.

Mike Moore admitted that a good part of the chaos in Seattle could be traced to the fact that he and his staff were barely in place during the key period of prepara-tions for the Ministerial Conference. His deputies had not met before the meeting, and his preparatory document to be used as the negotiation basis was an unwieldy thirty-two pages with seventy-nine actionable paragraphs, many of which had open-ended conclusions. On top of this were thirty-seven alternative texts from various countries and caucuses for consideration at the Ministerial Conference. As Moore began the two years of work leading up to the Doha Ministerial Conference, he had learned from this lack of focused preparation. In the end, he concluded that "preparation for Doha . . . was the mirror opposite and was largely responsible for its success."[1]

The geographic isolation and size of Qatar allowed its government to limit the visas available to protestors. Lack of hotel space was given as a reason to restrict outsiders. This limited the ability of the antiglobalization forces to disrupt the flow of the meetings. Street demonstrations were carefully restricted, and representative NGOs were invited to participate in the periphery discussions, allowing for a distinction between acceptable and unacceptable input into the deliberations.

There had been ninety new members admitted into the WTO since the Uruguay Round, most of which were developing states. This increased the pressures on the organization to deal with the complaints from developing states that had contributed to the deadlock in Seattle and continued to chaff. Increasingly, the United States and EU had begun to lose dispute settlement cases brought by developing countries, and this caught the attention of both. The issues left over from Seattle's failure to launch the new round brought great pressure on Doha to produce an agreement for a new round of negotiations or risk serious setbacks to the international free trade movement.

The strategy of the major states and the WTO secretariat, led by Moore, was to engage all views in a series of preliminary meetings aimed at molding discussions and to use preliminary texts to produce cooperative discussions in Doha. Special efforts were made to include key G77 members and to emphasize their issues. Crucial, however, were the issues that divided the two Atlantic powers.

Nothing concrete was agreed before the November 13–15, 2001, meeting, but there was agreement on the inclusion of key issues in the round's agenda. These issues were to include industrial goods, agriculture, services, as well as the attempt to build the beginnings of a framework to deal with the new, so-called *Singapore issues* dealing with investment, competition policy, trade facilitation, and government procurement. These last issues, sponsored especially by the EU and Japan, are called the Singapore issues because they were first introduced at the 1996 Ministerial Conference in that city. All these issues nested within the need for transparency and inclusion as far as the G77 was concerned.

Agriculture continued to be a central issue for both the Atlantic powers and many of the developing states: "Agriculture was always going to be a deal-maker or deal breaker," claimed Moore.[2] The EU and the United States, as we have seen in our case studies, continued to clash over agriculture. African and Latin American countries, though not united on specific views, saw agriculture as their central concern.

As the meeting began, facilitators of the separate working groups (the way WTO meetings are organized to ease negotiations) were carefully chosen for their prestige, representation, and tact. Frequent breaks to allow for consultations and caucus meetings were arranged. Exclusion from the crucial Green Room negotiations was a key complaint of developing countries at Seattle and as far back as the Uruguay Round; therefore, care was taken to include representative ministers from developing countries in Green Room consultations. Moore claims that they were always a majority in the room. In the negotiations over the final text for the conference, of the twenty-two ministers, six were from developed and sixteen from developing countries—split between Asia, Africa, and Latin America.[3]

Still, most agree that the key to the success of the Doha negotiations rested in the relationship between the U.S. and EU trade representatives (Robert Zoellick and Pascal Lamy, respectively). They had agreed to make concessions by placing in the final draft document wording that would pledge each of their entities to a significant reduction in agricultural supports as long as they were linked to access to markets. This reflected the agreement made by the G8 at its Canada meeting in July of 2002. As Tony Blair said on behalf of the group, they had committed to "comprehensive negotiations on agriculture aimed at substantial improvements in market access and reduction of all forms of export subsidies with a view to phase them out."[4] This is similar to the wording in the final Doha Declaration.

All this had the effect of raising expectations significantly for the consequent Doha Round on the part of the developing countries. The expectations were so high that they were to lead to the failure of the Cancun Ministerial Conference two years later. The early consultations and negotiations before and during Doha were to lead to the emergence of a leadership core for the developing states—a core not codeterminant with the least developed countries, incidentally. These leaders were those countries who were ahead in their development and needed or wanted concessions to protect their continued growth—countries like India, Nigeria, Brazil, Egypt, South Africa, and Kenya. The ministers from these countries were important within the Green Room negotiations and central in the acceptance of the final compromises. They would be the same ministers who would lead the revolt in Cancun and consolidate a power bloc among themselves and likeminded others. Not incidentally, the inclusion of China into the WTO at this meeting produced another leader for this emerging caucus.

The Doha negotiations were not easy. Besides the input made explicit by the core group of developing countries, African states had met in Zanzibar in early 2001 to push for concessions within the WTO for the least developed countries. The working text for the conference, hammered together by the WTO General Council chair and the director general after extensive consultations (and called a "clean text" under the assumption that only minimal changes would be made to it), was not received well by the African group or by other developing countries. They believed that the Zanzibar Declaration that had called for substantive action had been ignored.[5] The rich states liked what they saw because they had a large hand in producing the working text. The text was only forty-nine paragraphs long and was broad in its directives for negotiations to be conducted in the coming (Doha) round. It also was, rhetorically, very deferential to developing states. At least twelve of the paragraphs mentioned the needs of developing countries both substantively and in the need for technical help to aid in their understandings and availability for input into the complex WTO processes. The Africans still saw no action embodied in the declaration and thus remained skeptical.

The five-day schedule for the meeting was extended to a sixth day when agreement could not be reached. France, India, the Caribbean and African caucus, Honduras, and Ecuador all pushed the conference to the verge of collapse. (France, remember is a WTO member while the EU is not, though it negotiates for all its members. This does allow for the rare challenge of EU unanimity.) Each wanted to force specific concessions into the general document. Moore and conference leaders kept a core group of representative states (the Quad as well as those better-off developing countries mentioned above) in negotiations for forty-eight hours straight. A compromise was arrived at in the end. India continued to have some significant objections, though not enough for it to block approval of the compromise.[6]

In the final document, the developing countries got a commitment to negotiations on agriculture and service issues. However, the EU slipped into the final agriculture paragraph that nothing in the declaration would prejudge its outcome, a hedge on its subsidy concessions. If nothing could be "prejudged," then the EU's pledge to specific agriculture concessions made with the United States just before the conference opened seemed to be now up for negotiation. The United States was given credit for its leadership toward the continuation of negotiations and, indeed, for the success of the meeting, though it would have domestic difficulty getting political support for the implied and specific promises it made to get the deal done. The first step in inaugurating the Doha Round proved relatively easy; for members had only "agreed on broad goals and specific deadlines for liberalizing global commerce in agricultural goods and other products."[7] Specific implementation modalities would have to wait on the beginning of the round's actual negotiations. Nothing was decided except the areas on which to negotiate.

The final document came to be called the Doha Development Agenda, given its many nods to developing members. Development issues suffused the entire text. It opened a new round of negotiations centered on agriculture, services, implementation of specific areas, and investigations into the new so-called Singapore issues. Promised were serious negotiations to reduce and to phase out export subsidies and, with fewer assurances, domestic farm supports in agriculture as well as special exemptions in this area for developing countries. Service negotiations were to center on liberalization of telecommunications, finance, transport, and business services, with special help for developing countries.[8] It was an ambitious agenda. But the atmosphere of cooperation and concession was husbanded by the events of September 11, 2001, and the perceived need of the United States to gain support for its war on terrorism. Raised expectations would prove troublesome when it came time to deliver on the promises of Doha, however.

The World Bank said that a successful new round of opening trade plus other reforms would result in $2.8 trillion in increased global income and bring 320 million people out of poverty within fifteen years. However, others worried that empirical research did not substantiate the proposition that open trade helped the very poor. Still, even critics of the WTO said that by most accounts, the meeting was successful. Barry Coates, director of the liberal World Development Movement, was probably more accurate saying that "it was more an acquiescence than a consensus."[9] Most countries left Doha on November 15, 2001, after having approved the Doha Declaration, feeling that the frustration of Seattle had been erased and replaced by the anticipation of movement toward the first substantive negotiations on expanding the WTO accords since the Uruguay Round. Robert Zoellick was quoted as bragging, "We have removed the stain of Seattle."[10] The next regular two-year Ministerial Conference would be the first negotiating session of the new round. It was scheduled to be held in Cancun, Mexico in 2003. Cancun would prove that the stain was harder to remove than Zoellick had imagined.

THE CANCUN MINISTERIAL MEETING

If history were to be any kind of guide, storm clouds should have been seen on the Cancun horizon early on. One reason was that between Doha and Cancun, the WTO saw a change from Mike Moore to Dr. Supachai Panitchpakdi as director general of the WTO. This meant that at least some of the staff problems leading to Seattle were being repeated in the lead-up to Cancun. Much had to be done in a short period of time with a new leadership team.

The Doha Declaration had provided a long list of specific goals to be reached by the end of the round, which it pegged at a vastly optimistic January 2005. Given the contentious issues, this haste alone put undo pressures on the preparation processes. For example, in the area of services, states were to indicate which of the 160 specific service sectors they would offer for liberalization by March of 2002. Many developing countries hardly had the staff to attack the larger goals let alone deal with negotiations over a bevy of specifics.

As usual, preparations for the Cancun Ministerial Conference were complex and elaborate. Working groups and committees were set up in Geneva for preliminary negotiations and text preparation. A Trade Negotiations Committee was created to make the preparations for Cancun. It established "seven negotiating bodies, on agriculture, services, non-agricultural market access, rules, trade and environment, a multilateral register for geographic indications for wines and spirits [a European priority], and reform of the Dispute Settlement Understanding."[11] The General Council of the WTO oversaw the preparatory work. The challenges were formidable. Over a year and a half into these talks, no area of agreement seemed near. The crucial agricultural conflict between the United States and the EU continued to boil over rather than to simmer into some sort of consensus. The EU relies on subsidies more than the United States does, but the EU was pressured by the United States to fulfill at least some of the compromises promised at Doha. At the same time, the U.S. 2001 Farm Bill raised U.S. subsidies by $73.5 billion over a ten-year period.[12] The EU cried hypocrisy. When President Bush placed high tariffs on steel in 2003, the clash with Europe (and others as well) accelerated. In addition, the EU was intent on pushing the Singapore issues, either as a strategy to slow down the process or because they saw these issues as their future.

More clouds over Cancun could be foreseen because of the missed March 2002 deadlines for "modalities" to be completed by working groups. Stuart Harbinson, the WTO mediator for agriculture, for example, found it necessary to provide a compromise text in April only to have it heartily attacked by all sides, leaving competing texts on the table. Missed deadlines within most of the working groups left similar problems piled up to the very door of the opening of the conference on September 14, 2003.[13]

As the conference began, there were five thousand delegates from 146 countries (148 after the admissions of Cambodia and Nepal at the meeting) and a very large contingent of NGOs, some officially certified. The whole ranged from the moderate Oxfam to the more radical street demonstrators, many of whom were not officially sanctioned by the WTO. One group spelled out "No WTO" on the beach with their nude bodies, and a South Korean farmer stabbed himself to death as a protest. The stage was ready, but it had not been set very well. Though no one blames the street demonstrations or NGO presence for the failure of the conference, many pointed to NGO influence on developing countries and to the newly aggressive stance of the developing countries. NGOs provided a great deal of information (some valid, some not), especially to hard-pressed developing countries who had little staff and little ability to research in preparation for the trade talks.

Agriculture continued to be the focus for many of the developing countries and the caucus of developing countries led by African states. Even though a late August agreement on freeing farm trade was patched together and offered for the final draft text by the United States and the EU, it was not close to the promises of Doha or the expectations of poorer countries. The former president of Mexico, Ernesto Zedillo, reflected the views of these states when he indicated that if agriculture were the main problem, then the EU was the main villain along with Japan (it was intransigent on rice imports). He recognized the problem of the United States as well, since it had ruined the credibility garnered from its rhetoric and work in Doha with its Farm Bill and new steel tariffs.[14] Even pro–free trade writers became wary of U.S. strategy. They feared that the United States was making outside bilateral

Figure 9.1   The G21 member countries

Argentina	Ecuador	Paraguay
Bolivia	Egypt	Peru
Brazil	Guatemala	Philippines
Chile	India	South Africa
China	Indonesia	Thailand
Colombia	Mexico	Venezuela
Costa Rica	Nigeria	
Cuba	Pakistan	

and regional economic arrangements (in Latin America, for example) as a looming threat to recalcitrant WTO members. Bilateral and regional trade agreements could well create a spaghetti bowl of rules that simply makes trade more difficult, not easier.

Weeks before the Cancun opening, the G21 (see Figure 9.1) met to set demands for the ending of subsidies by the rich OECD countries that had held steady at more than three hundred billion dollars for the previous fifteen years.[15] This group of the better-off developing states that began to jell at Doha represented 51 percent of the world's population, 63 percent of its farmers, and one fourth of world farm exports. The insistence and unity of the G21 would remain unchanged to the end of the Ministerial Conference.

A small group of struggling West African states (Benin, Burkina Faso, Chad, and Mali) were also concerned about their singular cash crop, cotton. Curiously, this group was able to mobilize support from the G21 as well as the full African contingent in such a way that this dispute became a central conflict between rich and poor. Perhaps the great injustice of their case made it a clean example of developing country complaints. After all, the United States, the largest exporter of cotton, subsidizes its twenty-five thousand cotton farmers to the tune of three billion dollars a year. "There is no other American crop that causes more chaos and misery around the world," said Ken Cook of the Environmental Working Group.[16] In addition, the EU spends one billion dollars a year on cotton subsidies. Without these subsidies, U.S. and EU cotton producers would not be able to compete with these other states. With the subsidies, these poor states could not compete with the United States and EU. U.S. negotiators actually had the temerity to tell developing country representatives that they should get out of the cotton-growing business if they did not like U.S. subsidies. A better example of subsidies distorting world trade on a specific sector would be hard to find.

The rich states were not without their rebuttals. The theme of the U.S. Trade Representative Robert Zoellick was that developing countries need to open their markets to trade. Not only do they have a higher tariff average on industrial goods (13 percent on average as opposed to the rich country average of 3 percent), but tariffs on agriculture especially hurt fellow poor states more than the rich: "The trade barriers of the poor countries against one another are more significant restraints on their own development than those imposed by the rich countries."[17]

The final text of the Cancun draft declaration, while pointedly not mentioning subsidies, basically suggested that the West African cotton countries diversify their economies as a solution to their problems. The developing countries took this as a cue that the interests of poor states were not, as advertised, central to the conference goals. They decided to take a hard line on agriculture subsidies as well as on the EU's pet theme (with support from Japan), the inclusion of the Singapore issues. If the rich could be hardheaded, so could the less rich. In the middle of the conference, ninety states signed a letter saying they were not interested in including the Singapore issues into the Doha Round. Instead of a growing consensus, positions were grounded in rhetorical challenges and uncompromising positions.

Since the foundation of decision making at WTO ministerials is the creation of consensus, virtually by the time it was scheduled to begin, the conference teetered on the brink of collapse. Europe denied it ever promised to eliminate export subsidies; India and other poor states denied they ever wanted to negotiate the Singapore issues; and other poor states presented specific grievances rather than aiming at broad agreements. The United States seemed to be backsliding on its free trade positions; Japan wanted little but to protect its rice tariffs; and the G21, led by Brazil, simply expected the rich countries to come around in the end. In addition, there were protectionist states (Iceland, South Korea, Norway, and Switzerland) not happy about the stagnating situation: "Cancun means 'snake pit' in the local Mayan language, and it lived up to its name."[18]

As the Cancun Ministerial Conference opened on September 10, the draft text on the table that had been finished in July and finalized only on August 24 was already under fire. The Director General Supachai Panitchpakdi even broke out of his traditional neutral role by supporting the four African countries on cotton negotiations. The United States felt, reluctantly, that it had to negotiate, though nothing resulted. A broader attack came from the G21 that threw down the gauntlet early. Celso Amorim, the Brazilian minister, presented on behalf of the G21, which included cautiously aggressive China, an alternative proposed text on agriculture. It demanded large cuts in farm subsidies by the rich states and refused to let the conference negotiate purely on the early "official" draft text.

On September 11 and 12, the conference seemed to continue on its regular schedule, with working groups on all the key areas focusing on their draft text issues. Agriculture and the new issues dominated the key behind-the-scenes negotiations, however. NGOs and independent groups and individuals continued the demonstrations and marches outside, though the violence was not nearly of the scale of Seattle. Indeed, most were peaceful.

The conference was mired in petty disputes and hardened positions. There was no progress. After a flurry of secret negotiations between the advanced developing states and the rich states, the conference chair, Mexican Minister Luis Ernesto Derbez, produced a revised Draft Cancun Ministerial Text (Second Revision) on September 13. It attempted to give something to everyone, mainly by using language that glossed over major conflicts or that hid issues in annexes and addendums to the document. Developing countries were not pleased.

The EU and the American negotiating teams insisted that countries negotiate on the basis of the official draft texts that reflected rich country concessions. But the texts were limited ones, maintaining significant U.S. and EU subsidies.[19] Many, especially smaller countries not invited to the Green Room discussions, simply would not recognize the legitimacy of that text as the basis of negotiations. All sides had their own agendas, too many of which had more to do with the establishment of power positions rather than specific negotiation goals that would end up in the final text of the Ministerial Conference.

Derbez's attempt to move the conference forward only sowed confusion and resentment instead of a spirit of compromise. Before in negotiation rounds, last-minute compromise texts were greeted with relief and were the basis for a final text. Not this time. In the past, the rich countries simply prevailed over a fragmented developing and poor multitude. This time, the G21; the African, Caribbean, and Pacific countries; and specific issue-bound states refused to budge.

On September 13, Chairman Debrez called a Green Room session of a small number of participants (the United States, EU, Mexico, Brazil, India, China, Malaysia, Kenya, and South Africa). These consultations went on until four o'clock in the morning, at which time a break was called for members to talk with their constituent groups, especially about the issues proving most difficult at the time—the Singapore issues. The Green Room discussions would resume at eight thirty on the morning of September 14 with a much larger representative group of some thirty states. There appeared to be some movement as desperation set in. The EU conceded on its position on the Singapore issues. Instead of requiring that all be included, it was willing to go forward if just the investment issue was included. The EU and United States also pledged swifter movement on the elimination of agricultural export subsidies. However, representatives from the developing countries and the G21 had been met with resistance in their caucuses to any compromise that would include any Singapore issues or anything short of solving the cotton issue. And they demanded progress on the until-then quiet issue of labor movement, which was of strong concern to poorer countries.[20] Any compromise had come too little and too late.

There followed much confusion as news agencies announced that developing states had walked out of the talks. While this was denied later, few knew what was going to happen next. In point of fact, the conference chair had thrown up his hands at the seemingly insurmountable deadlock when African states refused to even talk about the EU's limited compromise. The G21 also would not budge on its demands on agriculture. The conference chair then summarily announced that the talks were irretrievably deadlocked and adjourned the conference. A six-paragraph Ministerial Conference statement was quickly drafted by Chairman Derbez and Director General Supachai Panitchpakdi to be approved by the ministers in a closing meeting at four o'clock in the afternoon on September 14, a day before deliberations were supposed to end. Derbez presented the statement to a relatively closed final conference session—closed specifically to the press and NGOs. After some glittering generalities, the statement pledged the members to "affirm the Doha Declaration and Decisions and recommit ourselves to working to implement them fully and faithfully."[21] The General Council was to coordinate the planning for future meetings to continue development of the Doha Round. By six o'clock, the Cancun Ministerial Conference had been officially adjourned.

As might be expected, each of the forces at the Ministerial Conference had their own view of what had happened and who was to blame. Lamy's report to the EU spread blame to all, though he thought the EU "paid the price" for wanting to succeed too much. The United States could have gone further with cotton and with EU concerns; the G21 misunderstood the subsidies issue; and the poorer states could not see their own interests in a successful negotiation.[22] Robert Zoellick put responsibility at the door of the G21 and other poor states for not compromising (on agriculture and open markets), focusing on too many specific problems, and not recognizing the larger need for open trade.[23] The United States seemed to be at a loss because its traditional influence within the structure of the organization's leadership and the Green Room did not prevail. The developing countries were happy to exert influence within the WTO for a change and blamed the rich for not fulfilling what they perceived to be the promises of the Doha Declaration. The Kenyan delegate to the conference, George Oduorong'wen, summed up these views when he said, "It's not our fault the talks collapsed, no deal is better than a bad deal."[24] The more militant NGOs virtually crowed over the collapse, seeing it as a vindication of their critiques of the organization if not of globalization as a whole.

One thing that everyone agreed on was that the processes of decision making within the WTO were the major overriding problem. The developing world sees the core deficiency as a lack of transparency and democracy that limits its effective participation. Pascal Lamy, the EU trade commissioner, reflected the frustrations of rich states with the consensus decision processes of the WTO, which he characterized as "medieval": "There is no way to structure and steer discussions among 148 members in a manner conducive to consensus," he stated.[25] The mechanisms of the negotiation process clearly need to be addressed if negotiations are to continue successfully. Putnam, as seen in Chapter 1, would most assuredly agree, given the absence of a core group he deems necessary to guide the decision process.

The United States, and to a lesser degree the EU, left the conference threatening to use the bilateral and regional approach to trade negotiation as a means to promote free trade—a method that favors their power positions. Clearly, Cancun reflected the continuing clash between much of the developing world (and its NGO allies) and the rich powers—the former centering its arguments around the theory of sovereign equality in international affairs and its consequent insistence on "democracy" and "humanitarian equality" within the WTO. The latter finds it hard to abandon its position of dominance wrapped around their national interest, defined in this case as the necessity for an expanded world of open trade modified by specific necessities. Robert Zoellick found the rest of the world to be just not practical enough: "The harsh rhetoric of the 'won't do' overwhelmed the concerted efforts of the 'can do.'"[26]

The *Economist*, showing its contempt for the Cancun conference mess, brandished on its cover a single fingered gesture in the form of a cactus, while editorializing that "the failure [of the conference] sprang not from principle, nor even from intelligent calculation, but from cynicism, delusion and incompetence."[27] The alternative view was that the conference simply tried to do too much too soon. Preliminary discussions showed significant distance between the positions of the major actors, both North and South as well as within these dimensions. All seemed to agree on contemplation that the Doha Round should be pursued, and most assured each other of a willingness to negotiate. Few could offer concrete suggestions as to exactly how progress was to occur or on what timetable. They did agree that the process of healing should begin with preliminary meetings at the end of 2003.

By July 31, 2004, tempers had calmed, and near panic over the possible collapse of the WTO itself brought all of the major players to agree to a seven-page framework agreement for completing the Doha Round. All sides made some compromises in order to get serious negotiations moving. The United States and the EU agreed to lower agriculture subsidies; developing countries agreed to tariff reductions; the G21 agreed to make deeper cuts in domestic subsidies; and everyone agreed to exempt the fifty poorest members from most everything. As in the past, loopholes were left in the language to satisfy both rich and poor on specific areas. Many sensitive areas like services were simply skimmed over. It was agreed that more negotiations were necessary and that they should begin on the basis of this framework immediately.

Large problems would remain if significant progress was to be made by the next scheduled Ministerial Conference held in Hong Kong in December of 2005. No one believed a final agreement would be ready before 2007, but this meeting was able to set the tone for progress toward such a completion. A crucial stumbling block was thought to be the replacement of key players in the negotiations. Mr. Lamy's term ended in October 2004; Mr. Zoellick left the U.S. position in early 2005; and the competition for the replacement of Director General Panitchpakdi, whose term ended in September 2005, was fierce. As it turned out, Pascal Lamy was elected the new director general of the WTO, providing a much needed continuity to the negotiations that continued with a stable, if unproductive, Ministerial Conference in Hong Kong in December of 2005.

ENDINGS

The discussion of the Doha Round's clumsy launch concludes the narrative sequence describing the birth, development, and politics of the WTO. Whether this has been a case study in world trade diplomacy or a simple continuation of the narrative is hard to distinguish. National interests of major countries molded the transformation of the GATT into the WTO on the assumption that the significant post–World War II growth in economic development through international trade could only continue with the maturation of a rule-based organization. While these assumptions were founded on liberal trade principles, they were fought for with more than a little neomercantilist ambition. As the WTO grew to enclose less developed countries, and as the realization that trade rules would need to apply equally to both rich and poor and between the rich countries themselves, national interest began to highlight the many protectionist elements within the policies and politics of even the most committed liberal trade states. As rich country economies transformed from manufacturing to service foundations, and as poorer countries scrambled to protect burgeoning cheap labor industries and to demand open markets for their agricultural products, the WTO has been increasingly looked to by both types of countries as a rule-based remedy—but a remedy sought selectively to balance the need to maintain the international liberal trade environment while protecting perceived endangered domestic economic sectors. What has to give in this tug of war is the remaining question undermining all of the conflicts coming together in the Doha Round of negotiations. Domestic politics as well as international diplomacy will determine the outcome of the negotiations. It is no wonder that the complexity of this modern dilemma has led to visceral opposition to all globalizing institutions as well as to bedrock confrontations between market interests, NGO objections, and the protection of national interests within a swiftly changing world.

CONCLUSIONS

FOUNDATIONS FOR THE NEW ROUND

LESSONS LEARNED SO FAR

Whether we champion the concept of a free market (liberal) international political economy or have sympathy for the necessity of states to protect their interests through a neomerchantalist philosophy, this text illustrates that all states in some circumstances act on the basis of perceived national interests. Clearly, we have seen this principle in action in each of the substantive chapters. We have seen how the interest of states led first to the creation of the GATT, to its expansion, and finally to its metamorphosis into the WTO. The WTO may champion free trade liberalism in the international marketplace, but it remains a creature of member interests. We noticed this in the consensus decision-making processes encouraged by and mostly used by the WTO. Each state is afraid that others may use the WTO to trample its interests; consensus keeps this from happening. Clumsy or not, in essence, every member can veto a decision that is harmful to its interests. Size and complexity may intervene in the coming rounds of negotiations to mitigate this principle with decisions made by hypermajorities. But it will not be easy to get the major states to surrender dominance in the processes of the organization.

State interests can also be seen in the WTO's dispute settlement process. Almost every state wanted a system that was rule-based and that could create greater certainty, but each was also afraid of creating an organization with the power to enforce the decisions it made. The result is a dispute process where the WTO acts as adjudicator, while the members themselves are responsible for enforcing the decisions. This makes the WTO far weaker than the world government some of its critics have imagined it to be, while still far stronger than many interests within and without the governments of many states want it to be.

This book also illustrates that member interests are at the heart of the politics represented within each case study. Putnam's two levels of politics are seen throughout the case studies. For instance, bananas became a dispute because U.S. leaders wanted to protect the interests of two U.S.-based multinational companies—Dole and Chiquita. On the European side, banana quotas were created to protect the colonial ties of England and France and to improve the position of several European-based companies. The EU was slow to comply with the eventual WTO decision because the costs of not complying were easier to bear than the political costs of compliance. Finding a solution to the conflict that bridged both the domestic and international interests of states was difficult and sometimes seemed impossible.

State interests, often reflecting domestic political forces, can be seen in conflict throughout the other four cases as well. Freer trade, it turns out, is just one interest of states that must be balanced against other interests. Each member of the WTO at times pushes for freer trade; each, at times, also pushes for more protection. Many find the magic to do both at once. Where a member sits depends on a variety of factors, including the member's domestic political situation, its relationships with other members, and the interests and values of its leaders.

We need to be quick to note that this does not mean that the WTO is merely a reflection of member interests and nothing more. The WTO can also have an impact on the behaviors of its members. This, too, can be seen clearly in the case studies. One reason many countries wanted China to become a member of the WTO is that they not only wanted stable access to its markets, but they also believed it would force China to liberalize not only its economy, but its political system as well. As China is tied into the dictates of the international political economy, it is hoped, as tariffs and other barriers to trade are lowered, that democratic institutions and Western-style human rights will cross into China much as new goods and services cross its borders. China's leadership, as we have seen, is worried about this prospect. Since the beginning of economic reform in the late 1970s, China has attempted to walk a path that would allow for economic openness without jeopardizing the Communist Party's control of the country, and it continues to strive for this balance. Here is a classic case of free trade and protectionism competing for the soul of a country's policies—and this competition reflecting the two-level politics so evident in all of international political economy.

The effect of the WTO on its members is evident through the high compliance rate with the Dispute Settlement Body's decisions, even though the enforcement mechanism for these decisions is comparatively weak, and only the hardest disputes are brought to the WTO table. Members worry about their reputations within the WTO. A member that develops a bad reputation within the organization will find negotiations over trade concessions more difficult, and more importantly, it will find that when it wins cases before the Dispute Settlement Body, others will refuse to comply. The impress of the WTO is so significant that even when a member refuses to comply with a WTO decision, it attempts to explain why it is not in compliance or attempts to negotiate some type of concession with the organization or the aggrieved party, depending on the locale of the dispute. We saw this clearly in the beef hormone case, for example. The EU waged a steady battle to convince others that hormones really were not safe for use in the fattening of cattle. In an effort to legitimize the continuance of the ban on beef from the United States, and to insure other members that its failure to comply should not be taken as a sign that the EU is a bad citizen within the organization, the EU emphasized the ethical argument over the mercantilist one.

This text also illustrates theories in action that are used to explain state behavior and the workings of the international system. The GATT/WTO sits on top of a foundation created to promote the liberal view of political economy. This view argues that tying states together through trade benefits everyone. All grow richer as trade relationships deepen, and the law of comparative advantage allows each to specialize in specific sectors of production. Some liberals believe that through free trade, armed conflicts between states are reduced and possibly eliminated altogether. The GATT/WTO process gives some support to this view. The reduction of trade barriers and the institutionalization of trade relationships by the WTO have led to sharp increases in trade among members over the last fifty years. Countries that plug into the international system, on average, do better economically than those that do not. Armed conflicts have also been nonexistent between the major states that created the GATT/ WTO, and this is true even among the secondary powers in the organization.

In contrast to liberal views are the mercantilist and neomercantilist views. These see states as motivated by survival and gain. As such, they must be constantly worried about the increases in power by other states. Under mercantilism and neomercantilism, a state should structure all trade relationships in a way that benefits itself more than those it is trading with. In this way, a state can grow in power relative to others, insuring that it survives. The problem is that if all states act this way, the development of trade relationships will be difficult. Gains from the relationship will have to be shared by all involved. This is difficult, if not impossible, to achieve. Economists talk about everyone winning from the law of comparative advantage, but they also admit that in reality some will win more than others, leading to changes in the distribution of relative wealth and power in the international system. This is unacceptable to those holding a mercantilist view of the world. To protect against serious uneven gains in trade, we have seen that some mercantilist values are embedded in the GATT/WTO. The norms of reciprocity and nondiscrimination were developed to help insure that all members would benefit from the lowering of tariff barriers. As the organization has grown, however, these norms have made negotiations over the expansion of the agreement and organization ever more difficult. Consensus decision making helps maximize the concept that each state is afforded equitable treatment, but as we have seen, consensus is hard to come by as the number of WTO members continues to grow.

Moreover, consensus has not prevented the strongest states within the WTO from exerting more influence than others. Ironically, the strongest states have even used the principle of consensus as a wedge to prevent caucuses of NICs and the poor to balance them. Reform of the decision process is a high priority of some in the Doha Round of negotiations.

The mercantilist and neomercantilist views help explain the actions of the United States and EU in both the banana and hormone cases, as well as their actions in the 2003 Cancun Ministerial Conference. Developing countries believed that both were attempting to skew the benefits of trade toward themselves for constituents within their domestic economies at the expense of the less developed. It is quite convenient that the ban on hormone-treated beef began just as huge beef surpluses were developing in the EU. It is also convenient that the EU banana regime in the 1990s led to the moving of market share from U.S.-based companies to European-based companies. The United States has been forceful in demanding changes in these EU policies, as well as broad agricultural policies, in the Doha Round by using liberal rhetoric in coordination with its own protectionist aspirations. The EU sees the Singapore issues as a wedge of advantage for their firms and thus pushes heavily for their inclusion into the WTO. The actions of Europe and the United States are not surprising to those who see the world through mercantilist eyes.

Antiglobalists, represented by the more aggressive forces seen in the streets of Seattle and Cancun, as well as some moderate NGOs who attack particular elements of the growing global free market system, see the structure of the international political economy as fundamentally skewed against the developing countries and toward the most developed and their multinational corporations.[1] These forces argue that the developed countries create rules and structures within the international political economy to insure and institutionalize their dominance. The WTO decision-making processes have given some support for this view. Green Room discussions, for example, have been historically dominated by the largest trading states—most of which are either developed industrial economies or the middle-range "developing countries." This text has noted that the African and other poor states at both Doha and Cancun specifically challenged this situation. The United States and EU also have more latitude within the WTO than smaller member states. Both the United States and EU find it easier to not comply with, or waffle on, WTO decisions that go against their interests, particularly if the protagonists are smaller powers. They are also able to use the size of their markets to force smaller states to grant concessions they might not otherwise wish to make during trade negotiations and to unduly influence them to comply with dispute panel decisions. As we saw in Chapter 4, the compliance rate of countries losing to the United States in a dispute panel decision is about 10 percent higher than the average compliance rate for dispute panel decisions on the whole. And even then, the United States tends to challenge any victory by poor states.

The antiglobalization forces also point to the fact that worldwide tariffs are lowest on the products produced by the developed countries. Developing countries constantly point out that many of their products do not have the same access into developed country markets as developed country products have into their markets. Many commentators in the developing countries believe that the GATT/WTO has been used to enrich the developed countries at the expense of the developing. For them, the WTO is not about making all countries better-off; it is about making the developed countries better-off at the expense of the developing. Many WTO critics argue that the developing countries should not have joined the WTO and should now leave the organization. But developing country leaders argue that they would be even worse-off if they did not participate. So they band together into various caucus groups, especially after Doha, in order to assert themselves in Cancun and beyond. The broad international shifts toward free market mechanisms have weakened the appeal of the more critical of the antiglobalization forces in developing countries. But depending on the responses to the collapse at Cancun, these forces along with more moderate NGOs might well turn developing countries toward more aggressive trade demands in future Doha Round negotiations.

CONTINUING ISSUES FACED BY THE DOHA ROUND

Having reviewed some basic insights demonstrated by our examination of the WTO, let us conclude by turning to the WTO and the issues and challenges it faces over the next several years.

The WTO has several issues on its plate that must be resolved if it is to fulfill its mission of providing for a stable, smoothly working, rule-based international trading system. If nothing else, Seattle and Cancun brought this fact home in a loud and clear voice. The configuration of this future depends on the outcome of the decisions made during the rehabilitation of the Doha Round that began at the Fourth Ministerial Conference in November 2001 in Qatar and derailed at the Fifth Ministerial Conference in Cancun in September 2003. There remains a list of issues left unresolved from (1) the built-in agenda included in the first generation of negotiations, (2) new issues untouched by GATT/WTO, and (3) the list of second-generation new issues referred to as the Singapore issues. The organization must also deal with the corollary, but fundamental, issues of institutional reform, including mechanisms for input from the civil society organizations that remain essential for building public understanding and legitimacy. These NGOs provide the foundation for continued opposition to the WTO, but also the potential for grassroots support.

The Doha Round had been scheduled to last at least three years, with late 2004 as the target for a new agreement. This date came and went with only the promise of progress in coming years. If the history outlined in this text has any application at all, the new issues will prove difficult to deal with, considering the expanded definition of trade and its more public application. The Cancun clashes have extended the round. Though interrupted by the collapse of the session, some progress has been made on the first-generation new issues through negotiations that have been continuous since Uruguay. Progress toward negotiations on the second-generation new issues will depend on the successful engagement with these issues over the near term of negotiations. Here, we simply want to briefly outline the fundamentals of the key continuing issues confronted by the Doha Round as a means of placing the reader in the next phase of the organization's development.

The *first-generation new issues* are generally identified as those dealing with trade in services, agriculture, and intellectual property rights. Squeezed in-between the first and second generation is the economically dynamic area of e-commerce. Following is a summary of the fundamental concerns for this grouping of issues.

TRADE IN SERVICES

This area is a built-in concern because its rules were outlined in the GATS that was concluded as part of the Uruguay Round. This agreement set up a series of responsibilities and expectations in the realm of "the interaction between providers and consumers" of services.[2] The two core principles of the agreement are MFN and national treatment obligations, which simply expand the basic rules of GATT to the area of services. What GATS added was a limited market access obligation that demands that each member list the service areas that they are willing to open to mutual access. This opening of only selective services by each country obviously limits the availability of many markets that are not on a state's list—thus the necessity for continuing negotiations to make sure "trade in services are fully transparent, and secur[ing] the progressive removal of measures [like selective lists] which discriminate against foreign service suppliers."[3]

What is defined as services is rather broad and includes the financial sector (insurance and banking), telecommunications, labor mobility (nationals working abroad), tourism, construction, and air and sea transportation. It is not hard to see why this area is such a difficult one to fully fold into international free trade, which is why the GATS agreement included a built-in schedule of continuing negotiations on a broad front separate from the Ministerial Conferences. Progress has been made on several fronts (financial services and telecommunications, especially), but the Doha Round puts a variety of sector issues in this category into a potpourri of a single undertaking in an attempt to increase bargained trade-offs. Cancun was to be the kick-off point to allow states to list their specific openings in services. Services, however, proved too complex an arena to effectively structure at Cancun. This complexity may well plague the negotiation processes during the Doha Round to the point where specific service sectors may have to be separated and dealt with individually.

AGRICULTURE

As we have seen, this has proven to be the single most contentious sector in the history of the WTO. We need only revisit the chapters on the Uruguay Round, bananas, beef, and the review of the early Doha Round to see the continuing tension between and among a combination of states on agricultural issues. Even though progress was made through the Uruguay Round on reducing domestic and export subsidies and replacing nontariff barriers with bound tariffs, barriers and tariffs remain. As developing states argued at Cancun, many practices are difficult to distinguish as trade barriers. For example, American and EU farm support programs that are designed to meet domestic goals inevitably echo onto export markets. The EU's Common Agricultural Policy is its largest budget item, and EU expansion complicates its use. Both U.S. and EU programs are vulnerable to increased limitations on subsidies if the WTO should act aggressively. Developing states provide added conflict in the area of agriculture, demanding access on favorable terms to developed markets. But they too discriminate against each other in this and other trade areas.

Another example of conflict is Canada's tariff on over-quota dairy products. These have a low quota with a small tariff, but dairy products over that quota are taxed at 200–300 percent.[4] Japan and Korea maintain high barriers in agriculture as well. The Cairns Group of agricultural exporters consistently opposes all these measures and wants completely open trade in agriculture. Even the U.S. legislation in 2000, granting access to some markets for African agriculture, hardly dented the marketplace for the key African products, since many, including cotton, are conveniently exempt from the access legislation. The resumption of the Doha Round negotiations, after the Geneva meetings that patched together preliminary compromises, especially on agriculture, were unsuccessful. Agriculture, especially the support policies of the United States and the EU, remains the key stumbling block to Doha progress.

INTELLECTUAL PROPERTY RIGHTS

The Uruguay Round produced another side agreement called the 1994 Agreement on Trade-Related Aspects of Intellectual Property (TRIPS), as was discussed in Chapter 3. With the rapid development in knowledge-based products and services, this agreement was needed to fill a gap in the old GATT agreements that concentrated almost exclusively on traditional products. The agreement itself authorizes continuing multinational negotiations, as well as a review of the agreement every two years—thus the built-in nature of continuity in this sector. The United States has been particularly aggressive in protecting such areas as entertainment copyrights; patents of all sorts, including in computer software; and pharmaceuticals.

Developing countries want to protect their ability to utilize technology, their own indigenous technology and folkways as well as the newer Western technology, without sacrificing large amounts of capital or losing access to these assets. Low-cost access to generic pharmaceuticals, for example, has been a central issue as a result of AIDS epidemic pressures. Alleviating developing country concerns a bit, the United States and EU agreed to allow some violations of pharmaceutical rights in an attempt to attack the AIDS epidemic. Because of resistance from poor countries and continuing problems with violations from China and other transitional countries, "the issue of the effective implementation of the TRIPS is destined to become one of the greatest causes of conflict among WTO member countries."[5] The American compromises on key pharmaceuticals in 2003 opened the door for more cooperative progress in this area, but Cancun showed that it did not buy cooperation throughout this sector from developing states.

E-COMMERCE

Electronic commerce exploded as an element of international trade after the conclusion of the Uruguay Round. The 1998 Ministerial in Geneva began consideration by the WTO of e-commerce through passage of a Declaration on Global Electronic Commerce that "established a working programme to analyze trade-related issues . . . and to make recommendations for action in Seattle."[6] A moratorium on customs duties began in 1998 at the insistence of the United States and has been extended until hard decisions are made. It applies only to services delivered over the Internet, however, not to goods ordered that must cross borders to be delivered. There is speculation that regulation might be left under the GATS, which had kept a "technology neutrality" on service provisions. The Doha Round may need to attack this issue before it is concluded.

Second-generation new issues are not new to the international trading system. They were, however, new to multinational attempts to bring them into a rule-dominated, codified system of agreements. Most take the trade negotiations further away from the concentration on simple direct tariff solutions. They include the so-called Singapore issues that are more public in nature and less amenable to elite decision making in Green Rooms. These new issues are competition policies, investment policies, environmental standards and trade, labor and trade, government procurement, and antidumping. In addition to these, there remains great pressure for adjustments to be made in the procedural elements of the WTO dispute settlement system.

COMPETITION POLICIES

This term refers to whether or not there is a need for a comprehensive approach to antitrust regulations through multinational agreement. The question is, can the WTO reach a single, multilateral antitrust agreement within the context of the GATT/WTO accords? What would be the principles used to establish standards? Many, if not most, states have some sort of means to regulate large business entities, but the principles and methods used vary greatly. Developing states are very interested in multinational rules to govern what they perceive to be anticompetitive practices of multinational corporations (MNCs). Their monopolistic tendencies often overwhelm domestic competitors. The liberal nature of the WTO agreements that champion free trade competition would seem to clash with this protectionist regulatory goal. Although, monopoly within states is seen by liberals as a form of market failure requiring state action and regulation. Minimum standards would be difficult to negotiate as a part of a rule-based multinational system within the WTO. One way suggested to do this would be to make international rules that would be enforced at the national, rather than international, level. There are multiple problems with this solution, given the different national enforcement mechanisms. Add to this the enormous influence of MNCs within domestic politics. Since solutions are hard to come by, this area is left open to bilateral agreements. These agreements, however, do not become multinational since they are outside the scope of the WTO. Competitive policies continue to be highly decentralized and increasingly cumbersome for WTO mechanisms to deal with.

INVESTMENT POLICIES

Many states, including the United States, see foreign domestic investment (FDI) limitations through multilateral agreement as a threat to national sovereignty. It is a complex economic matter, and because of this, there has been little progress in the sector. As with other second-generation new issues, the Uruguay Round produced a modest document in an attempt to deal with domestic content requirements and certain export-performance requirements that foreign investment must meet. The document was the Agreement on Trade-Related Investment Measures (TRIMS). Built into the agreement, commencing in 2000, is a self-review by the members who signed it.[7]

The topic of a multilateral agreement on investment (MAI) has been batted around for two decades, but states are reluctant to give up additional domestic independence for taxing, regulating, and placement of special conditions on foreign investment. Foreign investment problems include not just conflicts between developing and developed states, but among developed states themselves. For it must be remembered that most FDI flows between rich countries. Illustrating the difficulty of dealing with investment policies, in 1998 the OECD separately tried to deal with the issue but failed to make any progress. This issue may provide developing states with some trade-off value in the Doha Round of negotiations if they continue to demand use of joint venture and technology sharing on the part of MNCs. But little is expected in the way of progress toward a new MAI; for even these developing states were happy to see the Singapore issues set aside in Cancun.

ENVIRONMENTAL STANDARDS AND TRADE

Environmental issues bring some of the most intense lobbying activity to WTO deliberations. Business groups and developing states both fear that domestic environmental protection measures are being used as hidden trade protectionism. Developing states want to insure that environmental restrictions do not hamper their efforts at development. WTO rules do allow exceptions to general trade liberalization for protection of animals, human safety, and the environment; but these are all too susceptible to protectionist motivations that have made them sensitive for states to use. Environmentalists claim that the WTO rules fail to recognize environmental standards and thus endanger the planet.[8] Three cases not described in this text have continued to motivate many environmentalists. All went against U.S. domestic rules, and all were virtually ignored. One concerned tuna fishers whose nets catch dolphins; another dealt with shrimp nets that catch and kill turtles; and the third dealt with gasoline standards and imported oil. Each was proclaimed by the GATT/WTO dispute settlement systems to be in violation of the GATT/WTO agreements; each was taken by environmentalists as proof positive that the organization ignores environmental protection. The simple fact is that other environmental issues, like pollution control and natural resource management, increasingly intersect with trade and economic policy.[9]

One early attempt at dealing with the problem began in 1994 by the WTO ministers when they set up the Committee on Trade and the Environment (CTE). Its assignment was to study the relationship between the two and offer suggestions. Like most governmental attempts to make progress by setting up a "study group," the CTE met with decidedly mixed reactions.[10] Some suggested that one area for progress would be to free all environmental equipment and services from all trade barriers as a means of demonstrating commitment to the environment.[11]

There are Multilateral Environment Agreements (MEA) like the Kyoto Agreement on global warming, but it is not clear what the relationship is or should be between these and the WTO. What is clear is that Seattle and Cancun demonstrated the determination of environmentalists to attack the WTO as a penultimate example of destructive globalization. And they are making headway with the public at large if the claims of support by NGOs involved in Seattle have any validity. As one expert put it, "The WTO cannot become an environmental organization, but the trading rules can be made more environmentally friendly."[12] Resistance among government trade ministers remains strong, however, particularly within developing countries.

LABOR AND TRADE

A social dimension of international trade, labor and trade, is another one of the controversial sectors of a more public nature. The Seattle chapter of this text has noted the significant opposition to the WTO that has come from some labor unions and the extent to which they are willing to lobby against its influence in the United States. EU members and the United States have taken up the argument of the unions. Indeed, it was President Clinton's untimely prolabor statement that helped to torpedo the Seattle meeting. Developing countries perceive any GATT/WTO rules on labor standards, like environmental standards, to be merely a means to take away their comparative advantage by attacking their cheap labor base. They argue that poverty and indigenous culture determine the extent of labor laws, child labor, minimum wage, and workplace safety; and thus domestic policy should rule this relationship, not international regulation. Developed countries, it is claimed, are using this issue to protect their more expensive labor-intensive industries (particularly in manufacturing and textiles), even though in their formative years of development their work conditions were similar.

There is a growing sense that public opinion in developed countries and in the upper tier of developing countries supports the incorporation of "core labor values" into the multilateral economic system. There are four core values identified by the International Labor Organization (ILO), one of the oldest and more universal of international organizations: (1) the right to collective bargaining, (2) freedom from forced labor, (3) abolition of child labor, (4) and nondiscrimination in employment.[13] Since this organization has long championed these principles, many believe that the ILO is the proper venue for dealing with labor standards in international trade, not the WTO. The EU wants to find a means to combine the secretariats of the two organizations for the purpose of dealing with labor and trade.[14] The Singapore Ministerial Conference Declaration supported the core values but stated that the ILO should be the place to deal with these issues. This pressure was part of the resistance to the whole Singapore package by developing countries at Cancun.

GOVERNMENT PROCUREMENT

The question of whether or not to allow businesses from outside the country to bid for government procurement contracts has been a contentious one. "Buy local" campaigns are aimed at constituencies that believe their tax dollars should be spent to hire one's own nationals. Influential domestic business and labor interest groups also want to direct government spending to their members. For many states, government contracts and patronage tools are often centers of corruption. Liberalized free trade demands that governments follow the principle of nondiscrimination against foreign firms in all economic endeavors, including government spending. Clearly, this is a part of the GATT/WTO obligations, but at the same time specific provisions within the agreements provide for numerous exceptions. Given the protectionist nature of these loopholes, these exceptions point out the need for new negotiations on the topic. Progress is being made on an agreement on transparency in government procurement that will be proposed for WTO adoption. Note that the chapter on China illustrates the problems in government procurement for countries that have significant numbers of enterprises still owned or controlled by the government.

ANTIDUMPING

"Dumping takes place when exporters sell their products at an unsustainable lower price than their own market."[15] Countries have the right under WTO rules to retaliate against this practice, usually by placing additional duties on the goods involved. "Antidumping is one of the few legal ways for countries to impose protection unilaterally [that is, without WTO approval]."[16] Too often, however, a state's claim of having a good "dumped" on them has more to do with protectionism than with free trade. Antidumping complaints, correctly or wrongly put forward, are so prevalent that the number of cases filed before the WTO has climbed to over two hundred a year—most of these against the stronger developing countries.[17] Settling disputes often becomes either a very technical matter over whether dumping has occurred, or a very political matter of balancing domestic producer interests with the overall trade relationship between the states involved. The WTO Antidumping Agreement has many ambiguous elements to its rules on both the determination of antidumping and calculating levels of legitimate response. The Doha Round may need to investigate tightening and redefining these antidumping rules and for consequent safeguard measures that counter unfair trade practices.

If first- and second-generation new issues are not enough to crowd the agenda of a rejuvenated Doha Round, there is a necessity to find ways to deal with nonstate actors (the civil society), the opening up of the organization to broad scrutiny (the so-called transparency issue), and finding ways to be more efficient in the administrative operation of the organization (decision-making processes). More often than not, the dispute settlement system becomes a central concern for these areas of *institutional reforms*. As the chapters on bananas and beef illustrate, there needs to be changes in the compliance provisions of the dispute settlement process so that the binding rulings of the system are carried out in a more timely manner. Civil society critics would also like to see much more transparency in these processes. They want procedures to be open to the public in a timely manner. They also would like to be able to actively participate in the process by testifying, giving amicus briefs to the dispute settlement panels and the appeals panels, and having representatives in community deliberations. Recent practice has allowed written input into dispute panel deliberations from select NGOs, though how seriously the panel members have taken this input is questionable. Many civil society groups add a demand for more representative dispute panels, ones that are not so heavily weighted toward just trade experts hearing the cases. By adding civil society advocates, or at least representatives with broader concerns, they believe the process would become more amenable to public support.

More broadly, civil society groups have pushed for representation in all of the trade deliberations of the WTO. Some even want voting rights for civil society within the General Council. Nearly all the WTO members are against any suggestion that the organization is anything other than a government-to-government organization. As such, it cannot allow NGO membership or official participation in formal deliberations. Civil society, governments argue, should work through domestic processes to affect WTO policy. This does not rule out the use of experts from civil society or the participation of WTO ministers in conjunction with NGO representatives in forums, symposia, trade conferences, or other forms of exchanges. It should be remembered that invited NGOs participated in WTO-sponsored events prior to and parallel with the Seattle, Doha, and Cancun meetings.

The GATT/WTO has a history of limited access to information about the substances of their meetings. Most meetings have been, more often than not, closed to all but ministers, and minutes were not available in any timely manner. Often, ministers or secretariat representatives were not readily available for comment either. Some elements of the process have been closed even to nonchosen member state ministers or representatives of caucuses (note the Green Room phenomenon and its closed-door nature). A call for greater transparency has come from civil society critics and developing countries that have felt out of the loop on crucial negotiations. News media increasingly find the WTO as newsworthy as its issues seem to touch on concerns that are salient to the public and affect domestic politics. Seattle was an eye-opener for both insiders and critics of the WTO system of operation in regards to the necessity for a political and public relations perspective of providing significantly more transparency to the whole organization. Eye-opening does not necessarily mean corrective action, however, as Cancun too dramatically illustrated. While there might have been more transparency in some areas of Doha and Cancun, there clearly was not enough. There is still much to be done if public and civil society understanding and support is to be realized.

Institutional reforms, then, will need to be part of the Doha Round agenda, not only in regards to transparency, but also in dealing with the increasing difficulty of the organization in accommodating its large membership while keeping a focus on accomplishing agenda goals. Many observers have suggested some sort of select group to act as a kind of consultation or focus center, as was earlier used by the GATT but fell into disrepute with the Green Room process. Jeffrey Schott, reinforced by British Prime Minister Tony Blair, suggested an eminent persons group (EPG) that would serve as a focal group for helping to clarify priority agenda items for Ministerial Conferences and for maintenance of priorities within the General Council and Ministerial Conferences.[18] The director general could appoint such a group and ask for periodic reports to the members. By focusing the discussions and providing a blueprint from which to work, the EPG could allow states to engage in informal negotiations early enough to set the parameters of potential agreements, thereby increasing the probability of success. Both Seattle and Cancun proved problematical from early on because the rich states and the WTO administrators had disproportionate influence on the agendas. This resulted in large and contentious preliminary texts, missed deadlines for member input and views, and dysfunctional negotiations at these Ministerial Conferences.

Constant vigilance is a necessity for any viable organization, and this is most certainly true for the WTO. It is trying to do something unique in human history. It is trying to create a worldwide rule-based economic system that satisfies the needs and interests of the entire spectrum of political/social/economic societies. Its success could increase the kind of economic cooperation that is a foundation for political cooperation in a contentious world. Its failure could bring the worst predictions of the globalization critics to fruition or to a fragmentation of the global economic order, returning us to the economic system that existed between the World Wars and perhaps its problems as well.

SUMMARY OF URUGUAY ROUND RESULTS

The Uruguay Round established a single institutional framework encompassing the GATT, as modified by the Uruguay Round, and all other agreements and arrangements concluded during the Uruguay Round. As part of this, the WTO was developed to administer and implement the GATT and other Uruguay Round agreements. Finally, membership in the WTO requires that a state agree to comply with all agreements falling under the WTO's purview.

MARKET ACCESS FOR NONAGRICULTURAL GOODS

The Uruguay Round reduced tariffs by 40 percent for developed countries on about $787 billion worth of trade in industrial goods. The percent of industrial goods traded by developed countries with zero tariffs rose from 20 percent to 44 percent. Average tariffs for developed countries fell from 6.3 percent to 3.8 percent. Finally, developed countries increased the level of bound tariffs from 94 percent of all goods to 99 percent of all goods. Developing countries agreed to an average tariff reduction of 20 percent covering more than $300 billion in goods. They also increased the percent of tariff bindings from 14 percent to 59 percent of products exported into their markets. Average tariff levels for developing countries fell from 15.3 percent to 12.3 percent.

AGRICULTURAL PRODUCTS

Trade in agricultural products was brought within the GATT for the first time with commitments on internal supports, export subsidies, and market access for imports. Internal support program levels were reduced by 20 percent, and the new levels were bound against future increases. Three categories of supports were created: red, amber, and green. Supports considered green were exempt from Uruguay Round requirements. Export subsidies were reduced by 36 percent in value over a six-year period with 1986–90 set as the base period for determining reductions. Reductions applied only to specific product groups. Finally, market access was improved through tariffication. All nontariff barriers to agricultural trade were to be eliminated, and a single fixed tariff was to be created by WTO members. Overall tariff levels were to be reduced by 36 percent for developed countries and 24 percent for developing countries in ten years from the signing of the agreement.

TEXTILES AND CLOTHING

The Uruguay Round began the integration of textiles into the GATT. Until 1995 trade in textiles fell under the purview of the Multi-Fibre Arrangement (MFA), which set quotas for most every type of textile traded in the world. Integration of textiles was completed in four stages, and it meant the elimination of quotas. In 1995 members agreed to eliminate quotas on 16 percent of textiles covered by the MFA. Three years later, an additional 17 percent were freed from quotas. Four years after that, 18 percent more were freed from quotas, and finally in 2005, all textiles covered by the MFA were freed from quotas. Members of the WTO also agreed to reduce tariffs on textiles by about 20 percent and to bind most tariffs on textiles. Safeguards were included to allow members to reinstate quotas to avoid damaging surges in imports, but there were tight rules for their use.

SERVICES

The GATS was a significant outcome of the Uruguay Round. There are three major components to the agreement. The first is the framework agreement that contains the basic obligations applying to all member countries. These include MFN treatment for services, transparency requirements, safeguards, dispute settlement procedures, and the free flow of payments and transfers. The second contains the schedule of national commitments. These lay out exactly what each country has agreed to do in regards to opening access to services trade—they are much like the specific tariff levels countries agree to as part of the GATT. The last section contains annexes to the main agreement and creates rules and exceptions to the main agreement for specific service sectors. Finally, the agreement requires that members meet every five years to discuss expansion of the agreement's coverage.

TRADE-RELATED INVESTMENT MEASURES

This agreement recognizes that certain policies or measures created by states to govern investment can distort trade. The agreement prohibits any measure or policy that is inconsistent with Article III of the GATT—this is the norm of nondiscrimination that means that countries should treat foreign and domestic firms the same. It also prohibits any quantitative restrictions on investment. A specific list of measures that are incompatible with the agreement are appended to the text. All developed country members of the WTO agreed to eliminate any incompatible measures by 1997, while developing countries agreed to their elimination by 2000. The least developed members of the WTO were given until 2002 to eliminate these policies. A committee was created to monitor implementation of the agreement.

ITELLECTUAL PROPERTY RIGHTS

The Trade Related Intellectual Property Rights Agreement (TRIPS) was created to reduce the amount of conflict over the protection of the full range of property rights by member states due to different standards. The agreement requires that intellectual property receive national treatment by all members. In order to end conflict, minimum standards of protection were included as part of the agreement. The agreement also defines what types of materials members must protect. Finally, the agreement creates "obligations for members to provide procedures and remedies under their domestic laws to ensure that intellectual property can be effectively enforced by foreign right holders as well as their own nationals."[1]

OTHER OUTCOMES OF THE ROUND

The Uruguay Round tightened the procedures and rules concerning antidumping measures and the safeguards that members could use in protecting themselves from surges in imports due to the opening of their markets. An agreement was also added covering government procurement by members. Members of the WTO must create transparent procurement processes and inform losing bidders promptly of their decisions. The procurement agreement also expanded coverage of previous agreements to services. An additional agreement was added covering the sanitary and phytosanitary standards of members. (This agreement receives fuller coverage in Chapter 6.) Finally, the agreement expanded or tightened rules dealing with import licensing procedures, customs valuation, preshipment inspection, rules of origin, and technical barriers to trade.[2]

Notes

Chapter 1

1. Hoekman, Matoo, and English, *Development, Trade and the WTO*. For an extensive bibliography on the WTO, see Fulton, *The World Trade Organization*.
2. Danaher and Burbach, *Globalize This!*; Wallach, Woodall, and Nader, *Whose Trade Organization?*
3. Smith, *The Wealth of Nations*, 436.
4. Ibid., 180-81.
5. Putnam, *Hanging Together*.
6. Ibid., 10.
7. Milner, *Interests, Institutions and Information*, 118.
8. Derber, *People before Profit*.
9. Shoch, *Trading Blows*.
10. Putnam, *Hanging Together*, 10.
11. Ibid., 11.
12. Rodrik, "Trading in Illusions", 54-63.
13. Putnam, *Hanging Together*, 4.
14. Gilpin, *The Political Economy of International Relations*.
15. See, for example, James, *The End of Globalization*.
16. Putnam, *Hanging Together*, 6-7.
17. Narlikar, *International Trade and Developing Countries*.

Chapter 2

1. Gilpin, *The Political Economy of International Relations*, 2.
2. Hoekman and Kostecki, *The Political Economy of the World Trading System*.
3. Ibid., 14.
4. Eckes, *Opening America's Markets*, 1.
5. Zeiler, *Free Trade, Free World*.
6. Rhodes, *Reciprocity, U.S. Trade Policy*.
7. Ibid., 52.
8. Zeiler, *Free Trade, Free World*, see Chapter 1.
9. Rhodes, *Reciprocity, U.S. Trade Policy*, 53.
10. Zeiler, *Free Trade, Free World*.
11. Rhodes, *Reciprocity, U.S. Trade Policy*, 63.
12. Ruggie, "International Regimes."
13. Pease, *International Organizations*, 143.
14. Rhodes, *Reciprocity, U.S. Trade Policy*, 72.
15. Odell, *Negotiating the World Economy*, 162.

16. Culbert, "War-Time Anglo-American Talks"; Odell, *Negotiating the World Economy*.
17. U.S. Department of State, "Proposals for the Expansion," 13.
18. Odell, *Negotiating the World Economy*, 162.
19. Ibid., 163.
20. High and Lodge, "The World Trade Organization," 2.
21. World Trade Organization, "GATT 1947," Preamble.
22. Ibid.
23. Conklin, "From GATT to the World," 1.
24. John H. Jackson, as quoted in Conklin, "From GATT to the World," 383.
25. Ibid., 382.
26. Zeiler, *Free Trade, Free World*, 173.
27. Hoekman and Kostecki, *Political Economy of the World Trading System*, 18.
28. Eckes, *Opening America's Markets*, 181–83.
29. Evans, *From Trade Surplus to Deficit*, 1–17.
30. Eckes, *Opening America's Markets*, 181–83.
31. Kaplan, *American Trade Policy*, 9.
32. Barton, et al., *The Evolution of the Trade Regime*.
33. Baldwin, "The Tokyo Round," 231; Cline et al., *Trade Negotiations in the Tokyo Round*, 10.
34. Eckes, *Opening America's Markets*, 204.
35. Gilpin, *The Political Economy of International Relations*, 192.
36. Low, *Trading Free*, 24–26, 56–57; Golt, *Trade Issues*, chapter 4.
37. Low, *Trading Free*, 72.
38. Hoekman and Kostecki, *Political Economy of the World Trading System*, 18.
39. Low, *Trading Free*, 182.
40. Golt, *Trade Issues*, 2.
41. Odell, *Negotiating the World Economy*, 176.
42. Kaplan, *American Trade Policy*; Lovett, Eckes, and Brinkman, *U.S. Trade Policy*.
43. Odell, *Negotiating the World Economy*. For more on this point, see Narlikar, *International Trade and Developing Countries*.
44. Golt, *GATT Negotiations*, 3.
45. Zeiler, *Free Trade, Free World*, 196–97.
46. Baldwin, "The Tokyo Round," 249.
47. Low, *Trading Free*, 182.
48. Ibid., 183.
49. Baldwin, "The Tokyo Round," 239.
50. World Trade Organization, "GATT 1947," Article XXIII.
51. Quoted in Rhodes, *Reciprocity, U.S. Trade Policy*, 213.
52. Jackson, *Restructuring the GATT System*.
53. Quoted in Golt, *Trade Issues*, 8.
54. Baldwin, "The Tokyo Round," 248.

CHAPTER 3

1. Russett, Starr, and Kinsella, *World Politics*, 140.
2. Burtless, et al., *Globalphobia, Confronting Fears*.
3. Low, *Trading Free*.
4. Ibid.

5. Keohane, *After Hegemony*, 72–73.

6. Low, *Trading Free*.

7. Grieder, *Secrets of the Temple*, 724.

8. International Monetary Fund, *World Economic Outlook*.

9. Grieder, *Secrets of the Temple*, 545–54.

10. Low, *Trading Free*.

11. World Trade Organization, *International Trade Statistics 2005*, 31.

12. Dunkley, *The Free Trade Adventure*

13. Preeg, *Traders in a Brave New World*, 94–95.

14. Hillman, "The U.S. Perspective," 30.

15. Winters, "The Road to Uruguay," 1297.

16. Ibid.

17. Preeg, *Traders in a Brave New World*, 63–64.

18. Ibid., 4.

19. Hillman, "The U.S. Perspective," 30.

20. Rayner, Ingersent, and Hine, "Agriculture in the Uruguay Round: An Assessment," 1514–15.

21. Underhill, "Negotiating Financial Openness," 124–29.

22. Dunkley, *The Free Trade Adventure*, 187.

23. Low, *Trading Free*.

24. Moyer, "The European Community and the GATT," 104–5.

25. Paarlberg, "How Agriculture Blocked," 34.

26. The countries were Argentina, Australia, Brazil, Canada, Chile, Colombia, Fiji, Hungary, Indonesia, Malaysia, New Zealand, Philippines, Thailand, and Uruguay. The nominal leader of the group became Australia as the Uruguay Round progressed. Canada eventually became a marginal member due to its extensive reliance on dairy and livestock supports.

27. Tyers, "The Cairns Group Perspective," 90–91.

28. Winters, "The Economic Consequences," 47–48.

29. Tyers, "The Cairns Group Perspective," 99.

30. Raghavan, *Recolonization, GATT*, 110–11; Whalley, *The Uruguay Round and Beyond*, 23–24.

31. Preeg, *Traders in a Brave New World*, 70–74; Raghavan, *Recolonization, GATT*, 192, 199–204.

32. The first of a series of agreements regulating trade in textiles was created in the early 1960s as textiles from Japan and other lesser-developed countries began inundating U.S. and European Markets. These agreements eventually became the Multi-fibre Arrangement in 1974. Hoekman and Kostecki, *The Political Economy of the World Trading System*.

33. Raghavan, *Recolonization, GATT*, 184–88.

34. Ibid., 114–34.

35. Ibid.

36. Rapkin and George, "Rice Liberalization and Japan's."

37. Ibid., 63–64.

38. Ibid., 77.

39. The following sections on the negotiations in the Uruguay Round draw heavily on histories of Croome, *Reshaping the World*, and Preeg, *Traders in a Brave New World*.

40. Preeg, *Traders in a Brave New World*, 34.

41. Low, *Trading Free*, 192.

42. Croome, *Reshaping the World*, 18.

43. At the time, twenty-four countries made up the Organization of Economic Cooperation and Development. Five more countries joined in the 1990s. Member countries are the United States, the UK, Australia, Canada, New Zealand, Germany, France, Sweden, Norway, Denmark, Finland, Switzerland, Austria, Mexico, Japan, Hungary, Ireland, Iceland, the Czech Republic, Poland, Spain, Portugal, Greece, Turkey, South Korea, Belgium, Luxembourg, the Netherlands, and Italy.

44. Preeg, *Traders in a Brave New World*, 54.

45. Croome, *Reshaping the World*, 34–35.

46. Preeg, *Traders in a Brave New World*, 88.

47. Stewart, *The GATT Uruguay Round*, 194.

48. Preeg, *Traders in a Brave New World*, 115.

49. Ingersent, Hine, and Rayner, "The EC Perspective," 78.

50. Ibid., 74–75.

51. The EC became the EU in 1992 with implementation of the Single European Act. The name change was meant to signify that the members were now part of a seamless and unified market, and also moving toward greater political and social integration.

52. Preeg, *Traders in a Brave New World*, 140.

53. Webber, "Franco-German Bilateralism."

54. It should be noted that while the EC, and then EU countries, were represented by a single negotiator, each EU member country still had to ratify the Uruguay Round. EC, and then EU, members also had influence over negotiations through the EC and EU institutions.

55. Cloud, "Health Care's Painful."

56. Benenson, "GATT Pact Lurches."

57. Benenson, "GATT's Disappearing Act."

58. Ruzicka and Maggs, "Clinton Team Stands."

59. Rubin, "Dole, Clinton Compromise."

60. Benenson, "Free Trade Carries."

CHAPTER 4

1. World Trade Organization, *Annual Report 2006*, 92.

2. Jackson, *The World Trade Organization*, 42.

3. Sek, "Congressional Research Service Report for Congress: The World Trade Organization," 3.

4. Blackhurst, "The Capacity of the WTO," 35.

5. Ibid., 38–39.

6. World Trade Organization, *Trading into the Future*, 52–53.

7. Blackhurst, "The Capacity of the WTO," 39.

8. World Trade Organization, *Annual Report 2006*, 107.

9. Blackhurst, "The Capacity of the WTO," 39.

10. Michalopolos, "The Participation of the Developing," 7–8.

11. Blackhurst, "The Capacity of the WTO," 31–58.

12. Jawara and Kwa, *Behind the Scenes*.

13. Jackson, *World Trade Organization*, 64.

14. Stewart and Karpel, "Review of the Dispute," 601.

15. Jackson, *The World Trade Organization*, 72.

16. Cox, "WTO Turns Up," 3b.

17. World Trade Organization, *Trading into the Future*, 18.

18. U.S. General Accounting Office, "World Trade Organization," 7.

19. Stewart and Karpel, "Review of the Dispute," 625–26.

20. Jackson, *The World Trade Organization*, 76; Thomas and Meyer, *The New Rules*, 316.

21. U.S. General Accounting Office, "World Trade Organization," 7.

22. Jackson, *The World Trade Organization*, 71.

23. Lash, "The Limited but Important," 373.

24. Knox, "The World Trade Organization at a Crossroads," 34–42; Stewart and Karpel, "Review of the Dispute."

25. Busch and Reinhardt, "Bargaining in the Shadow," 161.

26. U.S. General Accounting Office, "World Trade Organization," 21.

27. Stewart and Karpel, "Review of the Dispute," 609–13.

28. Ibid., 641–43.

29. Ibid.

30. Anderson, "Peculiarities of Retaliation," 123–24.

31. Davies, "Reviewing Dispute Settlement," 34.

32. Michalopolos, "The Participation of the Developing," 8. For a discussion of how delegation size affected the Cancun ministerial, see Narlikar and Wilkinson, "Collapse at the WTO."

33. Blackhurst, "The Capacity of the WTO," 53.

34. Michalopolos, "The Participation of the Developing," 9–10.

35. Blackhurst, "The Capacity of the WTO," 52.

36. Busch and Reinhardt, "Bargaining in the Shadow," 172; Michalopolos, "The Participation of the Developing," 18.

37. Michalopolos, "The Participation of the Developing," 19; Stewart and Karpel, "Review of the Dispute," 627.

38. Pedersen, "The WTO Decision-Making," 104; Sutherland, Sewell, and Weiner, "Challenges Facing the WTO," 87.

39. Michalopolos, "The Participation of the Developing"; Pedersen, "The WTO Decision-Making."

40. World Trade Organization, *Annual Report 2006*, III.

41. Jawara and Kwa, *Behind the Scenes*.

42. Stewart and Karpel, "Review of the Dispute," 604.

43. Croome, "The Present Outlook," 19; Smith and Moran, "WTO 101," 68.

44. Croome, "The Present Outlook," 19.

45. Jawara and Kwa, *Behind the Scenes*.

46. McGillivray, "Democratizing the World Trade Organization."

47. Croome, "The Present Outlook," 19.

48. Pedersen 2006, "The WTO Decision-Making," 125–29; Sutherland, Sewell, and Weiner, "Challenges Facing the WTO," 99.

49. Blackhurst, "The Capacity of the WTO."

CHAPTER 5

1. This was the forerunner of the EU. It existed from 1957 until 1992. We use the name EC when describing activities before 1992 and EU when describing activities after 1992.
2. Martin, "Lomé Convention." The convention received its name from Lomé, Togo, the location of the meeting where it was negotiated.
3. Sutton, "The Banana Regime," 6.
4. Rosegrant, "Banana Wars," 4.
5. Sutton, "The Banana Regime," 13.
6. Ibid., 14–16.
7. ECU means European Currency Unit. This unit was used as an accounting mechanism before the creation of the Euro.
8. Rosegrant, "Banana Wars," 4–5.
9. Ibid., 6n13.
10. World Trade Organization, "European Communities—Regime for the Importation," 32.
11. Ibid., 224.
12. van de Kasteele, *The Banana Chain*, 14.
13. Sutton, "The Banana Regime," 18.
14. Brooke, "Forbidden Fruit."
15. U.S. Mission to the European Union, "USTR on 'Brief History of Banana Dispute.'"
16. Sutton, "The Banana Regime," 20.
17. Rosegrant, "Banana Wars," 8–9.
18. U.S. Mission to the European Union, "Outlines 'Fallacies.'"
19. van de Kasteele, *The Banana Chain*, 15.
20. Bowe, "Dole in Further Profit," 26.
21. Rosegrant, "Banana Wars," 9.
22. De Lombaerde, "Chiquita Brands Poised," 27.
23. Greenwald, "Banana Republican," 54.
24. DePalma, "Citing European Banana Quotas," A1.
25. Rosegrant, "Banana Wars," 9.
26. Common Cause, "American Financial Group."
27. Greenwald, "Banana Republican," 54.
28. Rosegrant, "Banana Wars," 10.
29. Weisskopf, "The Busy Backdoor Men," 40. Charles Lindner's donations also got him a stay in the Lincoln Bedroom of the White House and an invitation to have coffee with President Bill Clinton.
30. Rosegrant, "Banana Wars," 16.
31. Ibid.
32. Godfrey, "A Future for Caribbean."
33. "Expelled from Eden," 35–39.
34. Barclay, *The Trade Dispute Between*, 9.
35. Rosegrant, "Banana Wars," 15–16.
36. Ibid., 16.
37. World Trade Organization, "European Communities—Regime for the Importation."
38. Rosegrant, "Banana Wars," 19.
39. "EU Members Attack," 8.

40. EU Commission Directorate General for Trade, "Commission Proposes to Modify."
41. Rosegrant, "Banana Wars," 21.
42. Bates, "Going Bananas."
43. U.S. Mission to the European Union, "USTR on 'Brief History of Banana Dispute.'"
44. Rosegrant, "Banana Wars," 23.
45. Wolf, "Banana Dispute with the U.S.," B7A.
46. Cooper, "Why Does U.S. Pick," A1; Rosegrant, "Banana Wars," 24.
47. "The US/EU Banana Dispute."
48. U.S. Permanent Representative to the WTO, "Summary of the U.S. Legal Position."
49. Ibid.
50. EU Commission Directorate General for Trade, "Bananas: Background Note."
51. U.S. Permanent Representative to the WTO, "Summary of the U.S. Legal Position."
52. "The Beef Over Bananas," 65.
53. "The US/EU Banana Dispute."
54. Rosegrant, "Banana Wars," 23.
55. "Barshefsky Says."
56. "U.S. Attacks EU."
57. Freedman, "The U.S. Refuses to Budge."
58. Ibid.
59. Ibid.
60. Evans, "EU Slipped Up," C13.
61. EU Commission Directorate General for Trade, "Commission Proposes to Modify."
62. "Ecuador to Ask WTO."
63. DePalma, "Dole Says Trade," B2.
64. World Trade Organization, *Annual Report 2006*, 35.

CHAPTER 6

1. Thorn and Carlson, "The Agreement on the Application," 841.
2. World Trade Organization, "Sanitary and Phytosanitary Measures: Introduction."
3. Scott, "On Kith and Kine."
4. The EC became the EU with the implementation of the Single European Act in 1992. Therefore, we use EC before 1992 and EU thereafter.
5. World Trade Organization, "EC Measures Concerning Meat and Meat Products (Hormones)—Complaint by the United States—Report of the Panel," 9–13.
6. "Fattening Cattle," 84; "Campaign for Real Veal," 51.
7. "Veal Hormones: Ban Them All?" 45; "Veal Hormones: Down on the Pharm," 77; "Beefing Around the Bush," 78–79.
8. "Veal Hormones: Down on the Pharm," 77.
9. Castro, "Why the Beef," 44.
10. These are estradiol, melengestrol acetate, progesterone, testosterone, tenbolone acetate, and zeranol. They have been used in the fattening of cattle since the 1950s.
11. World Trade Organization, "EC Measures Concerning Meat and Meat Products (Hormones)—Complaint by the United States—Report of the Panel," 9.
12. Marshall, "Europe Bans Boeuf," 161–62.
13. Castro, "Why the Beef," 44.
14. Berger et al., *Politbarometer*.
15. Hanrahan, "CRS Issue Brief for Congress."

16. World Trade Organization "EC Measures Concerning Meat and Meat Products (Hormones)—Complaint by the United States—Report of the Panel," 10.

17. "Veal Hormones: Down on the Pharm," 77; "Veal Hormones: Ban Them All," 45.

18. World Trade Organization, "EC Measures Concerning Meat and Meat Products (Hormones)—Complaint by the United States—Report of the Panel," 10.

19. Marshall, "Europe Bans Boeuf," 161–62.

20. Freudenheim, "Beef Dispute Stakes High," sec. 1-1.

21. See Office of the U.S. Trade Representative, "WTO Hormones Report"; and Agriculture and Agri-Food Canada, "News Release: Canada Will," for the primary arguments.

22. U.S. Department of Agriculture: Foreign Agricultural Service, "A Primer on Beef Hormones."

23. World Trade Organization, "EC Measures Concerning Meat and Meat Products (Hormones)—Complaint by the United States—Report of the Panel," 7–8.

24. Freudenheim, "Beef Dispute Stakes High," sec. 1-1.

25. Hanrahan, "CRS Issue Brief for Congress."

26. The United States and Canada acted in 1986 to end the ban before it had began. In 1985 the EC informed importers that no beef would be allowed into the community that had been treated with hormones as part of the fattening process.

27. Hanrahan, "CRS Issue Brief for Congress."

28. World Trade Organization "EC Measures Concerning Meat and Meat Products (Hormones)—Complaint by the United States—Report of the Panel," 5–8. The Codex Alimentarius is a set of international food safety standards administered by the Codex Alimentarius Commission. Both the Codex and the commission are part of the United Nations through its Food and Agricultural Organization.

29. As quoted in World Trade Organization, "EC Measures Concerning Meat and Meat Products (Hormones)—Complaint by the United States—Report of the Panel," 11.

30. Hanrahan, "CRS Issue Brief for Congress."

31. World Trade Organization, "EC Measures Concerning Meat and Meat Products (Hormones)—Complaint by the United States—Report of the Panel," 1–2.

32. The positions of the United States, Canada, and the EU are drawn mainly from World Trade Organization, "EC Measures Concerning Meat and Meat Products (Hormones)—Complaint by the United States—Report of the Panel"

33. As quoted in World Trade Organization, "EC Measures Concerning Meat and Meat Products (Hormones)—Complaint by the United States—Report of the Panel," 34.

34. Peterson, "Hormones, Heifers, and High Politics," 460.

35. Castro, "Why the Beef," 44.

36. Peterson, "Hormones, Heifers and High Politics," 460.

37. World Trade Organization, "EC Measures Concerning Meat and Meat Products (Hormones)—Complaint by the United States—Report of the Panel."

38. U.S. Department of Agriculture: Foreign Agricultural Service, "Chronology of the European."

39. World Trade Organization, "EC Measures Concerning Meat and Meat Products (Hormones)—AB-1997-4—Report of the Appellate Body."

40. McDonald, "Big Beef Up," 115–26; Wagner, "The WTO's Interpretation," 858–59.

41. EU Commission Health and Consumer Protection Directorate-General, "The Hormone Case."

42. EU Commission Health and Consumer Protection Directorate-General, "Euro-barometer 49."

43. EU Commission, "Eurobarometer Survey 55.1."

44. EU Commission Health and Consumer Protection Directorate-General, "The Hormone Case."

45. EU Commission, "Communication of the Commission."

46. European Commission Health and Consumer Protection Directorate-General, "Press Releases: Hormones First Commission Debate."

47. EU Commission Health and Consumer Protection Directorate-General, "The Hormone Case."

48. "U.S. Threatens Europe," C2.

49. Olson, "$253 Million Sanctions," C4.

50. EU Commission Health and Consumer Protection Directorate-General, "The Hormone Case."

51. Stout, "U.S. Raises Taxes," C4.

52. Andrews, "Europe Refuses to Drop," C4.

53. EU Commission, "White Paper on Food Safety," 3.

54. Public Citizen is a consumer, environmental, and labor interest group created by Ralph Nader. It has been a leading opponent of the WTO and a critic of globalization in general.

55. Wagner and Goldman, "Comments to the Appellate Body."

56. McDonald, "Big Beef Up," 115–26; Wagner, "WTO's Interpretation," 855–59.

57. Andrews, "In Victory for U.S.," A1; Public Citizen, "On the Trienniel Review."

58. U.S. Mission to the European Union, "Barshefsky Teleconference."

59. U.S. Mission to the European Union, "USTR Scher on WTO."

CHAPTER 7

1. Dreyer, *China's Political System*, 113.

2. Ibid., 145.

3. Ibid., 145–52.

4. Huang, "Sino-U.S. Relations," 159.

5. Pearson, "China's Integration in the International," 162.

6. Ibid.

7. Steinfeld, "Beyond the Transition," 272.

8. Keidel, "China's Economic System," 45–59.

9. Corbet, "Issues in the Accession of China," 14–34. See also "Balancing Act: A Survey of China," 3–20.

10. Hu and Khan, "Why is China Growing So Fast," 6.

11. Pearson, "China's Integration," 169–74.

12. Yong, "China's Stakes," 22.

13. Economy and Oksenberg, "Introduction: China Joins the World," 20.

14. Bottelier, "The Impact of WTO Membership," 1.

15. Lardy, "Statement at Hearing."

16. Economy and Oksenberg, "Introduction: China Joins the World," 28.

17. Bottelier, "Impact of WTO Membership," 3.

18. See Gruber, *Ruling the World*, ch. 3.

19. See World Trade Organization, "Accession to the World Trade Organization," for a complete summary of the process.
20. Magarinos, Long, and Sercovich, *China in the WTO.*
21. World Trade Organization Training Institute, *Training Manual,*" 23.3.
22. Ibid.
23. Panitchpakdi and Clifford, *China and the WTO*, 69–80; World Trade Organization—Secretariat, "Technical Note on the Accession."
24. Office of the U.S. Trade Representative, "USTR Releases 2001 Inventory."
25. World Trade Organization, "Fifteenth Session of the Working Party."
26. Groombridge and Barfield, *Tiger by the Tail.*
27. Groombridge and Barfield, *Tiger by the Tail*, 21; Barton, et al., *The Evolution of the Trade Regime*, 156–60.
28. Barshefsky, "Trade Policy and the Rule."
29. Biddulph, "Enhancing China's Rule of Law," 200.
30. "China Preparing for Entry into WTO: Minister."
31. MacLeod, "China-WTO Will Bind."
32. Zhongquo, "China in the World Press."
33. Morici, "Barring Entry?" 275–76.
34. Yong, "China's Stakes," 26–30.
35. Steinfeld, "Beyond the Transition," 272.
36. Barshefsky, "Trade Policy and the Rule." See also Hufbauer and Rosen, "American Access to China's Market," for a summary of the agreement.
37. See Devereau, Lawrence, and Watkins, *Case Studies in U.S. Trade Negotiations*, ch. 6 for a good discussion of the politics surrounding PNTR.
38. See, for example, Barshefsky, "Trade Policy and the Rule"; and Barshefsky, "China's WTO Accession."
39. Hufbauer and Rosen, "American Access to China's Market," 1–2.
40. Telecommunications Industry Association, "China PTNR and WTO Accession."
41. "China's Entry into WTO Good."
42. "China: WTO Entry: Remedy," 4.
43. Southwick, "Addressing Market Access," 923–76.
44. Ministry of Foreign Affairs of Japan, "Position of the Government."
45. "Mexico Set to Restart China WTO Talks"; Peters, "Eastern Threat," 31.
46. Jintao, "Why China Loves Globalization"; Lynch, "Force of China's Impact Grows in USA," 1B.

Chapter 8

1. Falautano and Guerrieri, "New Trade Issues," 77–78.
2. Hillyard and Edmonds, "Millennium Trade Talks," 32.
3. Blackhurst, "Reforming WTO Decision Making," 295.
4. Raghavan, "After Seattle," 499.
5. Grady and MaccMillan, *Seattle and Beyond*, 8.
6. Odell, "The Seattle Impasse," 9.
7. Ibid., 14.
8. Hillyard and Edmonds, "Millennium Trade Talks." 8.
9. Ibid.
10. Raghavan, "After Seattle," 498.

11. Odell, "The Seattle Impasse," 18.
12. This is found in the preface of Schott, *The WTO After Seattle*, ix.
13. Barker and Mander, *Invisible Government*.
14. Wallach and Sforza, *Whose Trade Organization?*
15. Public Citizen, "Talking Points on WTO."
16. Dunning, "The Future of the WTO," 476.
17. Grady and MaccMillan, *Seattle and Beyond*, 14–15.
18. Hillyard and Edmonds, "Millennium Trade Talks," 12–19.
19. Finger and Schuler, "Developing Countries and the Millennium Round," 59.
20. Raghavan, "After Seattle," 500.
21. Quoted in Hillyard and Edmonds, "Millennium Trade Talks," 8.
22. Raghavan, "After Seattle," 501.
23. Paulson, "Clinton Says He Will," A1.
24. Buckley, "Collapse of Seattle Talks," 16.
25. Schott, "The WTO After Seattle," 6.
26. Odell, "The Seattle Impasse," 22.
27. Raghavan, "After Seattle," 502.
28. U.S. House of Representatives Subcommittee on Trade of the Committee on Ways and Means, "Report on World Trade Organization," 1.
29. World Trade Organization, "It is Vital to Maintain."
30. Preeg, "Reactions to Seattle: The South Rises in Seattle," 184.
31. Horlick, "Reactions to Seattle: The Speed Bump at Seattle," 167.
32. Schott, "The WTO After Seattle," 3–40.
33. Tyson, "What Really Sabotaged," 26.
34. "The Case Against the WTO," 8–11.
35. Sutherland, "Reality Check," 20.
36. EU Commission, "Report to the European Parliament," 4.
37. "Democracy Bites the WTO," 3.
38. Whitelaw, Yang and Perry, "Men in Black," 22.
39. Allen and Yang, "Trade's Battle Hits Seattle," 20–23.
40. Beck and Danaher, "Top Ten Reasons to Oppose," 102.
41. Mazur, "Labor's New Internationalism," 90–92.
42. For several examples, see James, "Conclusion: Ten Ways"; and Global Exchange, "Top 10 Reasons."
43. Robertson, "Civil Society and the WTO," 1126.
44. Dunning, "The Future of the WTO," 475.
45. Sampson, "The World Trade Organization After Seattle," 1102.
46. EU Commission, "Report to the European Parliament," 6.
47. "Clueless in Seattle," 17.
48. Erb-Leoncavallo, "The Road from Seattle," 31.
49. Robertson, "Civil Society and the WTO," 1131.
50. Danaher and Burbach, "Introduction: Making History," 9.

CHAPTER 9

1. Moore, *A World without Walls*, 97.
2. Ibid., 114.
3. Ibid., 129.

4. Blair, "G-8 Summit Statement," 2.
5. Tetteh, "Draft Declaration by WTO Chairman."
6. Timms, "Double Dealing in Doha," 68.
7. Norton, "'Doha Round' of Trade Agreements," 1340.
8. World Trade Organization, "Doha WTO."
9. Coates, "Analysis of the Final Ministerial Declaration."
10. Timms, "Double Dealing in Doha," 68.
11. World Trade Organization, "The Doha Development Agenda."
12. Norton, "'Doha Round' of Trade Agreements," 1340.
13. Ibid.
14. Zedillo, "To Be or Not to Be at Cancun," 45.
15. "The WTO Under Fire,"27.
16. Becker, "African Nations Press," A5.
17. Bhagwati, "The Poor's Best Hope," 24–26.
18. "The Cancun Failure," A24.
19. "The WTO Under Fire," 27.
20. World Trade Organization, "Summary of 14 September 2003." For a brief narrative on the negotiations and collapse of talks, see Khor, "The Collapse at Cancun," 25–29.
21. World Trade Organization, "Summary of 14 September 2003."
22. Lamy, "Result of the WTO Ministerial Conference," 2–4.
23. U.S. Department of Agriculture, "U.S. Secretary of Agriculture."
24. Becker, "Poorer Countries Pull Out," A1.
25. Denny, Elliot, and Munk, "Trade Summit," 15.
26. U.S. Department of Agriculture, "U.S. Secretary of Agriculture."
27. "Cancun's Charming Outcome," 11–12.

CHAPTER 10

1. For discussions of NGOs and the WTO, see Broad, *Global Backlash*; and Florini, *The Third Force*.
2. Falautano and Guerrieri, "New Trade Issues," 73.
3. Hillyard and Edmonds, "Millennium Trade Talks," 15.
4. Grady and MaccMillan, *Seattle and Beyond*, 9.
5. Falautano and Guerrieri, "New Trade Issues," 75.
6. Ibid., 77.
7. Moran, "Investment Issues," 223–24.
8. Wallach and Sforza, *Whose Trade Organization*.
9. Esty, "Environment and the Trading System," 251.
10. Wilson, "The World Trade Organization."
11. Esty, "Environment and the Trading System," 250.
12. Schott, "The WTO after Seattle," 28.
13. Elliot, "Getting Beyond No . . . !" 194.
14. Falautano and Guerrieri, "New Trade Issues," 81.
15. Hillyard and Edmonds, "Millennium Trade Talks," 11.
16. Schott, "The WTO after Seattle," 24.
17. Barton, *The Evolution of the Trade Regime*, 113–18.
18. Schott, "The WTO after Seattle," 38.

Appendix 3.1

1. World Trade Organization, "Legal Texts: The WTO Agreements."
2. Preeg, *Traders in a Brave New World*, 190–201; World Trade Organization, "Legal Texts: The WTO Agreements."

Bibliography

Agriculture and Agri-Food Canada. "News Release: Canada Will Request WTO Authority to Retaliate Against the EU." May 14, 1999. http://w01.international.gc.ca/
MinPub/Publication.aspx?isRedirect=True&publication_id=375005&Language=E&
docnumber=112 (accessed June 20, 2007).

Allen, Jodie T., and Dori Jones Yang. "Trade's Battle Hits Seattle." *U.S. News and World
Report*, December 13, 1999, pp. 20–23.

Anderson, Kym. "Peculiarities of Retaliation in WTO Dispute Settlement." *World Trade
Review* 1.2 (2002): 123–34.

Andrews, Edmund L. "Europe Refuses to Drop Ban on Hormone-Fed U.S. Beef." *New
York Times*, May 25, 2000, sec. C.

———. "In Victory for the U.S., Europe Ban on Treated Beef Ruled Illegal." *New York
Times*, May 9, 1997, sec. A.

"Balancing Act: A Survey of China." *Economist*, March 25, 2006, pp. 3–20.

Baldwin, Robert E. "The Tokyo Round of Multilateral Trade Negotiations." In *International Trade and Finance: Readings*. Edited by Robert E. Baldwin and David J. Richard-
son. 2nd ed., 231–61. Boston: Little Brown, 1981.

"Banana Wars: A Trade Fight Over Fruit Threatens to Spread to Other Food Groups."
Time, February 8, 1999, p. 42.

Barclay, Christopher. *The Trade Dispute Between the EU and USA Over Bananas*. House of
Commons Library Research Paper 99/2–028. March 12, 1999. House of Commons
Library, London.

Barker, Debi, and Jerry Mander. *Invisible Government. The World Trade Organization:
Global Government for the New Millennium*? San Francisco: International Forum on
Globalization, 1999.

Barshefsky, Charlene. "China's WTO Accession in American Pacific Strategy." Speech at
Asia Society, New York, February 29, 2000. http://www.asiasociety.org/speeches/
barshefsky.html (accessed March 6, 2007).

———. "Trade Policy and the Rule of Law: The Case of China's WTO Accession."
Speech at American University School of Law, Washington DC, April 3, 2000. http://
canberra.usembassy.gov/hyper/2000/0403/epf103.htm (accessed March 6, 2007).

"Barshefsky Says Europe 'Shut Down' WTO to Block Banana Sanctions." *Agence Presse
France International*, January 25, 1999. http://0-web.lexisnexis.com.csulib.ctstateu
.edu (accessed June 12, 2007).

Barton, John H., Judith L. Goldstein, Timothy E. Josling, and Richard H. Steinberg. *The
Evolution of the Trade Regime: Politics, Law, and Economics of the GATT and the WTO*.
Princeton, NJ: Princeton University Press, 2006.

Bates, Jenny. "Going Bananas: The United States, The European Union and a Slippery
Slope in the World Trade System." *Progressive Policy Institute Backgrounder*. January 1,
1999. http://www.ppionline.org/ppi_ci.cfm?knlgAreaID=108&subsecID=128&con
tentID=747 (accessed March 6, 2007).

Beck, Juliet, and Kevin Danaher. "Top Ten Reasons to Oppose the World Trade Organization." In *Globalize This! The Battle Against the World Trade Organization and Corporate Rule*, edited by Kevin Danaher and Roger Burbach, 98–102. Monroe, ME: Common Courage, 2000.

Becker, Elizabeth. "African Nations Press for an End to Cotton Subsidies in the West." *New York Times*, September 12, 2003, sec. A.

———. "Poorer Countries Pull Out of Talks Over World Trade." *New York Times*, September 15, 2003, sec. A.

"Beefing Around the Bush." *Economist*, December 24, 1988, pp. 78–79.

"The Beef Over Bananas." *Economist*, March 6, 1999, p. 65.

Benenson, Bob. "Free Trade Carries the Day As GATT Passes Easily." *Congressional Quarterly Weekly Report*, December 3, 1994, pp. 3446–50.

———. "GATT Pact Lurches Off Course As Hollings Hits the Brake." *Congressional Quarterly Weekly Report*, October 1, 1994, pp. 2761–64.

———. "GATT's Disappearing Act." *Congressional Quarterly Weekly Report*, November 5, 1994, pp. 3144.

Berger, M, W. G. Gibowski, D. Roth, and W. Schulte. *Politbarometer*. Mannheim, Germany: Forschungsgruppe Wahlen, 1998. http://www.gesis.org/en/data%5Fservice/politbarometer/data/studienprofile.htm (accessed March 6, 2007).

Bhagwati, Jagdish. "The Poor's Best Hope." *Economist*, June 22, 2002, pp. 24–26.

Biddulph, Sarah. "Enhancing China's Rule of Law." In *China's Accession to the World Trade Organization*, edited by Heike Holbig and Robert Ash, 193–226. New York: Routledge Curzon, 2002.

Blackhurst, Richard. "The Capacity of the WTO to Fulfill Its Mandate." In *The WTO as an International Organization*, edited by Anne O. Krueger, 31–58. Chicago: University of Chicago Press, 1998.

———. "Reforming WTO Decision Making: Lessons from Singapore and Seattle." In *World Trade Organization Millennium Round: Freer Trade in the Twenty-First Century*, edited by Klaus Günter Deutsch and Bernhard Speyer, 295–310. New York: Routledge, 2001.

Blair, Tony. "G-8 Summit Statement." *Presidents and Prime Ministers* 11.5 (2002): 2–3.

Bomberg, Elizabeth, and Alexander Stubb. *The European Union: How Does it Work*? New York: Oxford University Press, 2003.

Bottelier, Pieter. "*The Impact of WTO Membership on China's Domestic Economy.*" Speech at Johns Hopkins School of Advanced International Studies, China Forum, Washington DC, November 14, 2000.

Bowe, Christopher. "Dole In Further Profit Warnings." *Financial Times*, December 20, 1999.

Broad, Robin. *Global Backlash: Citizen Initiatives for a Just World*. Lanham, MD: Rowman and Littlefield, 2002.

Brooke, James. "A Forbidden Fruit in Europe: Latin Bananas Face Hurdles." *New York Times*, April 5, 1993, sec. A.

Buckley, Neil. "Collapse of Seattle talks blamed on U.S. WTO Fall-Out EU Cites Looming U.S. Presidential Elections." *Financial Times*, December 7, 1999.

Burtless, Gary, Robert Z. Lawrence, Robert E. Litan, and Robert J. Shapiro. *Globaphobia: Confronting Fears about Open Trade*. Washington DC: Brookings Institution, 1998.

Busch, Marc L., and Eric Reinhardt. "Bargaining in the Shadow of the Law: Early Settlement in GATT/WTO Disputes." *Fordham International Law Journal* 24 (2000): 158–72.

"Campaign for Real Veal." *Economist*, October 18, 1980, p. 51.

"Cancun's Charming Outcome." *Economist*, September 20, 2003, pp. 11–12.

"The Cancun Failure." *New York Times*, September 16, 2003, sec. A.

"The Case Against the WTO." *Progressive*, January 2000, pp. 8–11.

Castro, Janice. "Why the Beef Over Hormones?" *Time*, January 16, 1989, p. 44.

"China Preparing for Entry into WTO: Minister." *Xinhua News Agency*, March 6, 2001. http://0-web.lexis-nexis.com.csulib.ctstateu.edu (accessed June 12, 2007).

"China: WTO Entry: Remedy for Sino-Japanese Trade Sag." *China Daily*, October 22, 1999. http://0-web.lexis-nexis.com.csulib.ctstateu.edu (accessed June 12, 2007).

"China's Entry Into WTO Good for China, EU and WTO: EU Official." *Xinhua News Agency*, February 19, 2001. http://0-web.lexis-nexis.com.csulib.ctstateu.edu (accessed June 12, 2007).

Cline, William, Noboru Kawanabe, T. O. M. Krosjo, and Thomas Williams. *Trade Negotiations in the Tokyo Round: A Quantitative Assessment*. Washington DC: Brookings Institution, 1978.

Cloud, David S., and Heather M. Fleming. "Health Care's Painful Demise Cast Pall on Clinton Agenda." *Congressional Quarterly Weekly Report*, November 5, 1994, pp. 3142–45.

———. "Senate Panel Narrowly Oks GATT Financing Package." *Congressional Quarterly Weekly Report*, July 30, 1994, pp. 2118–19.

"Clueless in Seattle." *Economist*, December 4, 1999, p. 17.

Coates, Barry. "Analysis of the Final Ministerial Declaration of the 4th Ministerial Conference of the WTO in Doha." *Global Policy Forum*, New York, November 14, 2001. http://www.globalpolicy.org/socecon/bwi-wto/wto/2001/1114wdm.htm (accessed March 6, 2007).

Common Cause, "American Financial Group 1995–1999." *Common Cause: Soft Money Laundromat*, Washington DC, 1998.

Conklin, John G. "From GATT to the World Trade Organization: Prospects for a Rule-Integrity Regime." In *International Political Economy: State-Market Relations in the Changing World Order*. Edited by C. Roe Goddard, John T. Passe-Smith, and John G. Conklin, 381–98. 1st ed. Boulder, CO: Lynne Rienner, 1995.

Cooper, Helene. "Why Does U.S. Pick on Pecorino in Flap with EU on Bananas?" *Wall Street Journal*, March 1, 1999, sec. A.

Corbet, Hugh. "Issues in the Accession of China to the WTO System." *Journal of Northeast Asian Studies* 15.3 (1996): 14–34.

Cox, James. "WTO Turns Up Heat on U.S. Trade Fight." *USA Today*, September 1, 2004, sec. B.

Croome, John. "The Present Outlook for Trade Negotiations in the World Trade Organization." Policy Research Working Paper. October 1998. World Bank, Washington DC. http://www-wds.worldbank.org/external/default/WDSContentServer/IW3P/IB/1998/11/17/000178830_98111703524520/Rendered/PDF/multi0page.pdf (accessed March 6, 2007).

———. *Reshaping the World Trading System: A History of the Uruguay Round*. Geneva: World Trade Organization, 1994.

Culbert, Jay. "War-Time Anglo-American Talks and the Making of GATT." *World Economy* 10.4 (1987): 381–407.

Danaher, Kevin, and Roger Burbach. *Globalize This! The Battle Against the World Trade Organization and Corporate Rule*. Monroe, ME: Common Courage, 2000.

———. "Introduction: Making History." In *Globalize This! The Battle Against the World Trade Organization and Corporate Rule*, edited by Kevin Danaher and Roger Burbach, 7–11. Monroe, ME: Common Courage, 2000.

Davies, Arwel. "Reviewing Dispute Settlement at the World Trade Organization: A Time to Reconsider the Roles of Compensation?" *World Trade Review* 5.1 (2006): 31–67.

De Lombaerde, Geert. "Chiquita Brands Poised to Turn Around Fortunes: EU Ruling Should Open Up Europe." *Business Courier Serving Cincinnati–Northern Kentucky*, August 8, 1997.

"Democracy Bites the WTO." *Nation*, December 27, 1999, p. 3.

Denny, Charlotte, Larry Elliot, and David Munk. "Trade Summit: Europe Urges Shakeup of 'Medieval' WTO." *Guardian*, September 16, 2003.

DePalma, Anthony. "Citing European Banana Quotas, Chiquita Says Bankruptcy Looms." *New York Times*, January 17, 2001, sec. A.

———. "Dole Says Trade Accord on Bananas Favors Rival." *New York Times*, April 14, 2001, sec. B.

Derber, Charles. *People Before Profit: The New Globalization in an Age of Terror, Big Money and Economic Crisis*. New York: Picador, 2003.

Devereau, Charan, Robert Z. Lawrence, and Michael D. Watkins. *Case Studies in U.S. Trade Negotiations*. Vol. 1. New York: Peter G. Peterson Institute for International Economics, 2006.

Dreyer, June Teufel. *China's Political System: Modernization and Tradition*. 3rd ed. New York: Longman, 2000.

Dunkley, Graham. *The Free Trade Adventure: The Uruguay Round and Globalism—A Critique*. Victoria, Australia: Melbourne University Press, 1997.

Dunning, John H. "The Future of the WTO: A Socio-Relational Challenge?" *Review of International Political Economy* 7.3 (2000): 475–83.

Eckes, Alfred E. *Opening America's Markets: U.S. Foreign Trade Policy Since 1776*. Chapel Hill: University of North Carolina Press, 1999.

Economy, Elizabeth, and Michel Oksenberg. "Introduction: China Joins the World." In *China Joins the World: Progress and Prospects*, edited by Elizabeth Economy and Michel Oksenberg, 1–41. New York: Council on Foreign Relations, 1999.

"Ecuador to Ask WTO for Sanctions Against European Union." *Agencia EFE*, November 10, 1999.

Elliot, Kimberly. "Getting Beyond No . . . ! Promoting Worker Rights and Trade." In *The WTO After Seattle*, edited by Jeffrey J. Schott, 187–204. Washington DC: Institute for International Economics, 2000.

Erb Leoncavallo, Ann Marie. "The Road From Seattle." *UN Chronicle* 37.1 (2000): 28–32.

Esty, Daniel C. "Environment and the Trading System: Picking Up the Post-Seattle Pieces." In *The WTO After Seattle*, edited by Jeffrey J. Schott, 243–52. Washington DC: Institute for International Economics, 2000.

"EU Members Attack Commission Banana Proposal to Settle WTO Fight." *Inside U.S. Trade*, February 13, 1998, p. 8.

EU Commission. "Communication of the Commission to the Council and Parliament: WTO Decision Regarding the EC Hormones Ban." COM (99) 81 final, Brussels, February 10, 1999. http://aei.pitt.edu/4972/01/003120_1.pdf (accessed June 20, 2007).

———. "Eurobarometer Survey 55.1." EB55.1. *European Commission Public Opinion Analysis Homepage*, May 2001. http://ec.europa.eu/public_opinion/cf/nationoutput_en.cfm (accessed February 7, 2007).

———. "Proposal For a Directive of the European Parliament and of the Council Amending Council Directive 96/22/EC Concerning the prohibition on the use in stockfarming of certain substances having a hormonal or thyrostatic action and of beta-agonists." COM (2000) 320 final—2000/0132 (COD). *Official Journal of the European Communities*, May 24, 2000. http://eurlex.europa.eu/LexUriServ/site/en/oj/2000/ce337/ce33720001128en01630166.pdf (accessed March 6, 2007).

———. "Report to the European Parliament on European Community Activities in the WTO 1999." Brussels: EU Commission, January 2000. http://trade.ec.europa.eu/doclib/docs/2003/september/tradoc_112418.pdf (accessed March 1, 2007).

———. "White Paper on Food Safety." Com (1999) 719 final, January 12, 2000. http://europa.eu.int/comm/dgs/health_consumer/library/pub/pub06_en.pdf (accessed February 15, 2007).

EU Commission Directorate General for Trade. "Bananas: Background Note." Brussels, November 10, 1999.

———. "Commission Proposes to Modify the EU's Banana Regime." IP/99/828, Brussels, November 10, 1999. http://trade.ec.europa.eu/doclib/docs/2003/december/tradoc_114954.pdf (accessed June 20, 2007).

EU Commission Health and Consumer Protection Directorate-General. "Eurobarometer 49-Food Safety." September 3, 1998. European Coordination Office, Brussels. http://ec.europa.eu/dgs/health_consumer/library/surveys/eb49_en.html (accessed February 14, 2007).

———. "Press Releases: Hormones First Commission Debate." Health and Consumer Protection Directorate General Library, Press Releases, May 17, 1999. http://ec.europa.eu/dgs/health_consumer/library/press/press23_en.html (accessed February 15, 2007).

———. "The Hormone Case Background and History: WTO Dispute Settlement and Appellate Body Findings." European Commission, Brussels. May 24, 2000. http://trade.ec.europa.eu/doclib/docs/2003/november/tradoc_114718.pdf (accessed June 20, 2007).

Evans, John T. *From Trade Surplus to Deficit: The Impact of the Kennedy Tariff Round*. New York: Taylor and Francis, 1995.

Evans, Robert. "E.U. slipped up on banana trade rules: WTO: U.S. can impose sanctions: EU may appeal ruling it broke global trading rules." *Financial Post*, April 8, 1999. http://0-web.lexis-nexis.com.csulib.ctstateu.edu (accessed June 18, 2007).

"Expelled From Eden." *Economist*, December 20, 1997, pp. 35–39.

Falautano, Isabella, and Paolo Guerrieri. "New Trade Issues, Developing Countries and the Future of the WTO." *International Spectator* 35.2 (2000): 71–86.

"Fattening Cattle: Locked Horns." *Economist*, February 25, 1984, p. 84.

Finger, J. Michael, and Philip Schuler. "Developing Countries and the Millennium Round." In *The World Trade Organization Millennium Round: Freer Trade in the Twenty-First Century*, edited by Klaus Günter Deutsch and Bernhard Speyer, 58–71. New York: Routledge, 2001.

Florini, Ann. *The Third Force: The Rise of Transnational Civil Society*. Washington DC: Carnegie Endowment for International Peace, 2000.

Francks, Penelope. "Agriculture and the State in Industrial East Asia: The Rise and Fall of the Food Control System in Japan." *Japan Forum* 10.1 (1998): 1–16.

Freedman, Tani. "U.S. Refuses to Budge on Bananas Amid Strong Criticism at WTO Meeting." *Agence Presse France International*, March 8, 1999. http://0-web.lexis-nexis.com.csulib.ctstateu.edu (accessed June 12, 2007).

———. "U.S. Sanctions Against EU Averted in Short-Term in Banana Row." *Agence Presse France International*, January 29, 1999. http://0-web.lexis-nexis.com.csulib.ctstateu.edu (accessed June 12, 2007).

Freudenheim, Milton. "Beef Dispute Stakes High in Trade War." *New York Times*, January 1, 1989, sec. 1.

Fulton, Richard. "The World Trade Organization: A Bibliographic Guide." *Choice*, March 2007.

Gilpin, Robert. *The Political Economy of International Relations*. Princeton, NJ: Princeton University Press, 1987.

Global Exchange. "Top Reasons to Oppose the World Trade Organization." October 7, 2006. http://www.globalexchange.org/campaigns/wto/OpposeWTO.html (accessed March 3, 2007).

Godfrey, Claire. "A Future for Caribbean Bananas: The Importance of Europe's Banana Market for the Caribbean." Oxfam Trade Papers and Reports, London, March 1998. http://www.oxfam.org.uk/what_we_do/issues/trade/wto_bananas.htm (accessed March 6, 2007).

Golt, Sidney. *GATT Negotiations 1973–1979: The Closing State*. London: British-North American Committee, 1978.

———. *Trade Issues in the Mid-1980's*. London: British-North American Committee, 1982.

Grady, Patrick, and Kathleen MaccMillan. *Seattle and Beyond: The WTO Millennium Round*. Ottawa: Global Economics, 1999.

Greenwald, John. "Banana Republican: Ever wonder what businessmen get for campaign contributions? Take a look at Carl Lindner." *Time*, January 22, 1996, p. 54.

Greider, William. *Secrets of the Temple*. New York: Simon and Schuster, 1987.

Groombridge, Mark A., and Claude E. Barfield. *Tiger by the Tail: China and the World Trade Organization*. Washington DC: AEI, 1999.

Gruber, Lloyd. *Ruling the World: Power Politics and the Rise of Supranational Institutions*. Princeton, NJ: Princeton University Press, 2000.

Hanrahan, Charles E. "CRS Issue Brief for Congress: The European Union's Ban on Hormone Treated Beef." CRS Report RS20142. Washington DC: Congressional Research Service, December 19, 2000. http://ncseonline.org/NLE/CRSreports/Agriculture/ag-63.cfm (accessed March 6, 2007)

High, Jack, and George C. Lodge. "The World Trade Organization: Toward Freer Trade or World Bureaucracy?" *Harvard Business School Case 795-149*, August 16, 1995.

Hillman, Jimmye S. "The U.S. Perspective." In *Agriculture in the Uruguay Round*, edited by K. A. Ingersent, A. J. Rayner, and R. C. Hine, 265. New York: St. Martin's, 1994.

Hillyard, Mick, and Tim Edmonds. "Millennium Trade Talks and the 'Battle in Seattle.'" House of Commons Library Research Paper 99–107. December 15, 1999. House of Commons Library, London. http://www.parliament.uk/commons/lib/research/rp99/rp99-107.pdf (accessed June 21, 2007).

Hoekman, Bernard M., and Michel M. Kostecki. *The Political Economy of the World Trading System.* Oxford: Oxford University Press, 1995.

Hoekman, Bernard M., Aaditya Matoo, and Philip English, ed. *Development, Trade and the WTO: A Handbook.* Washington DC: World Bank, 2002.

Horlick, Gary. "Reactions to Seattle: The Speedbump at Seattle." *Journal of International Economic Law* 3.1 (2000): 167–72.

Hu, Zuliu, and Mohsin S. Khan. "Why is China Growing So Fast?" *Economic Issues* 8 (April 1997). Washington DC: International Monetary Fund. http://www.imf.org/external/pubs/ft/issues8/issue8.pdf (accessed February 10, 2007).

Huang, Yasheng. "Sino-U.S. Relations: The Economic Dimensions." In *In the Eyes of the Dragon: China Views the World,* edited by Yong Wang, Fei-Ling Garver, and John W. Deng, 159–82. New York: Rowman and Littlefield, 1999.

Hufbauer, Gary Clyde, and Daniel H. Rosen. "American Access to China's Market: The Congressional Vote on PTNR." *International Economics Policy Brief,* n. 00-3, The Peter G. Peterson Institute for International Economics, April 2000. http://www.petersoninstitute.org/publications/pb/pb00-3.pdf (accessed June 18, 2007).

Ingersent, K. A., R. C. Hine, and A. J. Rayner. "The E.C. Perspective." In *Agriculture in the Uruguay Round,* edited by K. A. Ingersent, A. J. Rayner, and R. C. Hine, 55–87. New York: St. Martin's, 1994.

Ingersent, K. A, A. J. Rayner, and R. C. Hine. *Agriculture in the Uruguay Round.* New York: St. Martin's, 1994.

International Monetary Fund. *World Economic Outlook.* Washington DC: International Monetary Fund, 1987.

Jackson, John H. *Restructuring the GATT System.* Chatham House Papers. New York: Continuum International, 1990.

———. *The World Trade Organization: Constitution and Jurisprudence.* Chatham House Papers. London: Pinter, 1998.

James, Deborah. "Conclusion: Ten Ways to Democratize the Global Economy." In *Globalize This! The Battle Against the World Trade Organization and Corporate Rule,* edited by Kevin Danaher and Roger Burbach, 203–8. Monroe, ME: Common Courage, 2000.

James, Harold. *The End of Globalization: Lessons from the Great Depression.* Cambridge, MA: Harvard University Press, 2001.

Jawara, Fatoumata, and Aileen Kwa. *Behind the Scenes at the WTO: The Real World of International Trade Negotiations/Lessons from Cancun.* Updated ed. London: Zed Books, 2004.

Jintao, Hu. "Why China Loves Globalization." *Globalist,* June 7, 2005. http://www.theglobalist.com/DBWeb/StoryId.aspx?StoryId=4606 (accessed March 6, 2007).

Kaplan, Edward S. *American Trade Policy, 1923–1995.* Westport, CT: Greenwood, 1996.

Keidel, Albert. "China's Economic System and Its Accession to the WTO." *Journal of Northeast Asian Studies* 15.3 (1996): 45–59.

Keohane, Robert O. *After Hegemony: Cooperation and Discord in the World Political Economy.* Princeton, NJ: Princeton University Press, 1984.

Khor, Martin. "The Collapse at Cancun: A Frontline Report on the Failed WTO Negotiations." *Multinational Monitor,* October 2003, pp. 25–29.

Knox, Andrea. "The World Trade Organization at a Crossroads." *World Trade* 12.10 (1999): 34–42.

Lamy, Pascal. "Result of the WTO Ministerial Conference in Cancún." Speech to the European Parliament, Strasbourg, September 24, 2003. http://europa.eu/rapid/press-ReleasesAction.do?reference=SPEECH/03/429&format=PDF&aged=1&language=EN&guiLanguage=en (accessed March 6, 2007).

Lardy, Nicholas. "Statement at Hearing on China's Accession to the World Trade Organization." U.S. Senate Committee on Finance. 106th Cong., 2nd sess., April 23, 2000.

Lash, William H., III. "The Limited but Important Role of the WTO." *CATO Journal* 19.3 (2000): 371–77.

Lovett, William A., Alfred E. Eckes, and Richard L. Brinkman. *U.S. Trade Policy: History, Theory and the WTO.* Armonk, NY: M. E. Sharp, 2004.

Low, Patrick. *Trading Free: The GATT and U.S. Trade Policy.* New York: Twentieth Century Fund, 1993.

Lynch, David J. "Force of China's Impact Grows in USA." *USA Today*, December 12, 2006, sec. B.

MacDonald, Jan. "Big Beef Up or Consumer Health Threat: The WTO Food Safety Agreement, Bovine Growth Hormone and the Precautionary Principle." *Environmental and Planning Law Journal* 15.2 (1998): 115–26.

MacLeod, Calum. "China-WTO will bind China to rule of law, says MOFTEC's Shi." *China Online*, March 13, 2001. http://0-web.lexis-nexis.com.csulib.ctstateu.edu (accessed June 12, 2007).

Magarinos, Carlos A., Yongtu Long, and Francisco Colman Sercovich. *China in the WTO: The Birth of a New Catching Up Strategy.* New York: Palgrave Macmillan, 2003

Maggs, John. "Last-Minute Deals Snare Senate Trade Pact Votes." *Journal of Commerce and Commercial*, December 2, 1994, sec. A.

Marshall, Eliot. "Europe Bans Boeuf a L'Estradiol." *Science* 243.4888 (1989): 161–62.

Martin, Guy. "Lome Convention." In *The Oxford Companion to Politics of the World*, edited by Joel Krieger, 548–50. New York: Oxford University Press, 1993.

Mazur, Jay. "Labor's New Internationalism." *Foreign Affairs* 79.1 (2000): 79–93.

McGillivray, Fiona. "Democratizing the World Trade Organization." *Hoover Institute Essays in Public Policy*, October 4, 2000. http://media.hoover.org/documents/epp_105b.pdf (accessed June 19, 2007).

"Mexico Set to Restart China WTO Talks." *Internet Securities*, June 26, 2001. http://0-galenet.galegroup.com.csulib.ctstateu.edu (accessed June 12, 2007).

Michalopolos, Constantine. "The Participation of the Developing Countries in the WTO." Policy Research Working Paper, World Bank and World Trade Organization, March 1998. http://www-wds.worldbank.org/external/default/WDSContentServer/IW3P/IB/1998/03/01/000009265_3980429111520/Rendered/PDF/multi0page.pdf (accessed June 19, 2007).

Milner, Helen. *Interests, Institutions and Information.* Princeton, NJ: Princeton University Press, 1997.

Ministry of Foreign Affairs of Japan. "Position of the Government of Japan on the Accession of the People's Republic of China to the World Trade Organization." Press Conference by the Press Secretary, July 6, 1999. http://www.mofa.go.jp/announce/press/1999/7/706.html#5 (accessed February 23, 2007).

Moore, Mike. *A World without Walls: Freedom, Development, Free Trade and Global Governance.* Cambridge: Cambridge University Press, 2003.

Moran, Theodore H. "Investment Issues." In *The WTO After Seattle*, edited by Jeffrey J. Schott, 223–42. Washington DC: Institute for International Economics, 2000.

Morici, Peter. "Barring Entry? China and the WTO." *Current History* 96.611 (1997): 274–78.

Moyer, H. Wayne. "The European Community and the GATT Uruguay Round: Preserving the Common Agricultural Policy at All Costs." In *World Agriculture and the GATT*, edited by William P. Avery, 95–119. Boulder, CO: Lynne Rienner, 1992.

Narlikar, Amrita. *International Trade and Developing Countries: Bargaining Coalitions in the GATT and WTO*. New York: Routledge, 2003.

Narlikar, Amrita, and Rorden Wilkinson. "Collapse at the WTO: A Cancun Post-Mortem." *Third World Quarterly* 25.3 (2004): 447–60.

Norton, Stephen J. "'Doha Round' of Trade Agreements Imperiled by Battle Over Subsidies." *Congressional Quarterly Weekly*, May 31, 2003, p. 1340.

Odell, John S. *Negotiating the World Economy*. Ithaca, NY: Cornell University Press, 2000.

———. "*The Seattle Impasse and Its Implications for the World Trade Organization.*" Paper presented at 42nd Annual International Studies Association Meeting, Chicago, February 21–24, 2001.

Office of the United States Trade Representative. "USTR Releases 2001 Inventory of Trade Barriers." USTR Press Releases, March 30, 2001. http://www.ustr.gov/Document_Library/Press_Releases/2001/March/USTR_Releases_2001_Inventory_of_Trade_Barriers.html? (accesed June 22, 2007).

———. "WTO Hormones Report Confirms U.S. Win." USTR Press Releases, August 18, 1997.

Olson, Elizabeth. "$253 Million Sanctions Sought in Beef Fight with Europe." *New York Times*, June 4, 1999, sec. C.

Paarlberg, Robert L. "How Agriculture Blocked the Uruguay Round." *SAIS Review* 12.1 (1992): 27–42.

Page, Susan. "Clinton tries to salvage trade talks President points to 'big picture.'" *USA Today*, December 2, 1999, sec. A.

Panitchpakdi, Supachai, and Mark L. Clifford. *China and the WTO: Changing China, Changing World*. New York: John Wiley and Sons, 2002.

Paulson, Michael. "Clinton Says He Will Support Trade Sanctions for Worker Abuse." *Seattle Post-Intelligencer*, December 1, 1999, sec. A.

Pearson, Margaret. "China's Integration in the International Trade and Investment Regime." In *China Joins the World: Progress and Prospects*, edited by Elizabeth Economy and Michel Oksenberg, 161–205. New York: Council on Foreign Relations, 1999.

Pease, Kelly-Kate S. *International Organizations: Perspectives on Governance in the Twenty-First Century*. 2nd ed. Upper Saddle River, NJ: Prentice Hall, 2002.

Pedersen, Peter N. "The WTO Decision-Making Process and Internal Transparency." *World Trade Review* 5.1 (2006): 103–32.

Peters, Gretchen. "Eastern Threat." *Business Mexico*, May 1, 2001, p. 31.

Peterson, John. "Hormones, Heifers and High Politics: Biotechnology and the Common Agricultural Policy." *Public Administration* 67 (1989): 455–71.

Preeg, Ernest H. "Reactions to Seattle. The South Rises in Seattle." *Journal of International Economic Law* 3.1 (2000): 183–86.

———. *Traders in a Brave New World*. Chicago: University of Chicago Press, 1995.

Public Citizen. "On the Triennial Review by the World Trade Organization on the Application of Sanitary and Phytosanitary Measures (The 'SPS Agreement')." Public Citizen Global Trade Watch, Comments, Washington DC, January 9, 1998. http://

www.citizen.org/trade/harmonization/comments/articles.cfm?ID=4358 (accessed February 14, 2007).

————. "Talking Points on WTO: Shrink or Sink 'Global NGO Campaign.'" Public Citizen Global Trade Watch, Washington DC, 1999.

Putnam, Robert. *Hanging Together: Cooperation and Conflict in the Seven Power Summits.* Cambridge, MA: Harvard University Press, 1984.

Raghavan, Chakravarthi. "After Seattle, World Trade System Faces Uncertain Future." *International Review of Political Economy* 7.3 (2000): 495–504.

————. *Recolonization: GATT, the Uruguay Round and the Third World.* London: Zed Books, 1990.

Rapkin, David P., and Aurelia George. "Rice Liberalization and Japan's Role in the Uruguay Round: A Two Level Game Approach." In *World Agriculture and the GATT*, edited by William P. Avery, 55–94. Boulder, CO: Lynne Rienner, 1992.

Rayner, A. J., K. A. Ingersent, and R. C. Hine. "Agriculture in the Uruguay Round: An Assessment." *Economic Journal* 103.421 (1993): 1513–27.

Rhodes, Carolyn. *Reciprocity, U.S. Trade Policy and the GATT Regime.* Ithaca, NY: Cornell University Press, 1993.

Robertson, David. "Civil Society and the WTO." *World Economy* 23.9 (2000): 1119–34.

Rodrik, Dani. "Trading in Illusions." *Foreign Policy* 123 (2001): 54–63.

Rosegrant, Susan. "Banana Wars: Challenges to the European Union's Banana Regime." Harvard University, John F. Kennedy School of Government Case Studies in Public Policy and Management, case n. 1534, March 1, 1999.

Rubin, Alissa. "Dole, Clinton Compromise Greases Wheels for GATT." *Congressional Quarterly Weekly Report*, November 26, 1994, p. 3405.

Ruggie, John G. "International Regimes, Transactions, and Change: Embedded Liberalism in the Postwar Economic Order." *International Organization* 36.2 (1982): 379–415.

Russett, Bruce, Harvey Starr, and David Kinsella. *World Politics: Menu for Choice.* 6th ed. New York: St Martin's, 2000.

Ruzicka, Milan, and John Maggs. "Clinton Team Stands Firm Against Delay in GATT Vote." *Journal of Commerce and Commercial*, November 17, 1994, sec. A.

Sampson, Gary P. "The World Trade Organization After Seattle." *World Economy* 23.9 (2000): 1097–117.

Schott, Jeffrey J. "The WTO After Seattle." In *The WTO After Seattle*, edited by Jeffrey J. Schott, 3–40. Washington DC: Institute for International Economics, 2000.

————, ed. *The WTO After Seattle.* Washington DC: Institute for International Economics, 2000.

Scott, Joanne. "On Kith and Kine (and Crustaceans): Trade and Environment in the EU and WTO." Harvard Jean Monnet Working Paper No.3/99. 1999. Jean Monnet Center for International and Regional Economic Law and Justice, NYU School of Law. http://www.jeanmonnetprogram.org/papers/99/990301.html (accessed February 14, 2007).

Sek, Lenore. "Congressional Research Service Report for Congress: The World Trade Organization: Background and Issues." CRS Report 98-928 E, Washington DC: Congressional Research Service, March 5, 2003.

Shoch, James. *Trading Blows: Party Competition and U.S. Trade Policy in a Globalizing Era.* Chapel Hill: University of North Carolina Press, 2000.

Smith, Adam. *The Wealth of Nations.* New York: Dutton, 1964.

Smith, Jackie, and Timothy Patrick Moran. "WTO 101: Myths About the World Trade Organization." *Dissent* 47.2 (2000): 66–70.

Smith, Peter J., and Elizabeth Smythe. "Sleepless in Seattle: Challenging the WTO in a Globalizing World." Paper presented at 42nd Annual Meeting of the International Studies Association, Chicago, February 21–24, 2001.

Southwick, James D. "Addressing Market Access Barriers in Japan Through the WTO: A Survey of Typical Japan Market Access Issues and the Possibility to Address Them Through WTO Dispute Resolution Procedures." *Law and Policy in International Business* 31.3 (2000): 923–76.

Steinfeld, Edward S. "Beyond the Transition: China's Economy at Century's End." *Current History* 98.629 (1999): 271–76.

Stewart, Terence P. *The GATT Uruguay Round: A Negotiating History (1986–1992),* Vol. 1. Boston: Kluwer Law and Taxation, 1993.

Stewart, Terence P., and Amy Ann Karpel. "Review of the Dispute Settlement Understanding: Operation of Panels." *Law and Policy in International Business* 31 (2000): 593–646.

Stout, David. "U.S. Raises Tax on Food from Europe." *New York Times,* July 20, 1999, sec. C.

Sutherland, Peter. "Reality Check: The WTO and Globalization After Seattle." *Harvard International Review* 22.1 (2000): 20–25.

Sutherland, Peter, John W. Sewell, and David Weiner. "Challenges Facing the WTO and Policies to Address Global Governance." In *The Role of the World Trade Organization in Global Governance,* edited by Gary P. Samson, 81–112. New York: United Nations University Press, 2001.

Sutton, Paul. "The Banana Regime of the European Union, the Caribbean and Latin America." *Journal of Inter-American Studies and World Affairs* 39.2 (1997): 5–36.

Telecommunications Industry Association. "China PTNR and WTO Accession: White House Summary of the Deal. November 15, 1999." Arlington, VA: Telecommunications Industry Association, December, 2000.

Tetteh, Hormeku. "Draft Declaration by WTO Chairman. Clean Text for WTO Ministerial; Dirty Slap in Face of Africans." *Global Policy Forum,* October 9, 2001. http://www.globalpolicy.org/socecon/bwi-wto/wto/2001/1010attac.htm (accessed March 2, 2007).

Thomas, Jeffrey S., and Michael A. Meyer. *The New Rules of Global Trade: A Guide to The World Trade Organization.* Toronto: Thomson Carswell, 1997.

Thompson, Ginger. "Protesters Swarm the Streets at WTO Forum in Cancun." *NYTimes.com,* September 13, 2003. http://www.nytimes.com/2003/09/14/international/americas/14TRAD.html (accessed March 2, 2007).

Thorn, Craig, and Marinn Carlson. "The Agreement on the Application of the Sanitary and Phytosanitary Measures and the Agreement on Technical Barriers to Trade." *Law and Policy in International Business* 31.3 (2000): 841–54.

Timms, Dave. "Double Dealing in Doha." *Ecologist,* February 2002, p. 68.

Tyers, Rod. "The Cairns Group Perspective." In *Agriculture in the Uruguay Round,* edited by K. A. Ingersent, A. J. Rayner, and R. C. Hine, 88–109. New York: St. Martin's, 1994.

Tyson, Laura D'Andrea. "What Really Sabotaged the Seattle Trade Talks?" *Business Week,* February 7, 2000, p. 26.

Underhill, Geoffrey R. D. "Negotiating Financial Openness: The Uruguay Round and Trade in Financial Services." In *Finance and World Politics: Markets, Regimes and States in the Post-Hegemonic Era*, edited by Philip G. Cerny, 114–51. Aldershot, Great Britain : Edward Elgar, 1993.

"U.S. Attacks EU in Banana Trade Dispute." *El Pais*, January 26, 1999.

U.S. Department of Agriculture. "U.S. Secretary of Agriculture Ann M. Veneman and U.S. Trade Representative Robert B. Zoellick: Final Press Conference: World Trade Organization Fifth Ministerial Meeting Cancun, Mexico." Press Releases, Release No. 0318.03, September 14, 2003. http://www.usda.gov/news/releases/2003/09/0318 .htm (accessed June 19, 2007).

U.S. Department of Agriculture: Foreign Agricultural Service. "Chronology of the European Union's Hormone Ban." FAS Online, November 18, 2005. http://www.fas .usda.gov/itp/policy/chronology.html (February 14, 2007).

———. "A Primer on Beef Hormones." FAS Online, February 24, 1999. http://stock-holm.usembassy.gov/Agriculture/hormone.html (accessed June 19, 2007).

U.S. Department of Commerce. "Survey of Current Business." Washington DC: U.S. Department of Commerce, April 2000.

U.S. Department of State. "Proposals for the Expansion of World Trade and Employ-ment." United States Department of State Publication 2411, Washington DC: GPO, November, 1945.

"The U.S./EU Banana Dispute: Unilateral U.S. Retaliation Not in Line With WTO Rules and Politically Unwise, Sir Leon Brittan Says." *PR Newswire*, November 10, 1998.

U.S. General Accounting Office. "World Trade Organization: Issues in Dispute Settle-ment." Washington DC: Government Printing Office, August 2000.

U.S. House of Representatives Subcommittee on Trade of the Committee on Ways and Means. "Report on World Trade Organization (WTO) Ministerial Meeting in Seat-tle." 106th Cong., 2nd sess., 1999, pp. 1–25. http://frwebgate.access.gpo.gov/cgi-bin/getdoc.cgi?dbname=106_ways_and_means_committee_prints&docid=f:wm010. pdf (accessed March 6, 2007).

U.S. Mission to the European Union, "*Barshefsky Teleconference on Beef Hormone Issue,*" Transcript from Federal News Service, Washington DC, May 14, 1999.

———. "Outlines 'Fallacies' in EU 'Fact Sheet.'" Brussels, March 18, 1999.

———. "USTR on 'Brief History of Banana Dispute.'" Brussels, December 21, 1998.

———. "USTR Scher on WTO Beef Hormone Case." Transcript excerpts from Federal News Service, Washington DC, July 13, 1999.

U.S. Permanent Representative to the WTO. "Summary of the U.S. Legal Position on Dispute in the WTO on E.C. Banana Regime." Geneva, January 12, 1999.

"U.S. Threatens Europe with Duties in Beef Dispute." *New York Times*, May 15, 1999, sec. C.

van de Kasteele, Adelien. *The Banana Chain: The Macro-Economics of the Banana Trade.* Paper presented at International Banana Conference, Amsterdam, February 1998. http://www.bananalink.org.uk/images/the_banana_chain_by_a_van_de_kasteele.pdf (accessed March 6, 2007).

"Veal Hormones: Ban Them All?" *Economist*, January1, 1981, p. 45.

"Veal Hormones: Down on the Pharm." *Economist*, March 27, 1982, p. 77.

Wagner, Martin J. "The WTO's Interpretation of the SPS Agreement Has Undermined the Right of Government to Establish Appropriate Levels of Protection against Risk." *Law and Policy in International Business* 31.3 (2000): 855–59.

Wagner, Martin J., and Patti Goldman. "Comments to the Appellate Body of the World Trade Organization: EC Measures Concerning Meat and Meat Products." *Public Citizen–Global Trade Watch*, October 31, 1997. http://www.citizen.org/trade/harmonization/comments/articles.cfm?ID=5582 (accessed February 14, 2007).

Wallach, Lori, and Michelle Sforza. *Whose Trade Organization? Corporate Globalization and the Erosion of Democracy*. Washington DC: Public Citizen, 1999.

Wallach, Lori, Patrick Woodall, and Ralph Nader. *Whose Trade Organization? A Comprehensive Guide to the WTO*. 2nd ed. New York: New Press, 2004.

Watson, Peter S., Joseph E. Flynn, and Chad C. Conwell. *Completing the World Trading System: Proposals for a Millennium Round*. The Hague: Kluwer Law International, 1999.

Webber, Douglas. "Franco-German Bilateralism and Agricultural Politics in the European Union: The Neglected Level." *West European Politics* 22.1 (1999): 45–67.

Weiskopf, Michael. "The Busy Backdoor Men." *Time*, March 31, 1997, p. 40.

Whalley, John. *The Uruguay Round and Beyond*. Ann Arbor: University of Michigan Press, 1990.

Whitelaw, Kevin, Dori Jones Yang, and Joellen Perry. "Men in Black." *US News and World Report*, December 13, 1999, p.22.

Wilson, Arlene. "The World Trade Organization: The Debate in the United States." CRS Report RL30521. Washington DC: Congressional Research Service, April 12, 2000. http://ncseonline.org/NLE/CRSreports/international/inter-42.cfm?&CFID=4550177&CFTOKEN=37908294 (accessed March 3, 2007).

Winters, Alan L. "The Economic Consequences of Agricultural Support: A Survey." *OECD Economic Studies* 9 (1987): 7–54.

———. "The Road to Uruguay." *Economic Journal* 100.403 (1990): 1288–1303.

Wolf, Julie. "Banana Dispute with the U.S., EU Hits New Stage." *Wall Street Journal*, December 14, 1998, sec. B.

World Trade Organization. "Accession to the World Trade Organization: Procedures for Negotiations under Article XII—Note by the Secretariat." WTO Report wt/acc/1. Geneva: World Trade Organization, January 1995. http://docsonline.wto.org/DDF-Documents/t/WT/ACC/1.WPF (accessed March 6, 2007).

———. "Agreement on the Application of Sanitary and Phytosanitary Measures." *WTO Legal Texts*. Geneva: World Trade Organization, 1994. http://www.wto.org/english/docs_e/legal_e/15sps_01_e.htm (accessed June 20 2007).

———. *Annual Report 2005*. Geneva: World Trade Organization, 2005. http://www.wto.org/english/res_e/reser_e/annual_report_e.htm (accessed March 6, 2007).

———. *Annual Report 2006*. Geneva: World Trade Organization, 2006. http://www.wto.org/english/res_e/reser_e/annual_report_e.htm (accessed March 6, 2007).

———. "The Doha Development Agenda : Doha Launches Negotiations, TNC Oversees Them." Cancun WTO Ministerial 2003, Briefing Notes, 2003. http://www.wto.org/english/theWTO_e/minist_e/min03_e/brief_e/brief02_e.htm (accessed March 1, 2007).

———. "Doha WTO Ministerial 2001: Ministerial Declaration." Geneva, November 20, 2001. http://www.wto.org/english/thewto_e/minist_e/min01_e/mindecl_e.htm (accessed June 22, 2007).

————. "EC Measures Concerning Meat and Meat Products (Hormones)–AB-1997–4— Report of the Appellate Body." WTO Report WT/DS26/AB/R. Geneva: World Trade Organization, January 16, 1998. http://docsonline.wto.org/DDFDocuments/t/WT/ DS/26ABR.WPF (accessed March 6, 2007).

————. "EC Measures Concerning Meat and Meat Products (Hormones)—Complaint by the United States—Report of the Panel." WTO Report WT/DS26/R/USA. Geneva: World Trade Organization, August 18, 1997. http://docsonline.wto.org/ DDFDocuments/t/WT/DS/26RUSA.WPF (accessed March 6, 2007).

————. "European Communities—Regime for the Importation, Sale and Distribution of Bananas—Complaint by Guatemala and Honduras—Report of the Panel." WTO Report WT/DS27/R/GTM, WT/DS27/R/HND. Geneva: World Trade Organiza- tion, May 22, 1997. http://docsonline.wto.org/DDFDocuments/t/WT/DS/27 RGTM.WPF (accessed March 6, 2007).

————. "Fifteenth Session of the Working Party on China: Statement by H.E. Vice Min- ister LONG Yongtu, Head of the Chinese Delegation." WTO News: 2001 News Items. Geneva, January 17, 2001. http://www.wto.org/English/news_e/news01_e/ wpchina_longstat_jan01_e.htm (accessed February 28, 2007).

————. "General Agreement on Tariffs and Trade 1947." *WTO Legal Texts*, Geneva: World Trade Organization, 1947. http://www.wto.org/english/docs_e/legal_e/legal_ e.htm (accessed March 6, 2007).

————. "General Agreement on Tariffs and Trade 1994." *WTO Legal Texts*, Geneva: World Trade Organization, 1994. http://www.wto.org/english/docs_e/legal_e/legal _e.htm (accessed March 6, 2007).

————. *International Trade Statistics 2005.* Geneva: World Trade Organization, 2005. http://www.wto.org/english/res_e/statis_e/its2005_e/its2005_e.pdf (accessed March 6, 2007).

————. "It Is Vital to Maintain and Consolidate What Has Already Been Achieved." WTO News: 1999 Press Releases, Press/160, December 7, 1999. Post Conference News Conference. http://www.wto.org/english/news_e/pres99_e/pr160_e.htm (accessed March 6, 2007).

————. "Legal Texts: The WTO Agreements." Geneva: World Trade Organization, 2007. http://www.wto.org/english/docs_e/legal_e/ursum_e.htm (accessed March 6, 2007).

————. "Sanitary and Phytosanitary Measures: Introduction: Understanding the Agree- ment on Sanitary and Phytosanitary Measures." Geneva: The World Trade Organiza- tion, 1998. http://www.wto.org/english/tratop_e/sps_e/spsund_e.htm (accessed June 20, 2007).

————. "Summary of 14 September 2003: Day 5: Conference Ends without Consensus." WTO OMC Cancún 03, September 14, 2003. http://www.wto.org/english/thewto _e/minist_e/min03_e/min03_14sept_e.htm (accessed June 20, 2007).

————. *Trading into the Future.* St. Juste-La Pendue, France: Imprimerie Chirat, 1995.

World Trade Organization—Secretariat. "Technical Note on the Accession Process." WTO Report WT/ACC/7/Rev.2. Geneva: World Trade Organization, November 1, 2001. http://docsonline.wto.org/DDFDocuments/t/WT/ACC/7R2.doc (accessed March 6, 2007).

World Trade Organization Training Institute. *Training Manual.* 2nd ed. Geneva: World Trade Organization, 2001. http://e-fpo.fpo.go.th/e-inter/WTO_training/t/tpc/Training %20Manual.htm (accessed March 1, 2007).

"The WTO Under Fire." *Economist*, September 20, 2003, 26–28.

Yong, Wang. "China's Stakes in WTO Accession: The Internal Decision-Making Process." In *China's Accession to the World Trade Organization: National and International Perspectives*, edited by Heike Holbig and Robert Ash, 20–40. New York: Routledge Curzon, 2002.

Zedillo, Ernesto. "To Be or Not to Be at Cancún." *Forbes*, September 1, 2003, 45.

Zeiler, Thomas W. *Free Trade, Free World: The Advent of GATT*. Chapel Hill: University of North Carolina Press, 1999.

Zhongquo, Q. B. "China in the World Press." *China Enterprise News*, January 5, 2001.

Zupnick, Elliot. *Vision and Revisions: The United States in the Global Economy*. Boulder, CO: Westview, 1999.

Index